PANDORA IN THE CRIMSØN SHELL

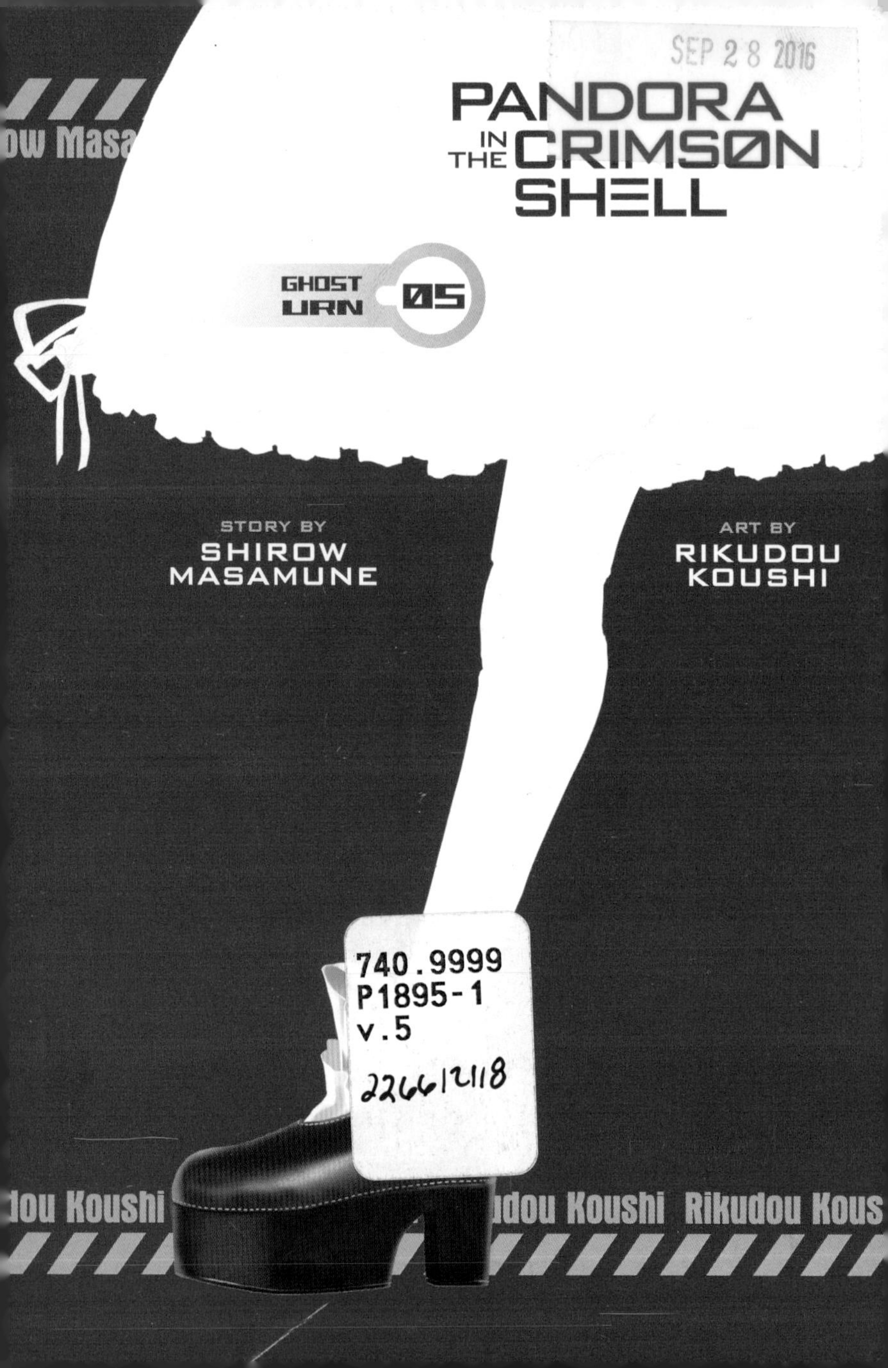
GHOST URN
05
ow Masa
dou Koushi
udou Koushi Rikudou Kous

STORY BY
SHIROW MASAMUNE

ART BY
RIKUDOU KOUSHI

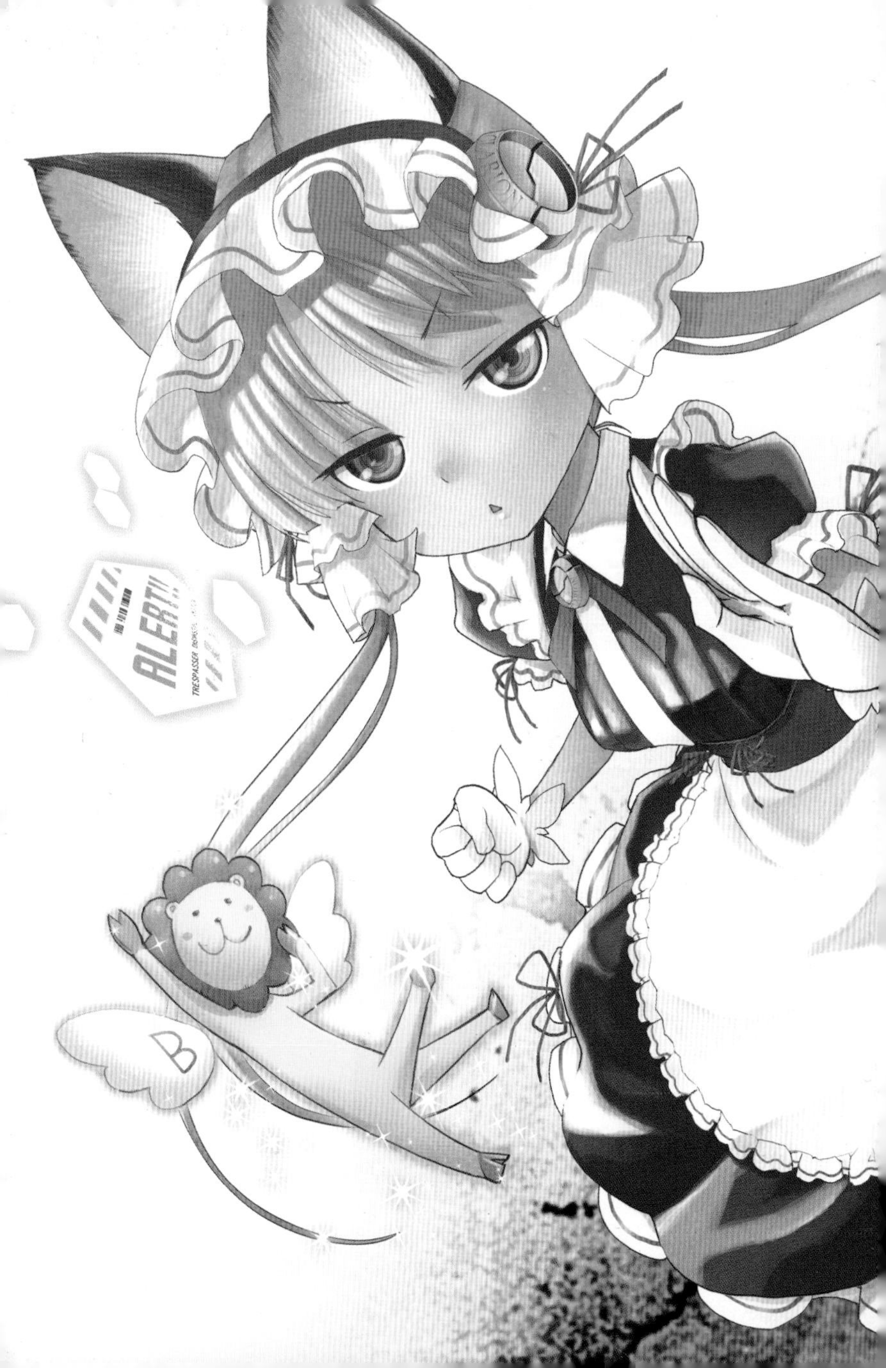
ALERT!!
TRESPASSER

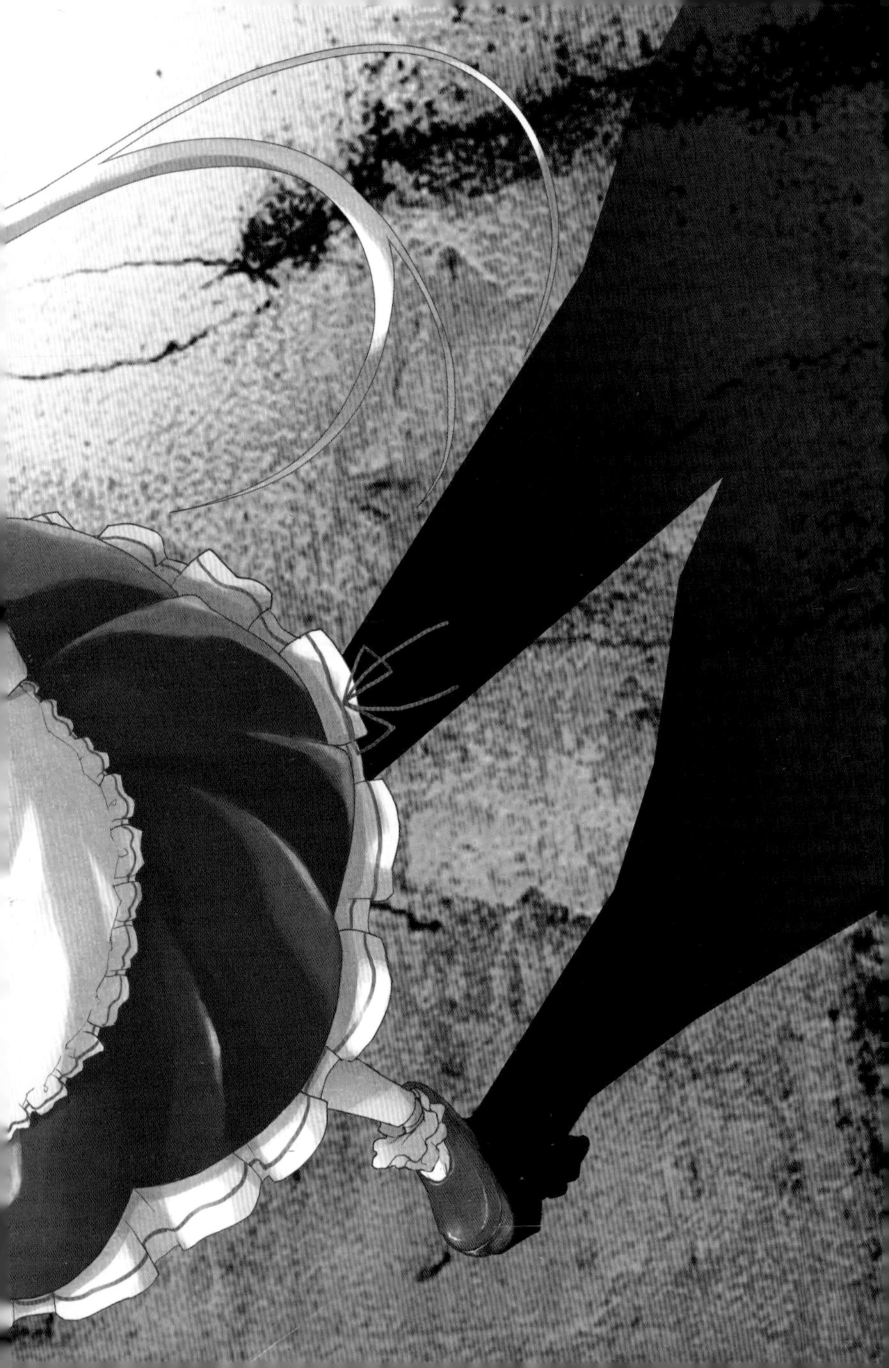

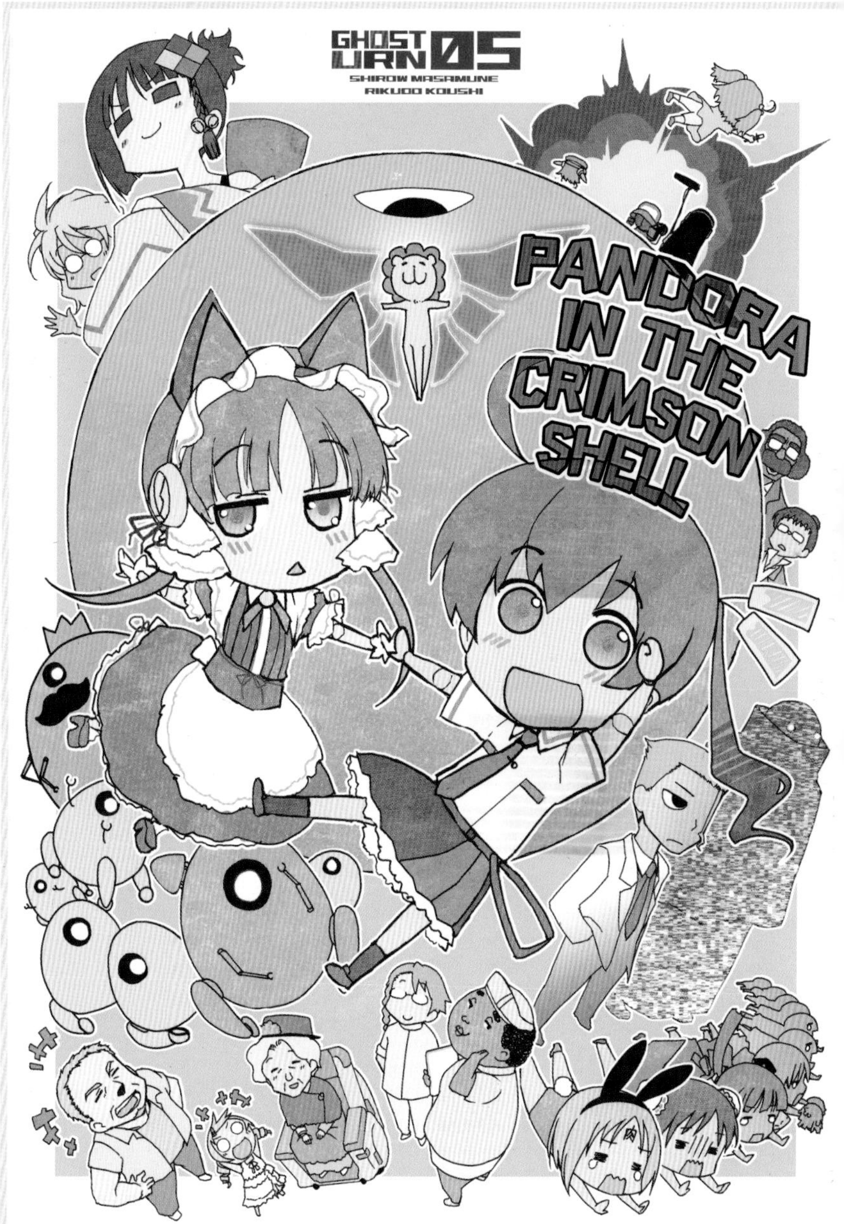
GHOST URN 05
SHIROW MASAMUNE
RIKUDO KOUSHI
PANDORA IN THE CRIMSON SHELL

ow Masamune Shirow Masamune Shirow Masamune Shirow Masan

GHOST URN-EPISODE.log —— The story so far!

Nanakorobi Nene, a girl who uses a full-body prosthetic, has a special ability: with help from her android partner Clarion, she's able to use the Pandora Device to install an endless variety of temporary abilities!

Nene and Clarion are settling into a routine on the artificial resort island of Cenancle, but things aren't as peaceful as they seem! Colonel Kurtz and his followers from the American Empire are continuing their attempts to unearth the massive boring machine Buer, putting everyone at risk...

dou Koushi Rikudou Koushi Rikudou Koushi Rikudou Koushi Rikudo

GHOST URN-CHARACTERS——Main Characters

■Nanakorobi Nene

A girl whose brain was implanted into an entirely artificial body after an accident when she was young. Nene has one of the few full-body prosthetics in the world!

■Clarion

A combat android owned by Uzal. Clarion has many top-secret, illegal programs tucked away inside her.

■Korobase Takumi

Age unknown. She heads up the Korobase Foundation, which controls cybrain marketing, but has a pathological fear of people.

■Massive boring machine Buer: Central Nervous Unit

The central control unit for the large multi-legged boring machine Buer. As Buer's actual body is currently dormant underground, the central nervous unit is accompanying Nene. This pompous-sounding entity provides a constant stream of perverted, leering commentary.

■Vlind ————

A perky, enthusiastic new Titan TV reporter who happened to be on the scene when the terrorist incident occurred. She miraculously survived! She currently has a part-time job, but she's working hard to move up in the world.

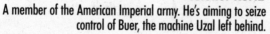

■Colonel Kurtz

A member of the American Imperial army. He's aiming to seize control of Buer, the machine Uzal left behind.

■Robert Altman

A captain with the Cenancle Defense Forces, currently under the command of Special Military Advisor Kurtz. A passionate tough guy who loves justice and peace.

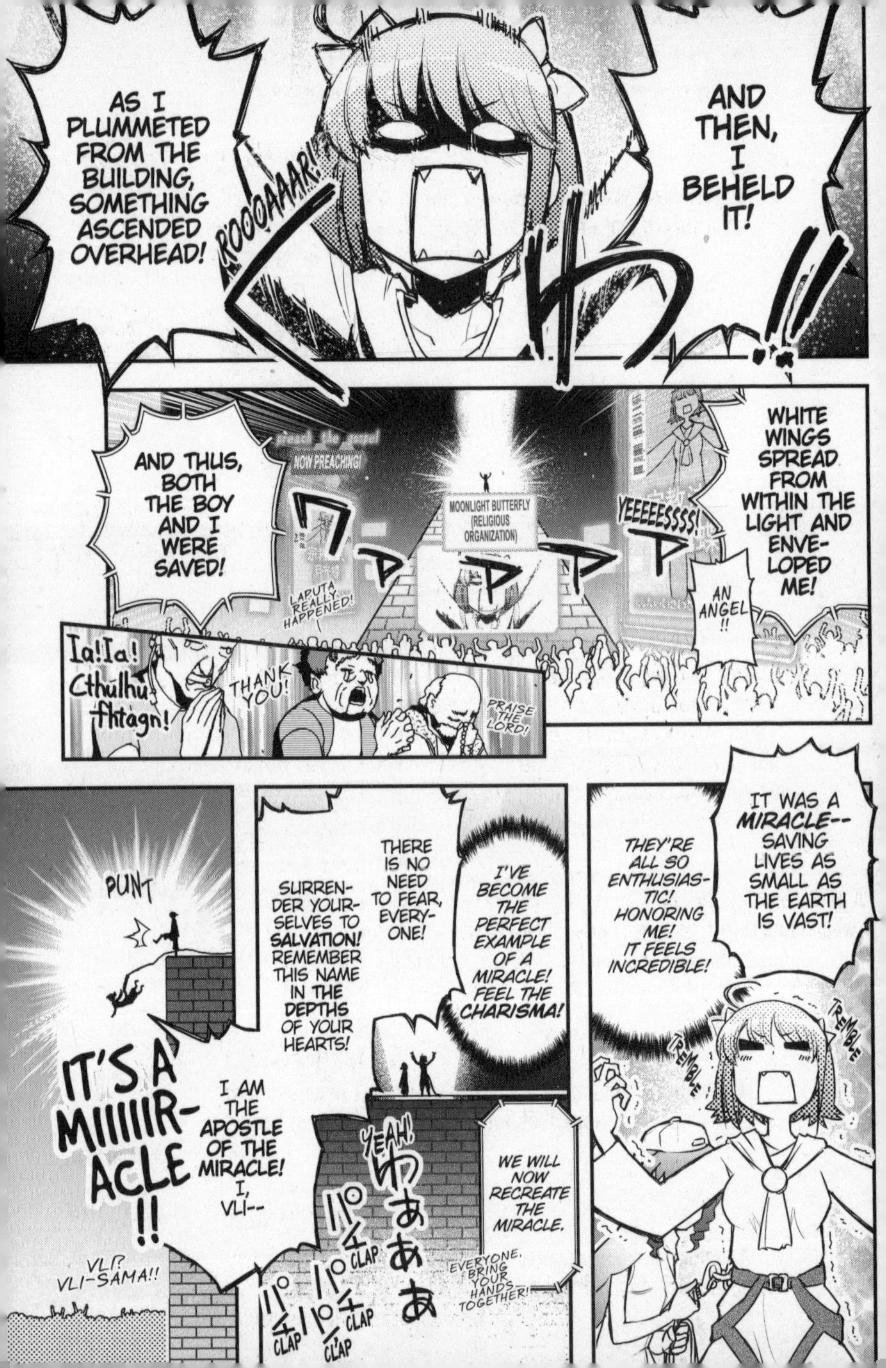
AND THEN, I BEHELD IT!
ROOOAAAR!!
AS I PLUMMETED FROM THE BUILDING, SOMETHING ASCENDED OVERHEAD!
WHITE WINGS SPREAD FROM WITHIN THE LIGHT AND ENVELOPED ME!
YEEEEESSSS!
AN ANGEL!!
MOONLIGHT BUTTERFLY (RELIGIOUS ORGANIZATION)
LAPUTA REALLY HAPPENED!
preach the gospel
NOW PREACHING!
AND THUS, BOTH THE BOY AND I WERE SAVED!
PRAISE THE LORD!
THANK YOU!
Ia! Ia! Cthulhu fhtagn!
IT WAS A MIRACLE-- SAVING LIVES AS SMALL AS THE EARTH IS VAST!
THEY'RE ALL SO ENTHUSIASTIC! HONORING ME! IT FEELS INCREDIBLE!
TREMBLE
TREMBLE
I'VE BECOME THE PERFECT EXAMPLE OF A MIRACLE! FEEL THE CHARISMA!
THERE IS NO NEED TO FEAR, EVERYONE!
SURRENDER YOURSELVES TO SALVATION! REMEMBER THIS NAME IN THE DEPTHS OF YOUR HEARTS!
WE WILL NOW RECREATE THE MIRACLE.
EVERYONE, BRING YOUR HANDS TOGETHER!
YEAH!
CLAP
CLAP
CLAP
CLAP
CLAP
I AM THE APOSTLE OF THE MIRACLE! I, VLI--
PUNT
IT'S A MIIIIIR-ACLE!!
VLI? VLI-SAMA!!

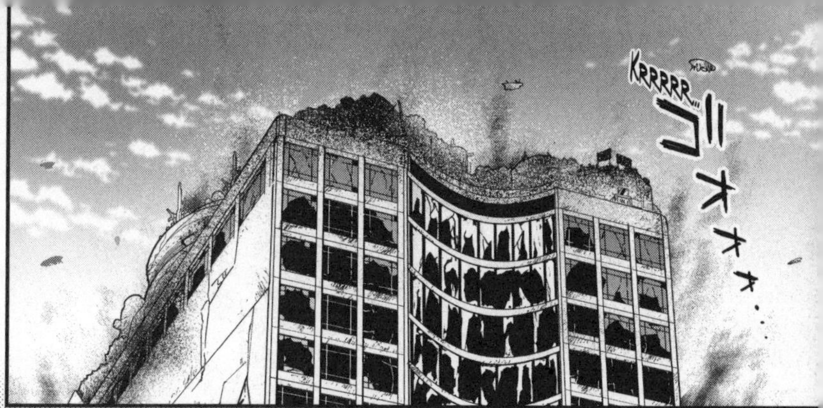
KRRRRR
ゴオォォ…
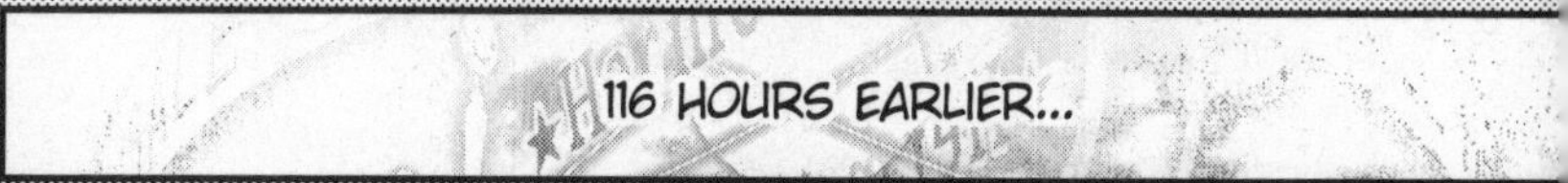
116 HOURS EARLIER...
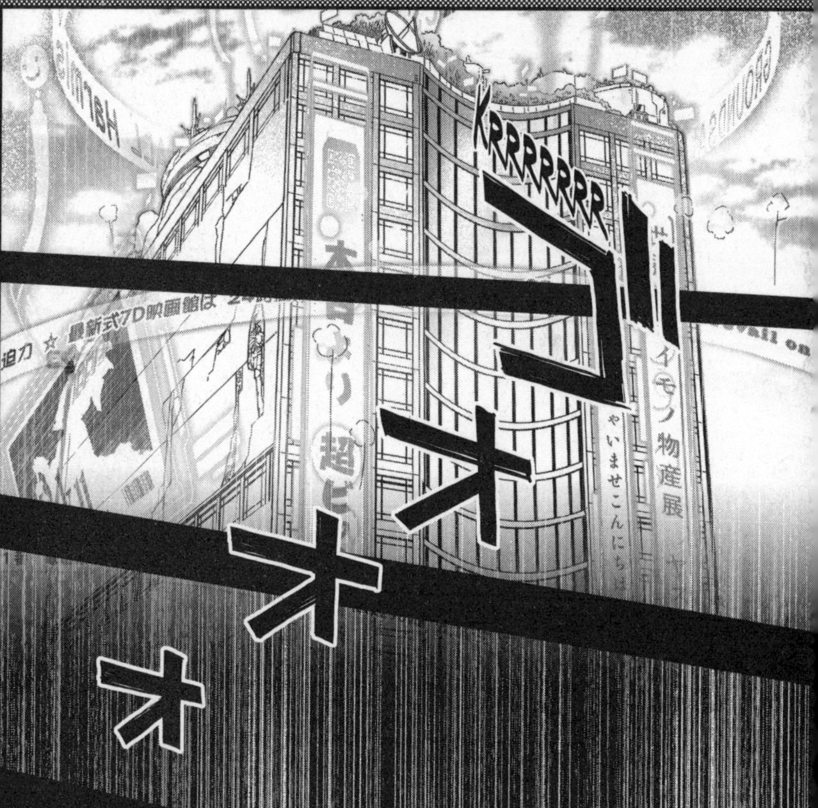
KRRRRRRR
ゴォォォ

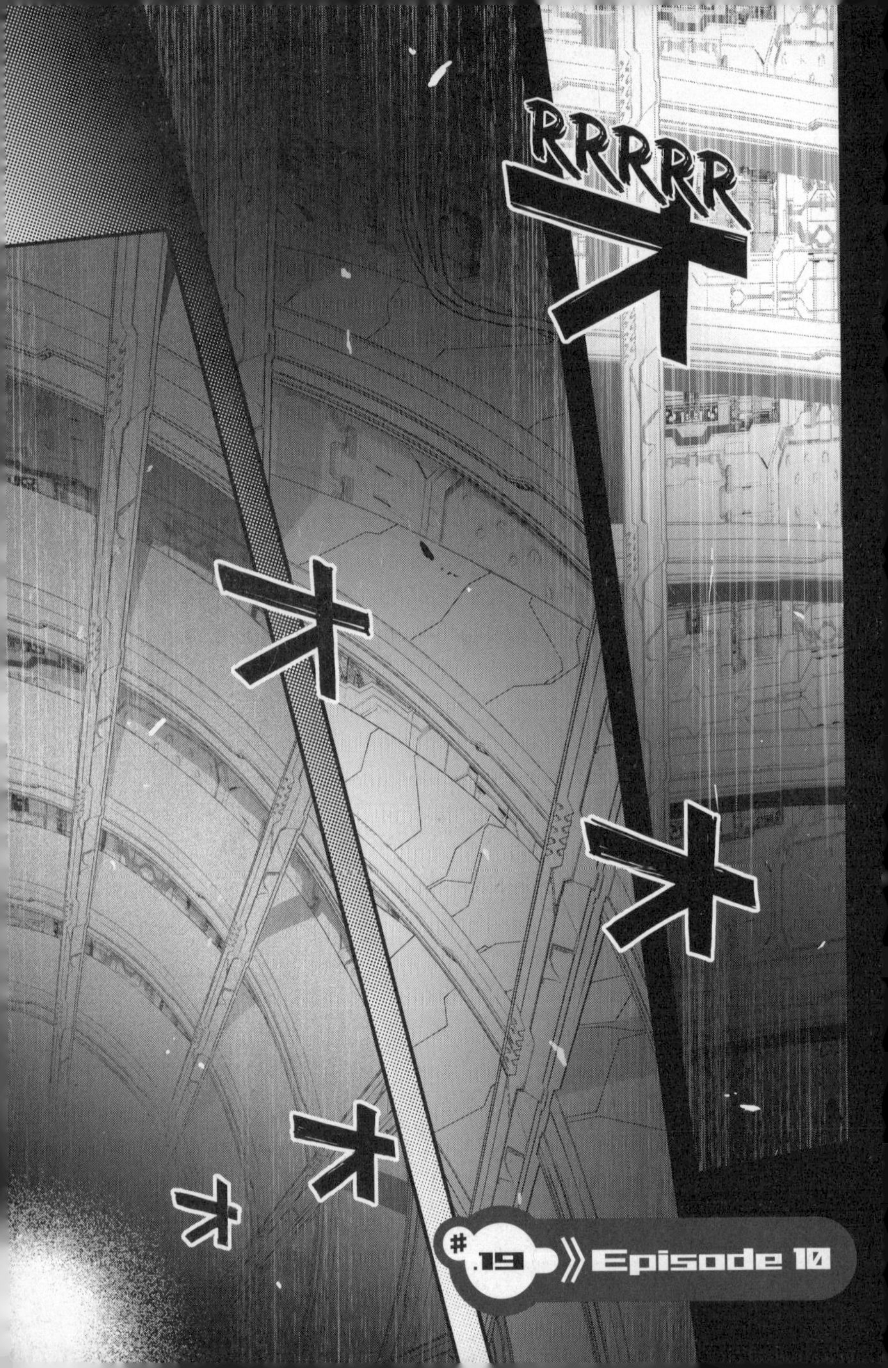

RRRRR
#.19 》Episode 10

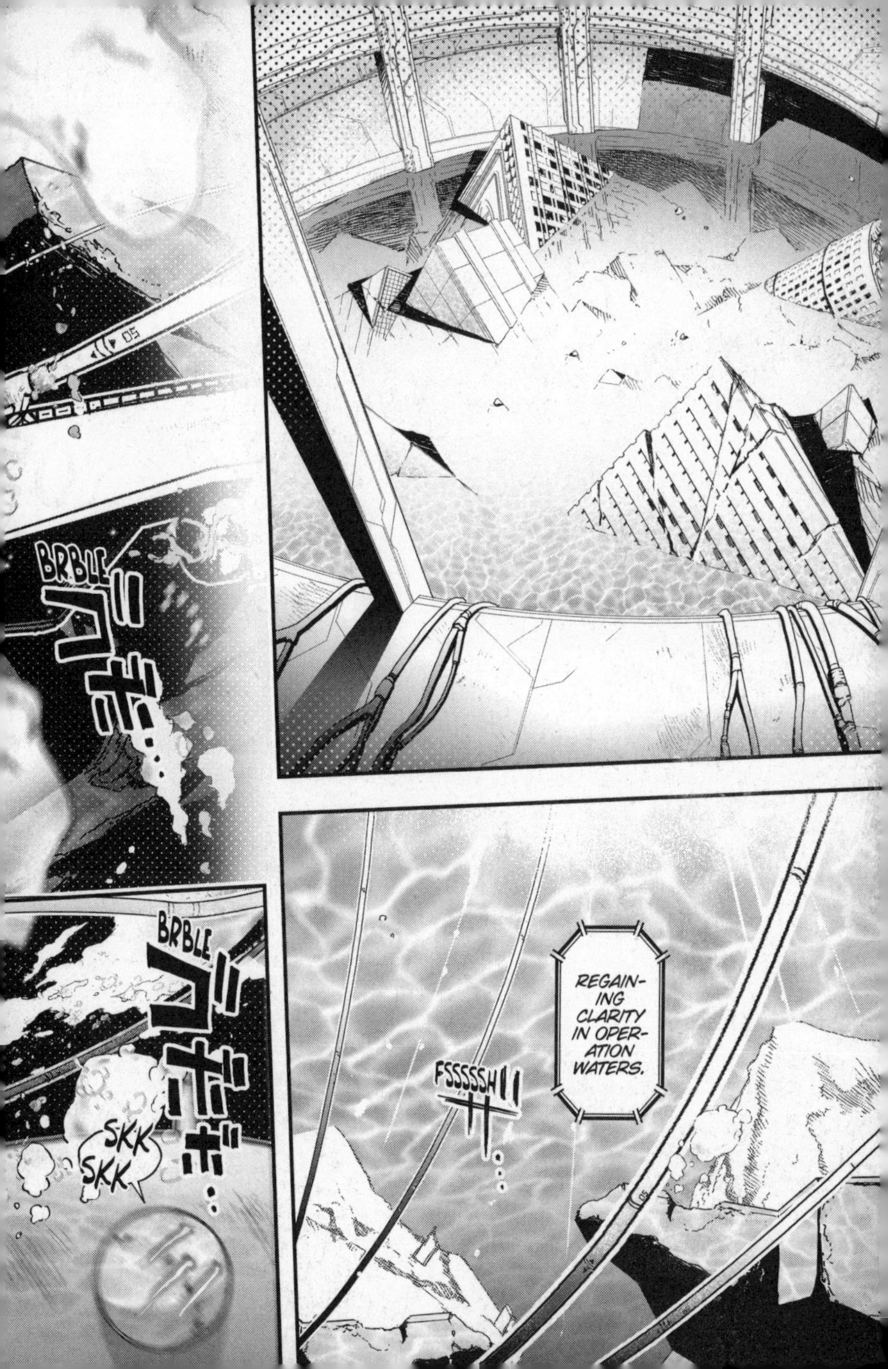
REGAINING CLARITY IN OPERATION WATERS.
FSSSSSH!!
BRBLE
ゴボ…
BRBLE
ゴボボ…
SKK SKK

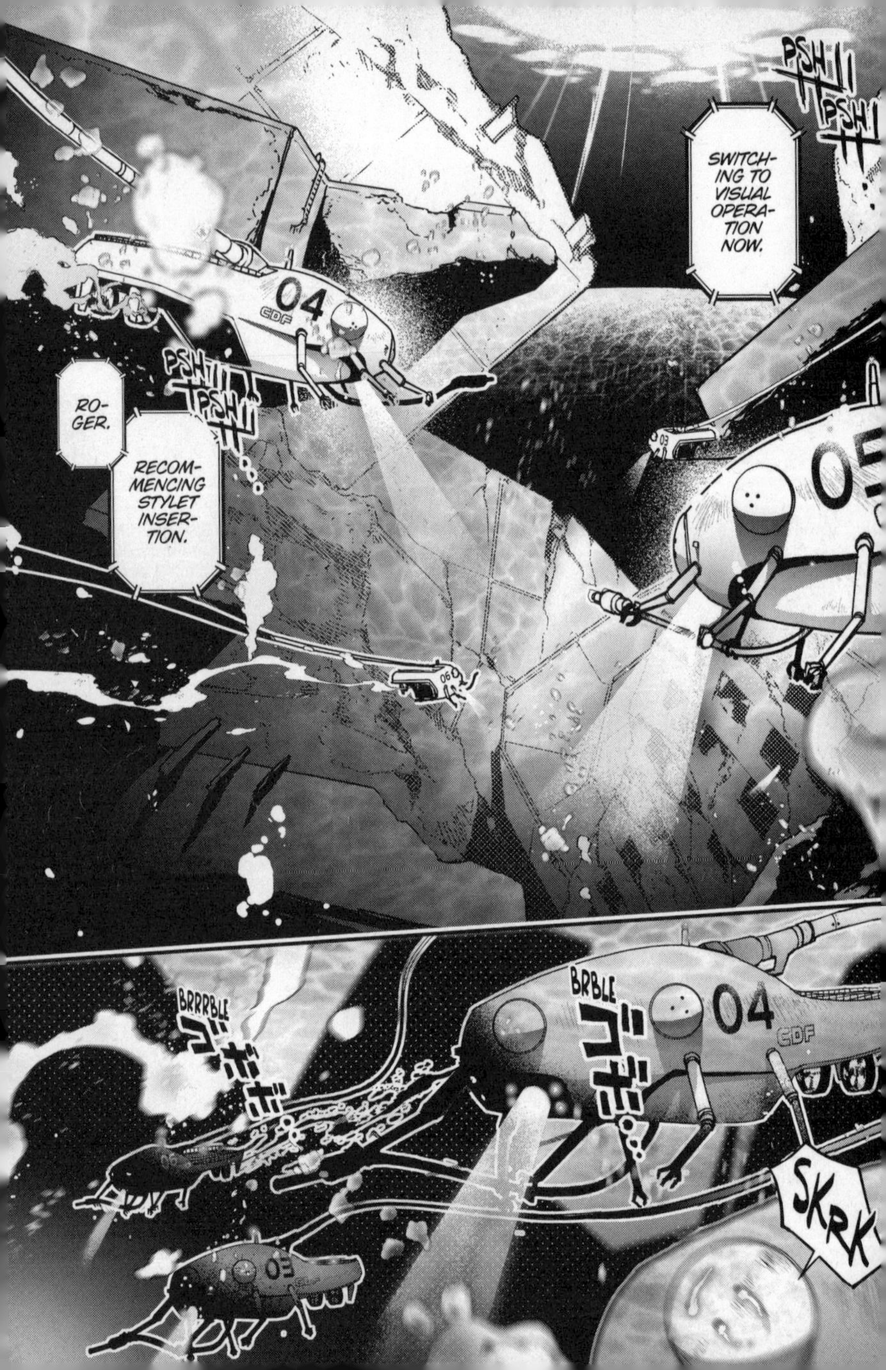
PSH PSH
SWITCHING TO VISUAL OPERATION NOW.
PSH PSH
ROGER.
RECOMMENCING STYLET INSERTION.
SKRK
BRBLE
ゴボ
BRRRBLE
ゴボボ

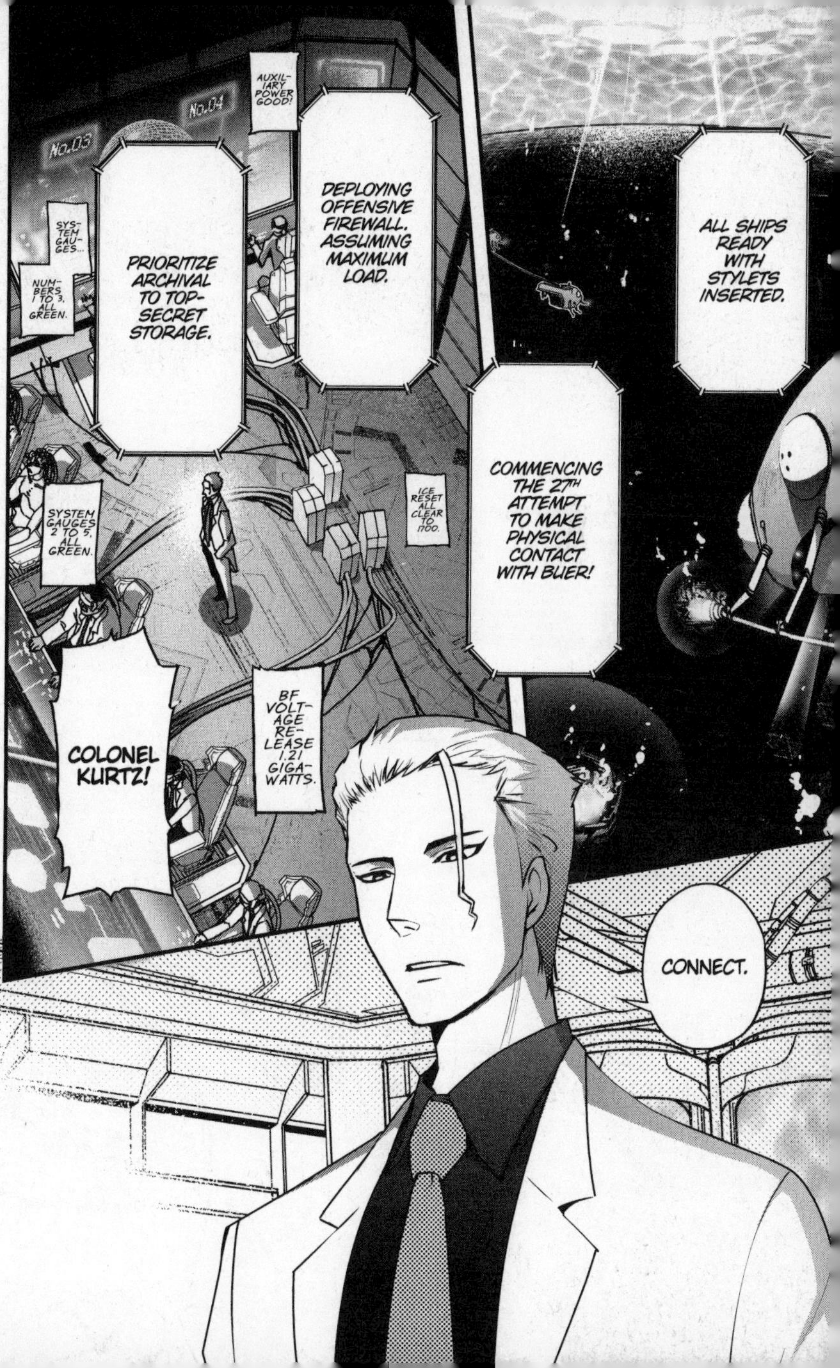
ALL SHIPS READY WITH STYLETS INSERTED.
COMMENCING THE 27TH ATTEMPT TO MAKE PHYSICAL CONTACT WITH BUER!
AUXILIARY POWER GOOD!
DEPLOYING OFFENSIVE FIREWALL. ASSUMING MAXIMUM LOAD.
PRIORITIZE ARCHIVAL TO TOP-SECRET STORAGE.
SYSTEM GAUGES...
NUMBERS 1 TO 3, ALL GREEN.
ICE RESET ALL CLEAR TO 1700.
SYSTEM GAUGES 2 TO 5, ALL GREEN.
BF VOLTAGE RELEASE 1.21 GIGAWATTS.
COLONEL KURTZ!
CONNECT.

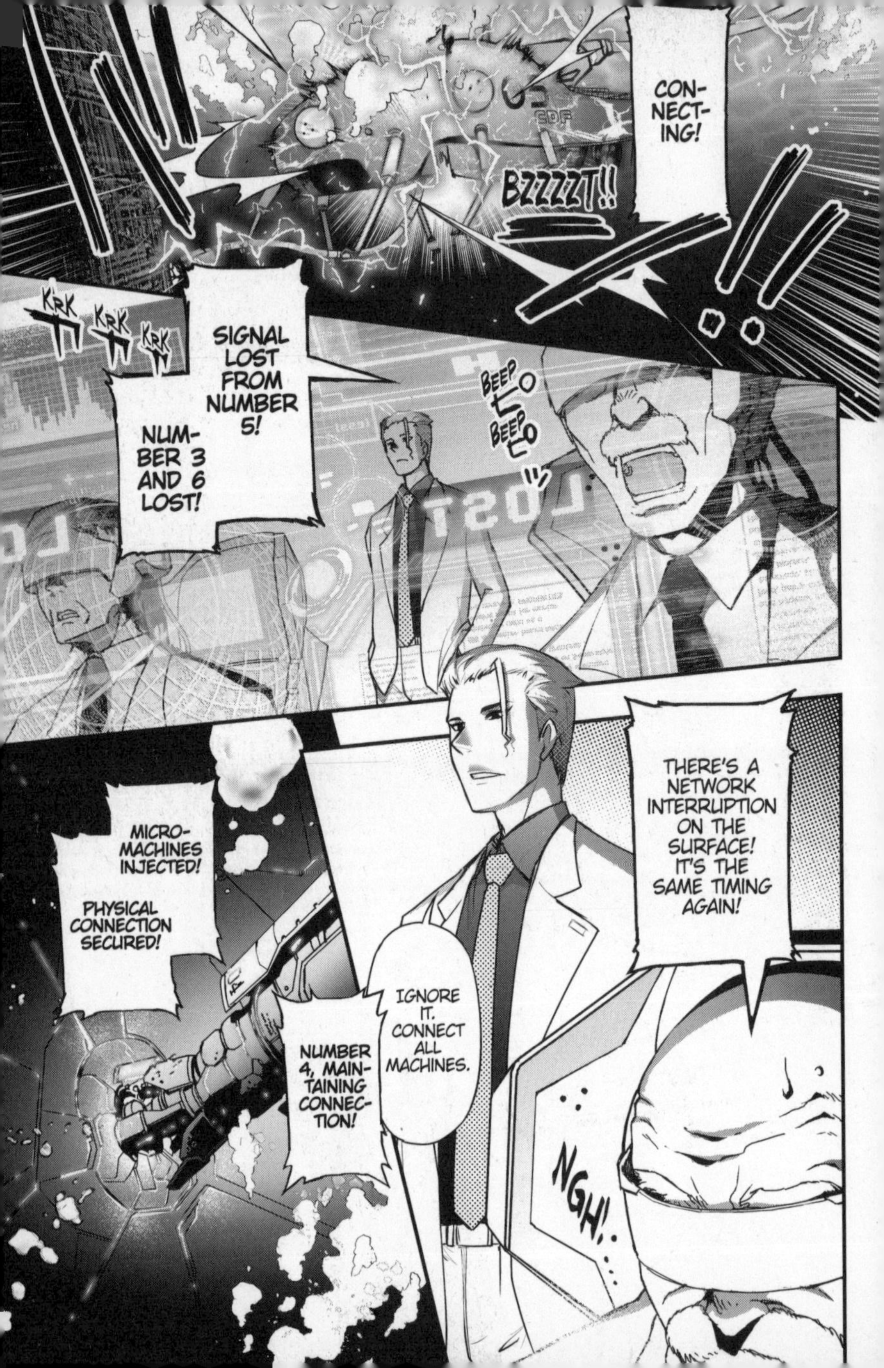
CON-NECT-ING!
BZZZZT!!
BEEP BEEP
KRK KRK KRK
SIGNAL LOST FROM NUMBER 5!
NUM-BER 3 AND 6 LOST!
LOST
THERE'S A NETWORK INTERRUPTION ON THE SURFACE! IT'S THE SAME TIMING AGAIN!
NGH!
IGNORE IT. CONNECT ALL MACHINES.
NUMBER 4, MAIN-TAINING CONNEC-TION!
MICRO-MACHINES INJECTED!
PHYSICAL CONNECTION SECURED!

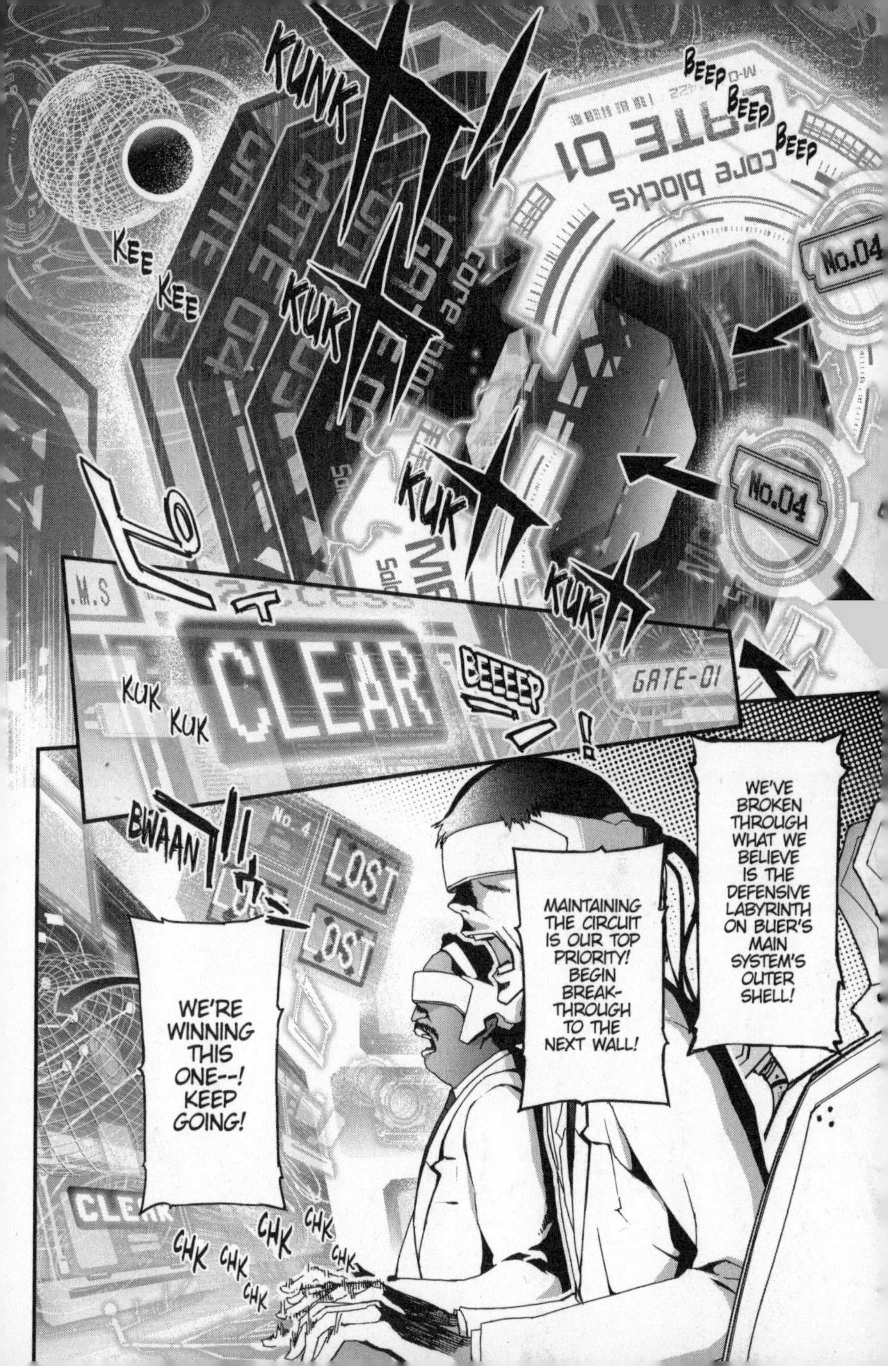
BEEP
BEEP
BEEP
GATE 01
core blocks
No.04
KUNK
KUK
No.04
KUK
KUK
KEE
KEE
GATE-01
BEEEEP
CLEAR
KUK
KUK
!
WE'VE BROKEN THROUGH WHAT WE BELIEVE IS THE DEFENSIVE LABYRINTH ON BUER'S MAIN SYSTEM'S OUTER SHELL!
MAINTAINING THE CIRCUIT IS OUR TOP PRIORITY! BEGIN BREAK-THROUGH TO THE NEXT WALL!
LOST
LOST
BWAAN
WE'RE WINNING THIS ONE--! KEEP GOING!
CLEAR
CHK
CHK
CHK
CHK
CHK
CHK

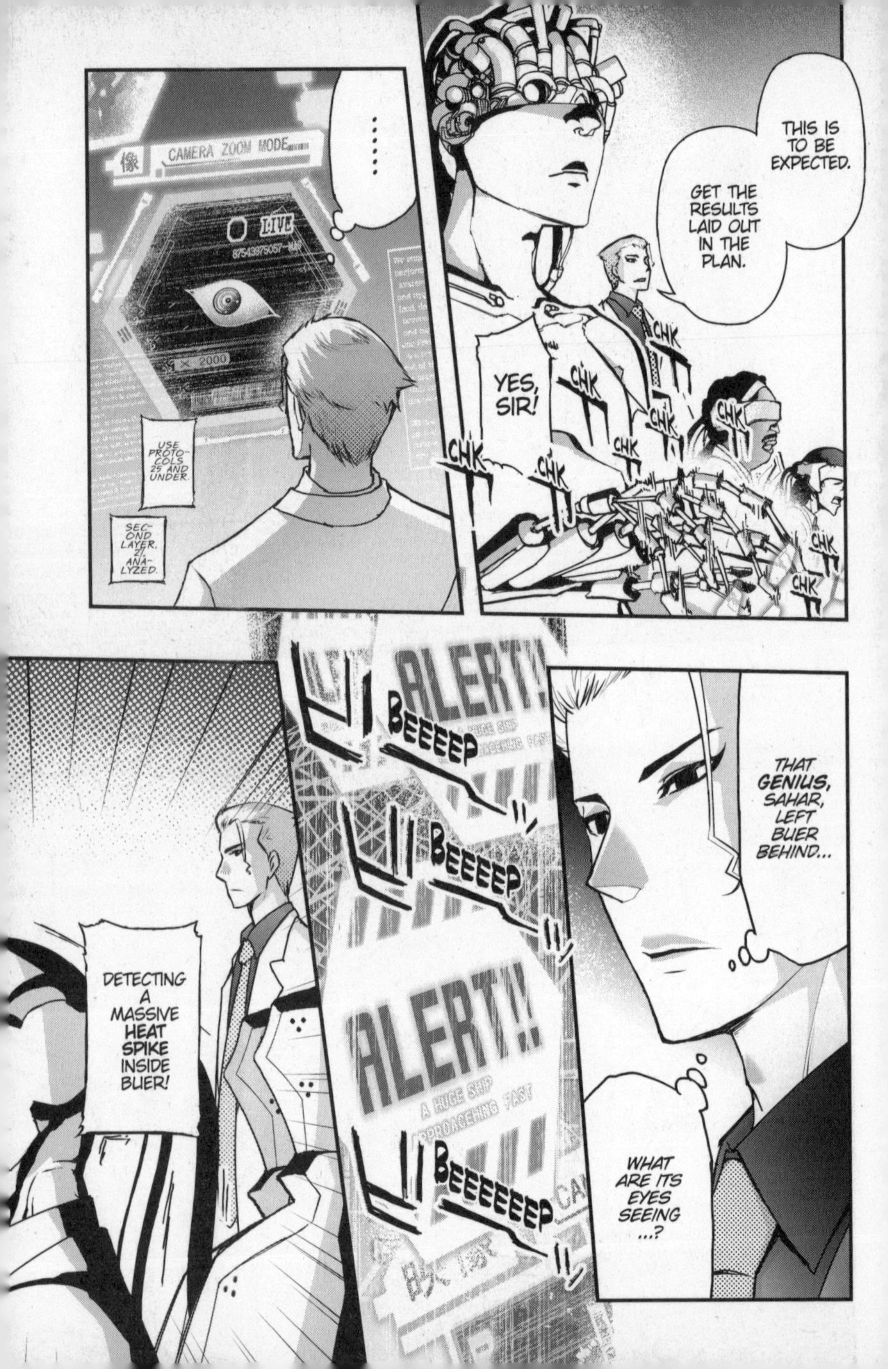
THIS IS TO BE EXPECTED.
GET THE RESULTS LAID OUT IN THE PLAN.
YES, SIR!
CHK
CHK
CHK
CHK
CHK
CHK
CHK
CHK
CAMERA ZOOM MODE
LIVE
......
USE PROTOCOLS 25 AND UNDER.
SECOND LAYER. 2% ANALYZED.
THAT GENIUS, SAHAR, LEFT BUER BEHIND...
WHAT ARE ITS EYES SEEING ...?
ALERT!!
BEEEEP!!
BEEEEP!!
ALERT!!
A HUGE SHIP APPROACHING FAST
BEEEEEEP!!
DETECTING A MASSIVE HEAT SPIKE INSIDE BUER!

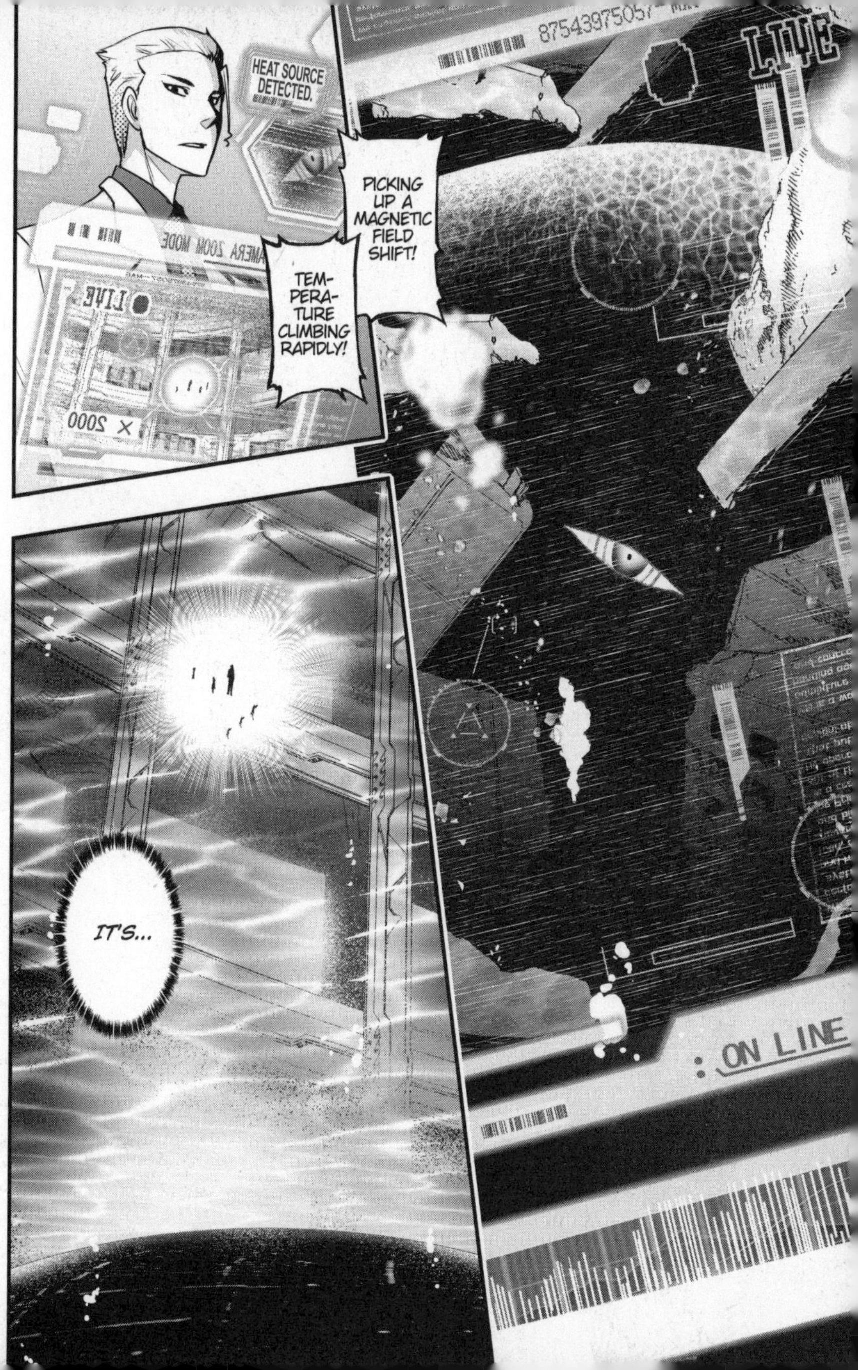
LIVE
87543975057
ON LINE
HEAT SOURCE DETECTED.
PICKING UP A MAGNETIC FIELD SHIFT!
TEM-PERA-TURE CLIMBING RAPIDLY!
IT'S...

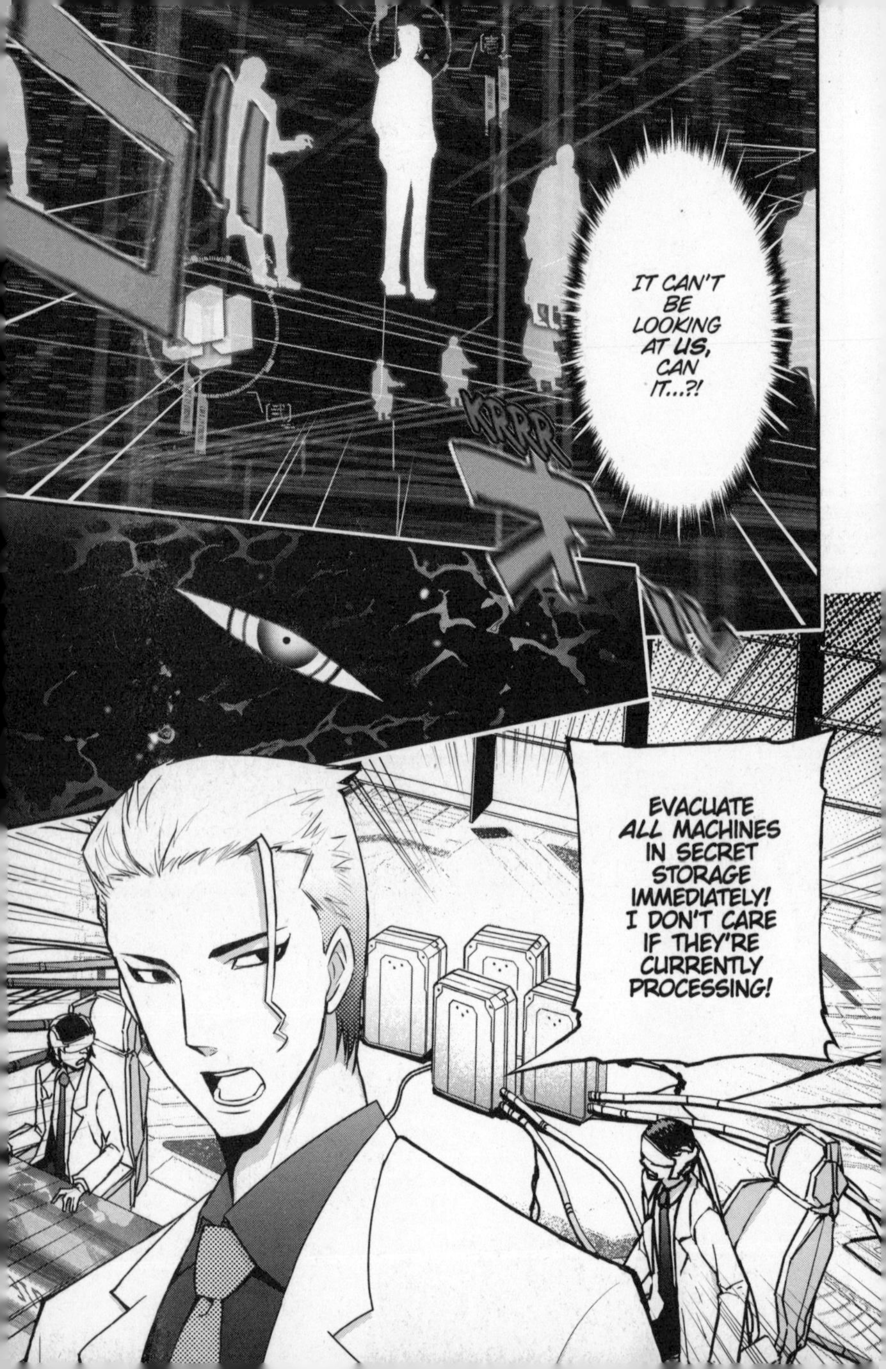
IT CAN'T BE LOOKING AT US, CAN IT...?!
KRRR
EVACUATE ALL MACHINES IN SECRET STORAGE IMMEDIATELY! I DON'T CARE IF THEY'RE CURRENTLY PROCESSING!

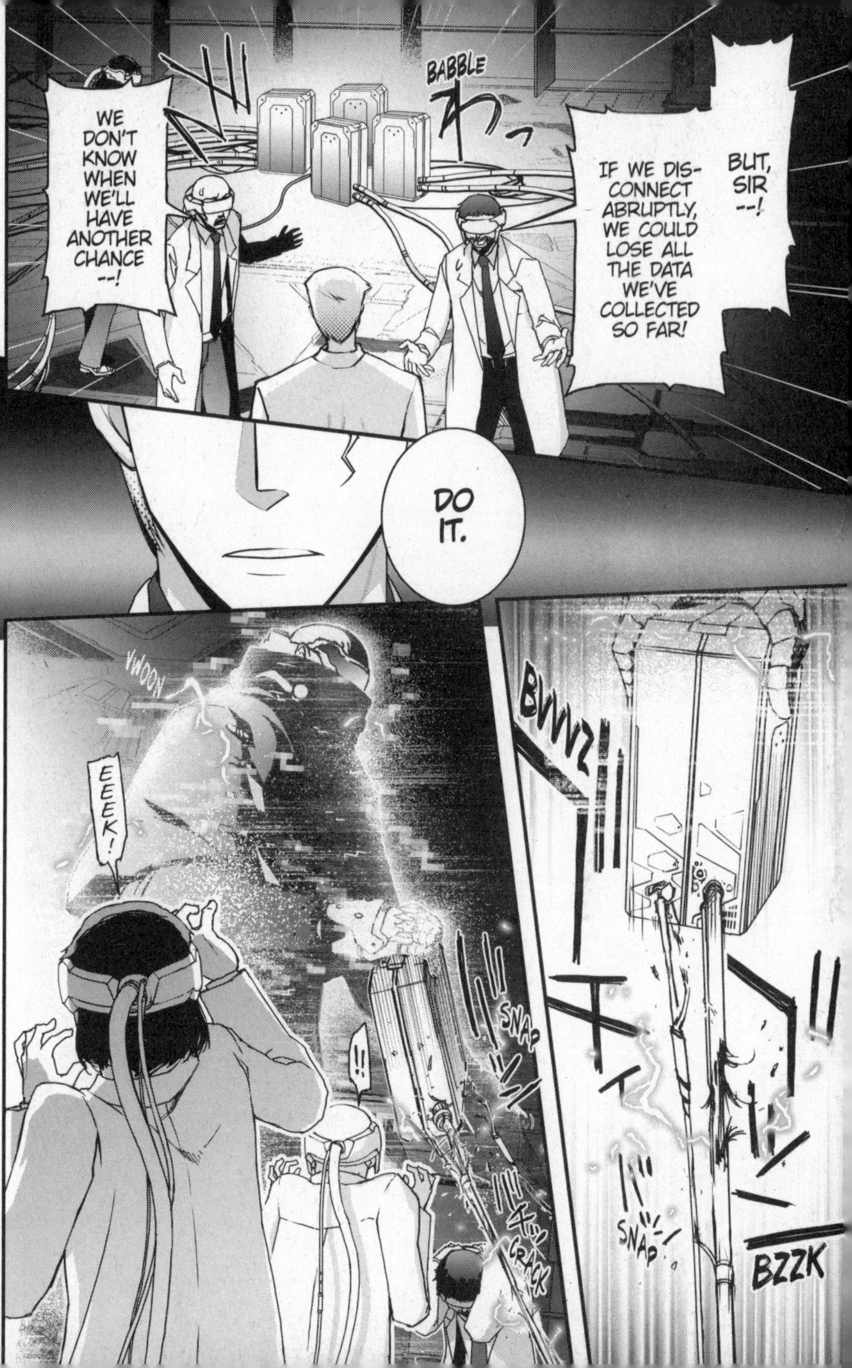
BUT, SIR --!
IF WE DIS-CONNECT ABRUPTLY, WE COULD LOSE ALL THE DATA WE'VE COLLECTED SO FAR!
BABBLE
WE DON'T KNOW WHEN WE'LL HAVE ANOTHER CHANCE --!
DO IT.
BVVVZ
SNAP
BZZK
VWOON
EEEK!
SNAP
!!
CRACK

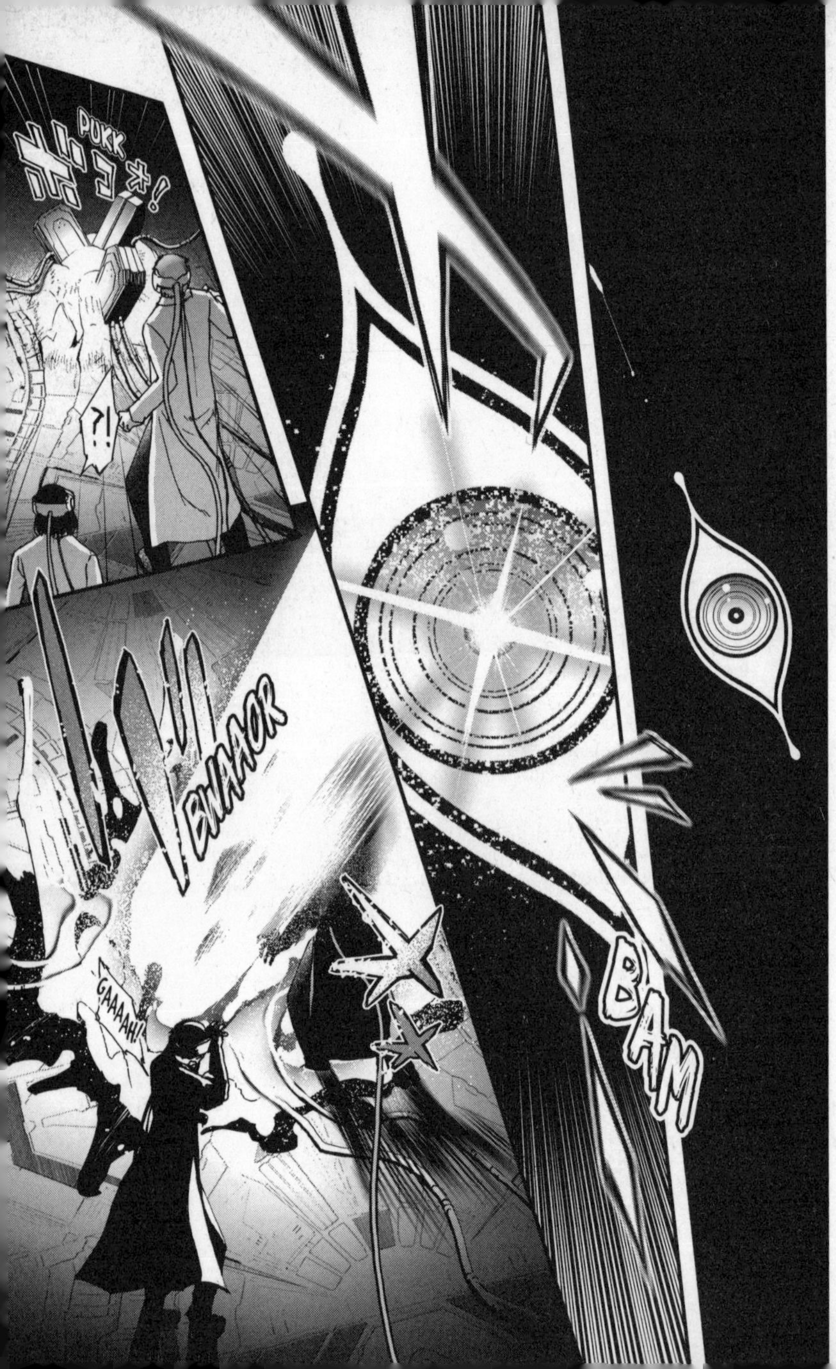
BAM
PUKK
?!
BWAAOR
GAAAAH!

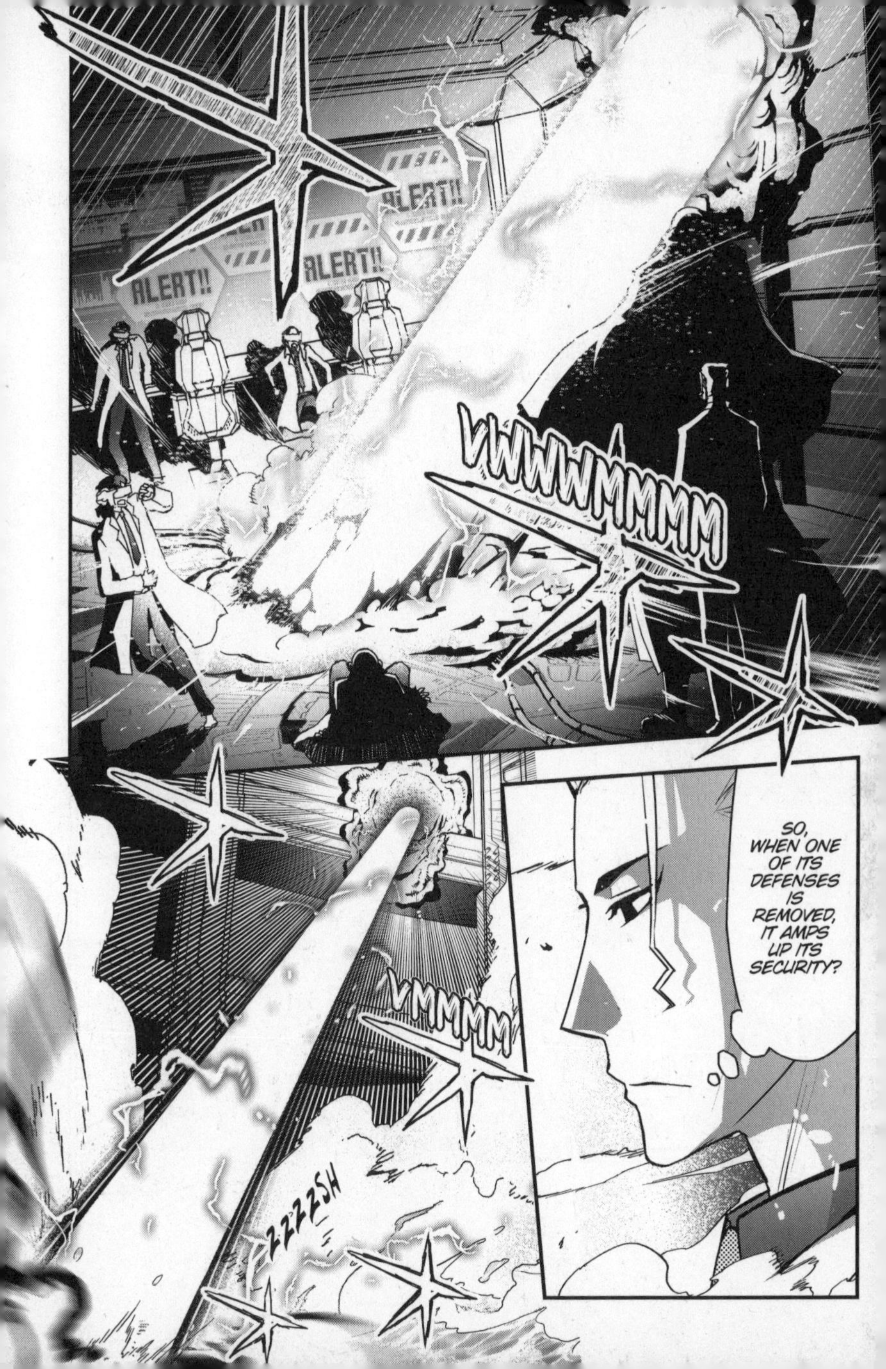
ALERT!!
ALERT!!
ALERT!!
VWWWMMMM
SO, WHEN ONE OF ITS DEFENSES IS REMOVED, IT AMPS UP ITS SECURITY?
VMMMM
ZZZZSH

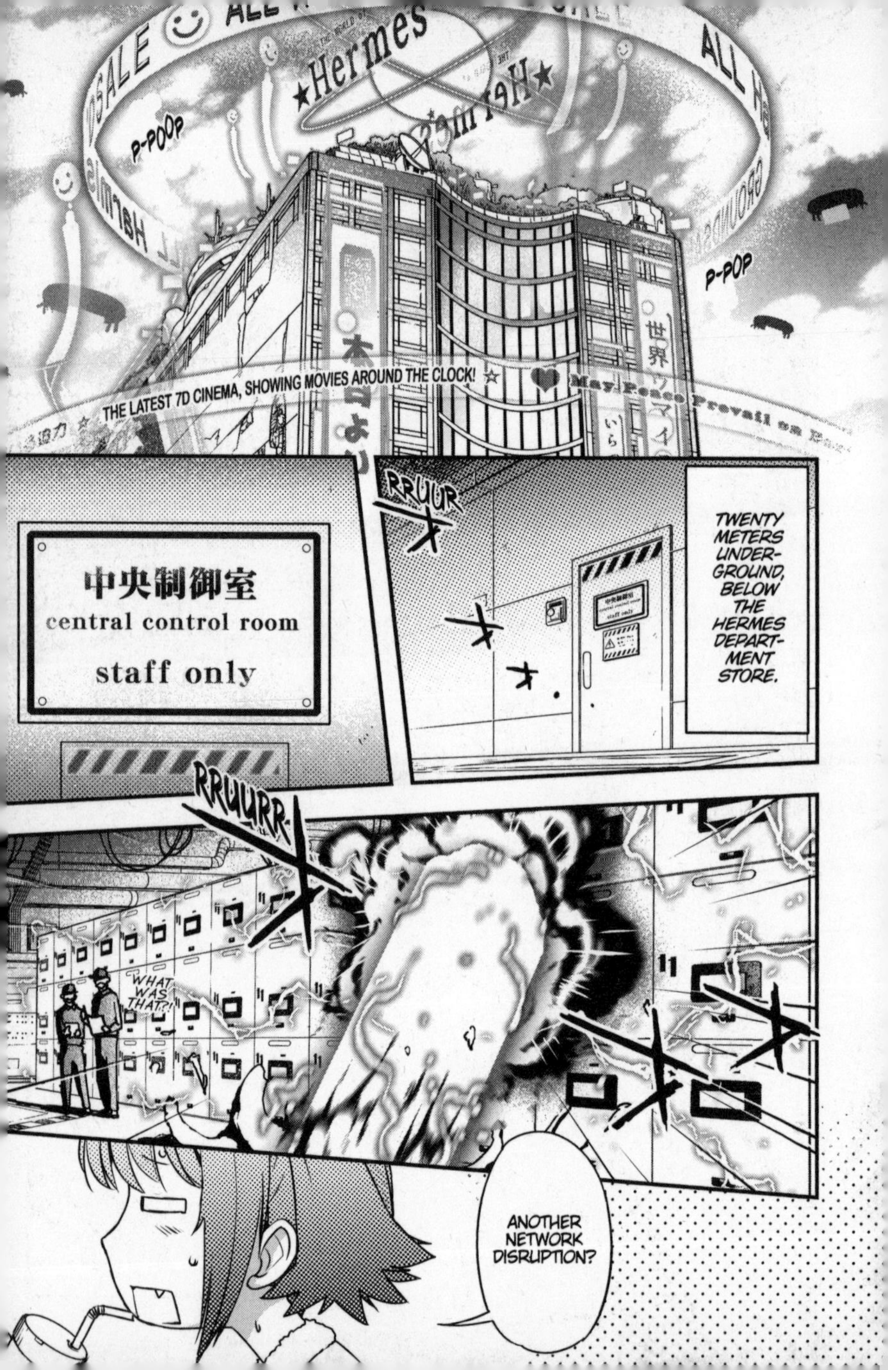
★Hermes★
P-POP
P-POOP
THE LATEST 7D CINEMA, SHOWING MOVIES AROUND THE CLOCK! ☆
RRUUR
TWENTY METERS UNDERGROUND, BELOW THE HERMES DEPARTMENT STORE.
中央制御室
central control room
staff only
RRUURR
WHAT WAS THAT?!
ANOTHER NETWORK DISRUPTION?

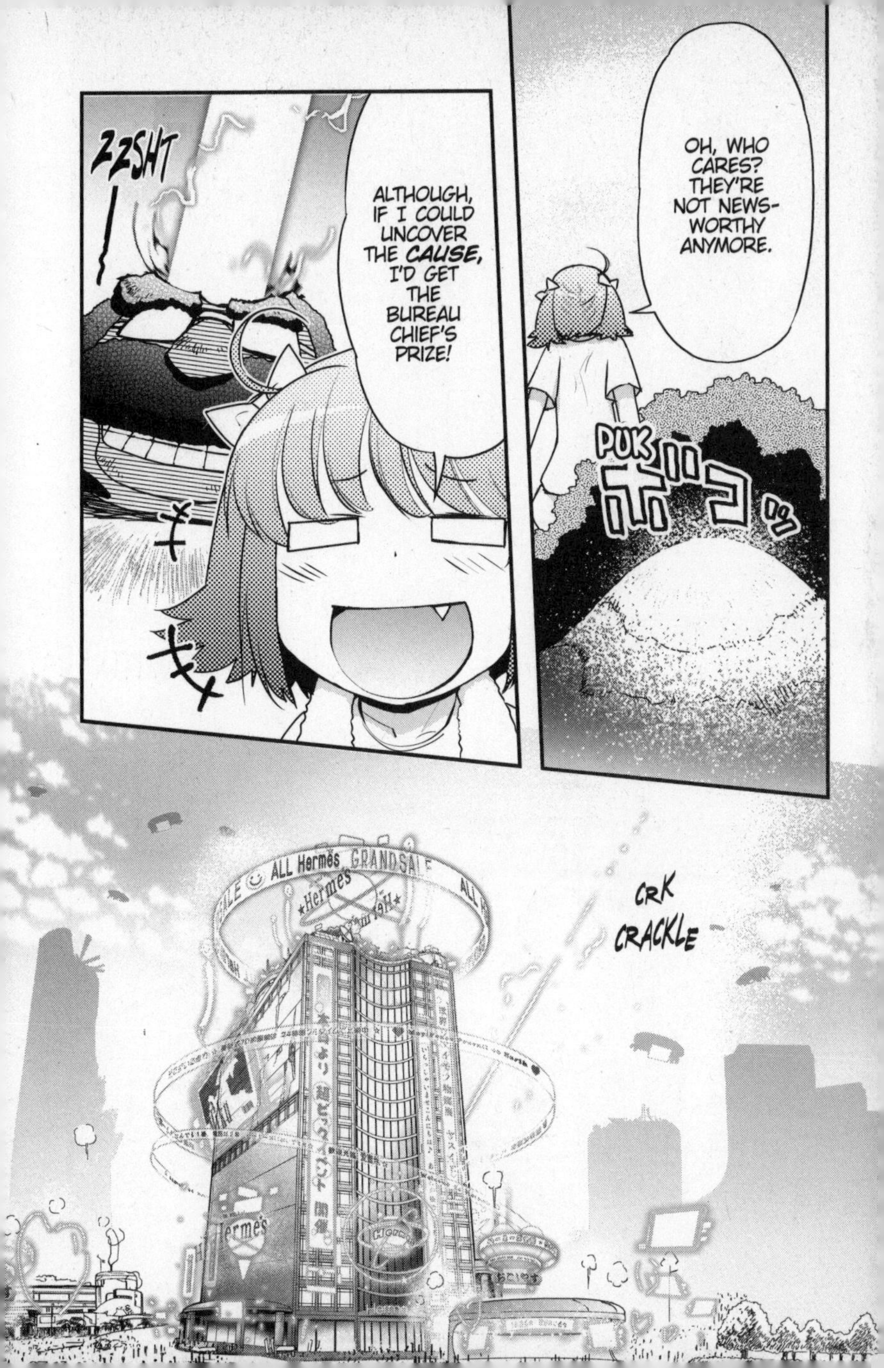
OH, WHO CARES? THEY'RE NOT NEWS-WORTHY ANYMORE.
PUK
ZZSHT
ALTHOUGH, IF I COULD UNCOVER THE *CAUSE,* I'D GET THE BUREAU CHIEF'S PRIZE!
CRK
CRACKLE

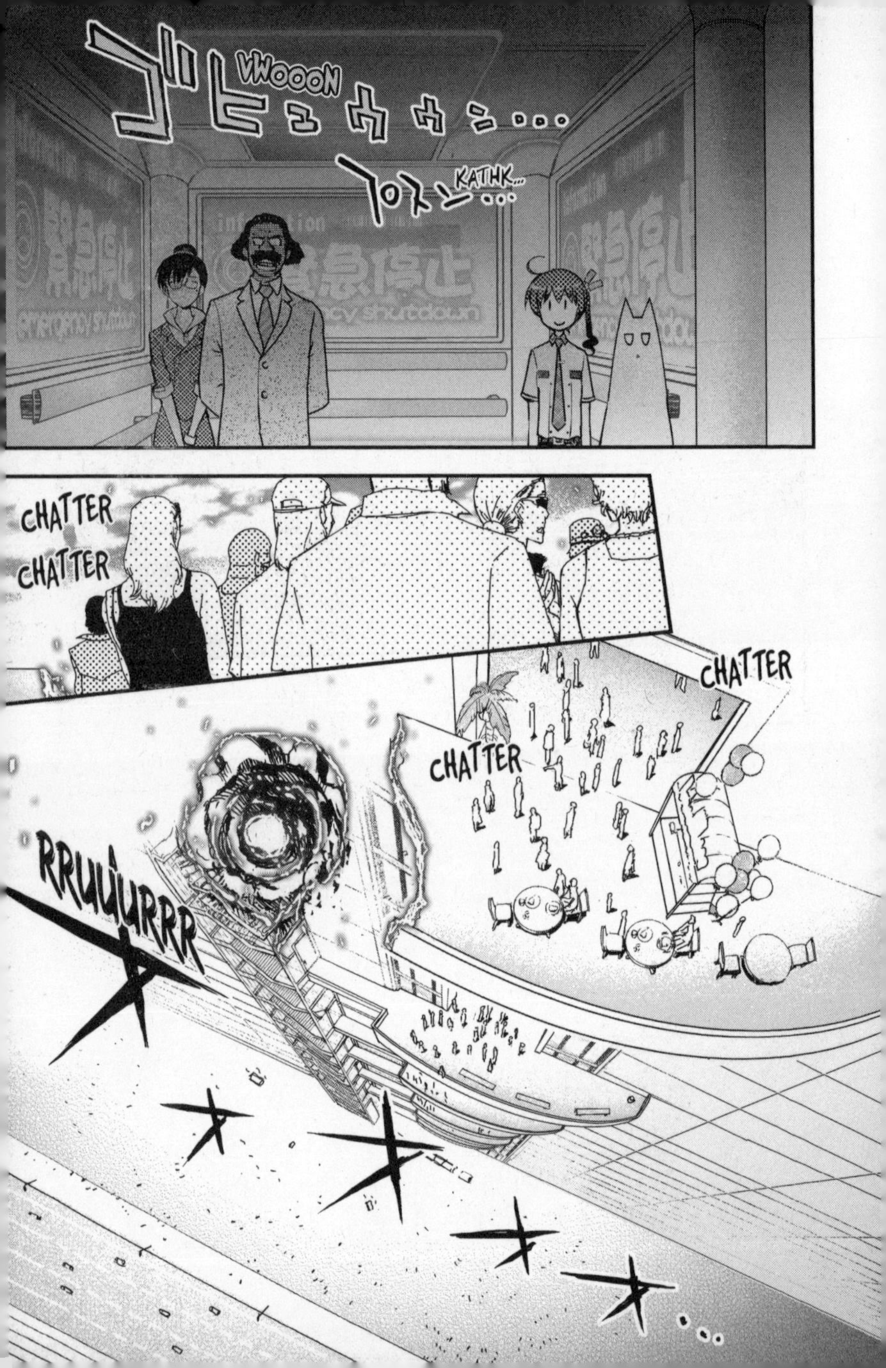
VWOOON
KATHK...
CHATTER
CHATTER
CHATTER
CHATTER
RRUUURRR
...

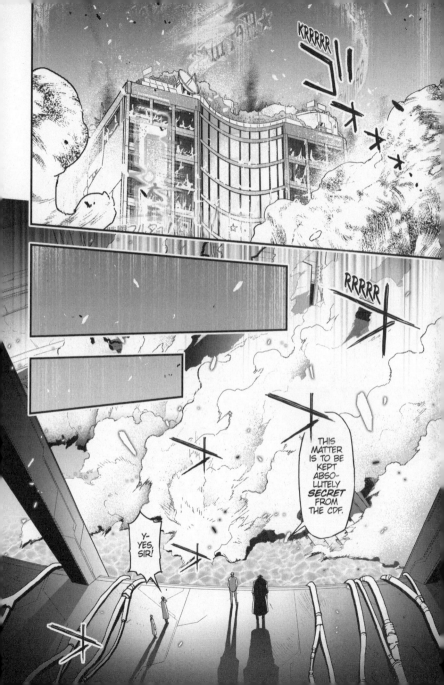

KRRRRR

RRRRR

THIS MATTER IS TO BE ABSO- LUTELY **SECRET** FROM THE CDF.

Y- YES, SIR!

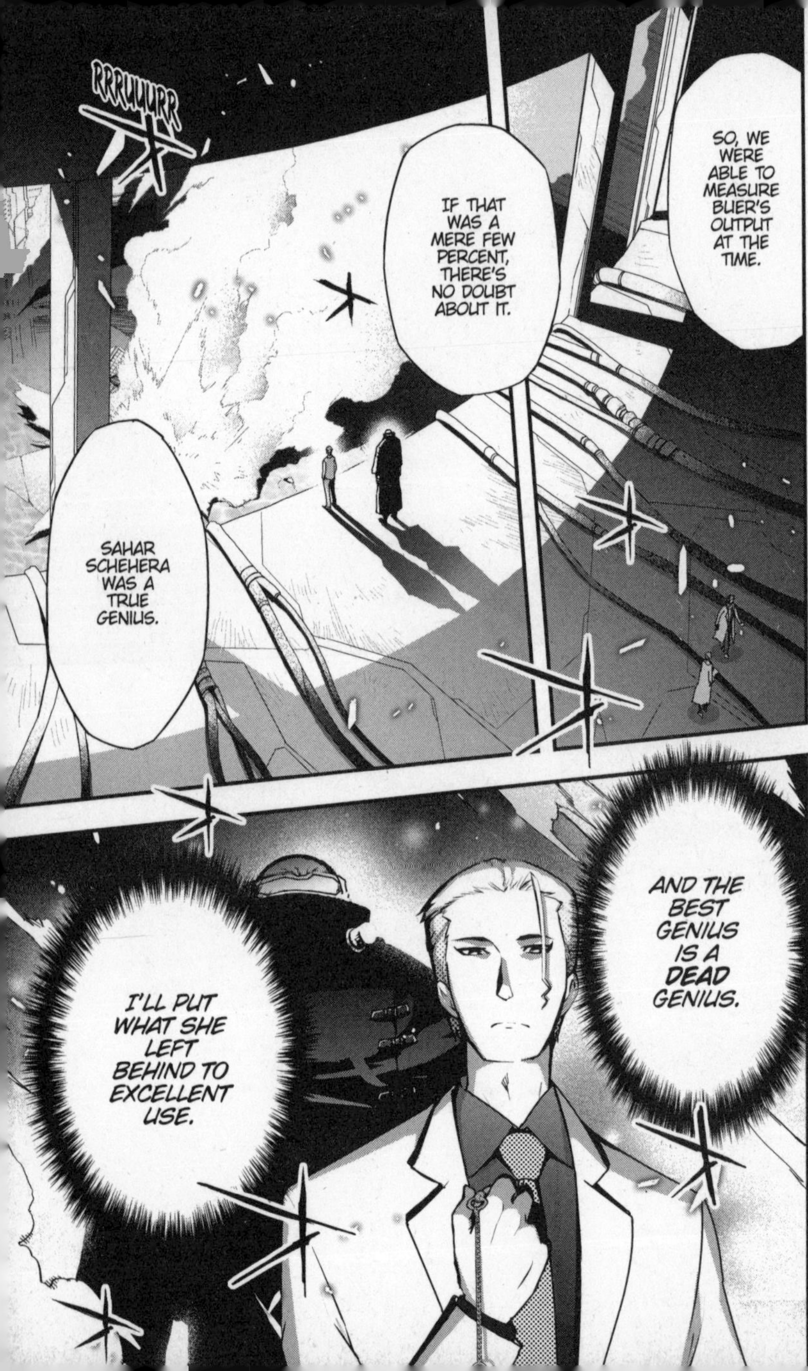
SO, WE WERE ABLE TO MEASURE BUER'S OUTPUT AT THE TIME.
IF THAT WAS A MERE FEW PERCENT, THERE'S NO DOUBT ABOUT IT.
RRRUUUURR
SAHAR SCHEHERA WAS A TRUE GENIUS.
AND THE BEST GENIUS IS A DEAD GENIUS.
I'LL PUT WHAT SHE LEFT BEHIND TO EXCELLENT USE.

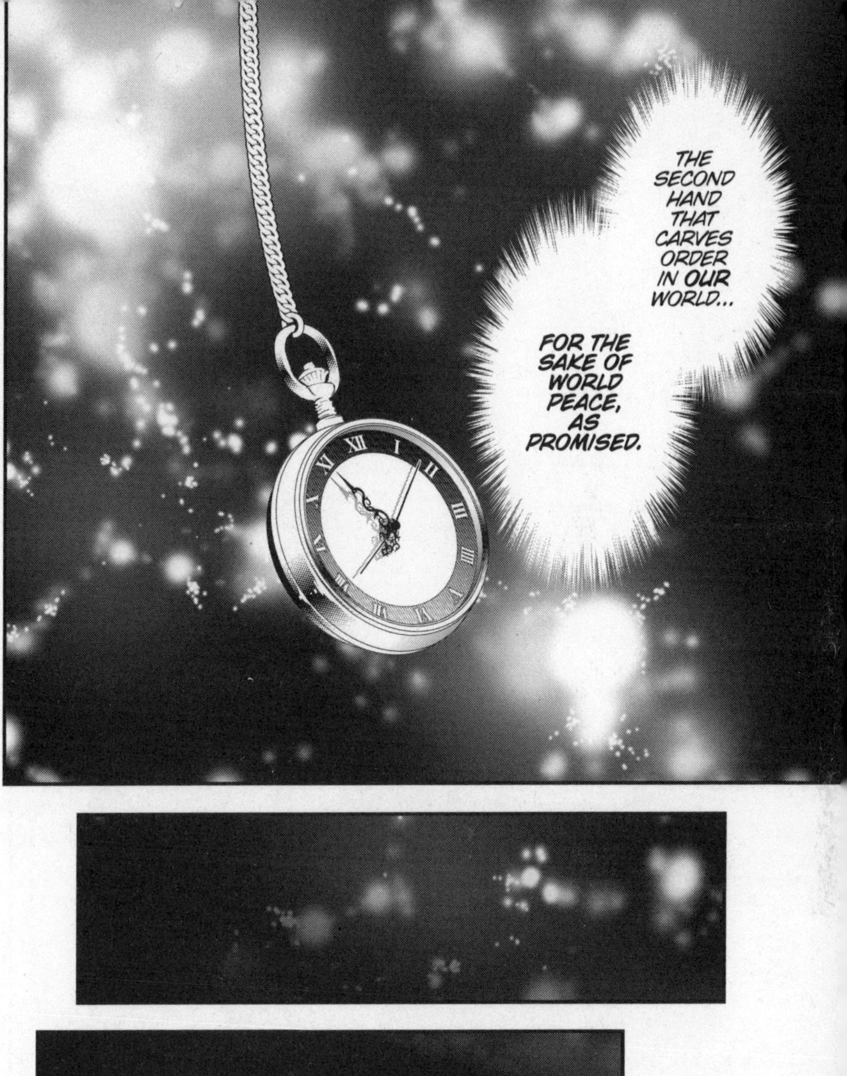
THE SECOND HAND THAT CARVES ORDER IN **OUR** WORLD...
FOR THE SAKE OF WORLD PEACE, AS PROMISED.

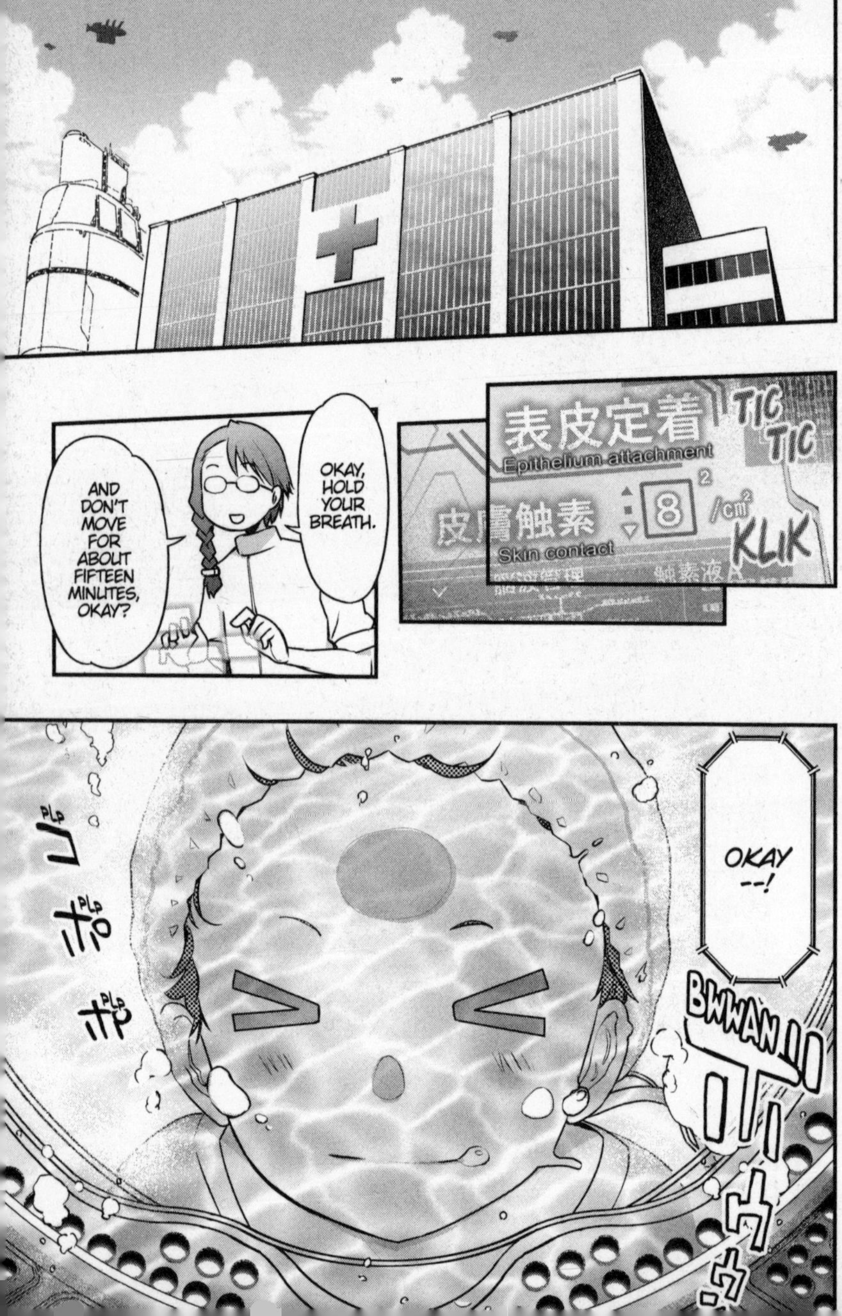
表皮定着
Epithelium attachment
TIC TIC
皮膚触素
Skin contact
8 /cm2
KLIK
OKAY, HOLD YOUR BREATH.
AND DON'T MOVE FOR ABOUT FIFTEEN MINUTES, OKAY?
OKAY --!
BWWAN!!
PLP
PLP
PLP

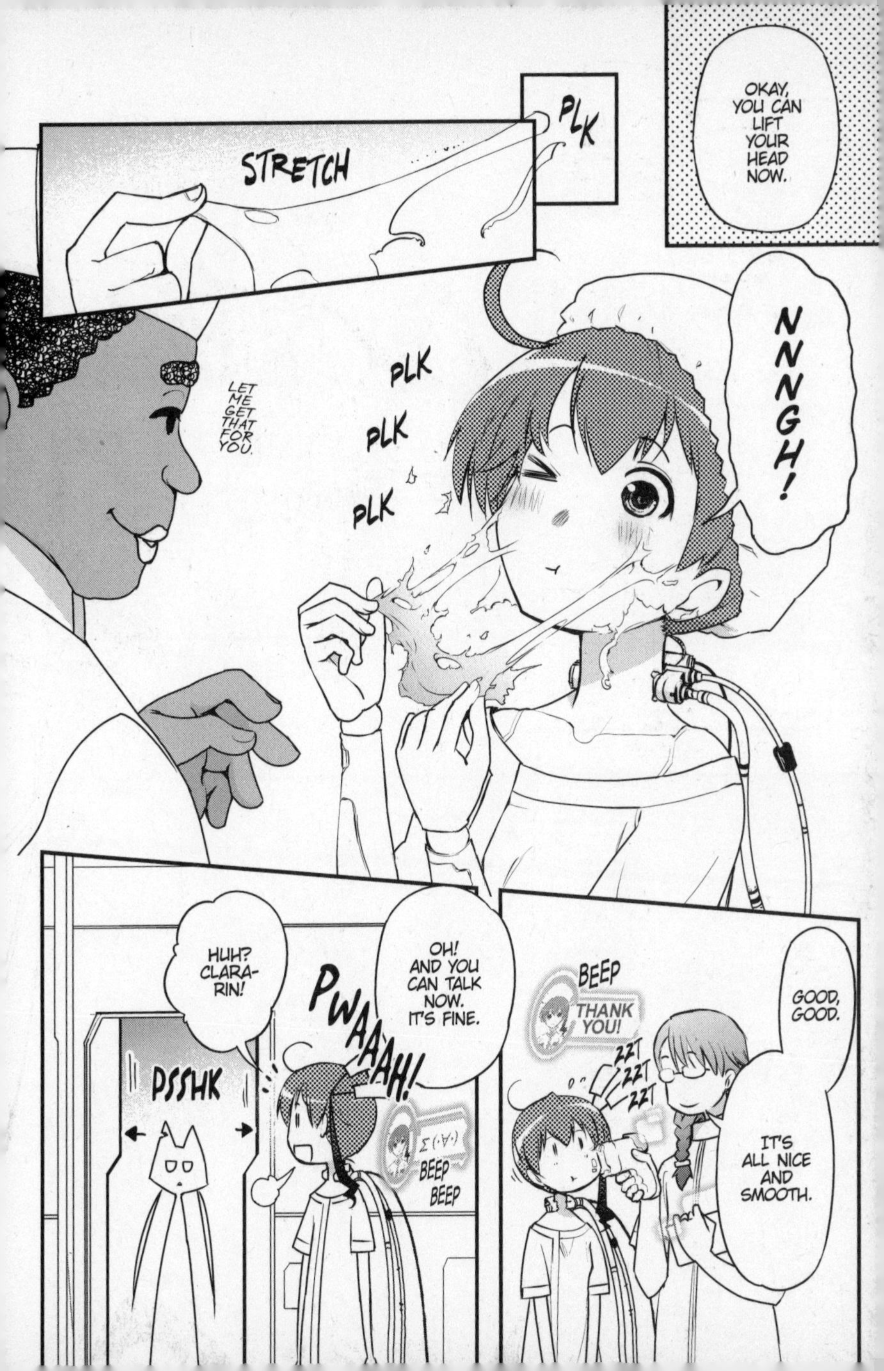
OKAY, YOU CAN LIFT YOUR HEAD NOW.
PLK
STRETCH
NNNGH!
PLK
PLK
PLK
LET ME GET THAT FOR YOU.
GOOD, GOOD.
IT'S ALL NICE AND SMOOTH.
BEEP
THANK YOU!
ZZT
ZZT
ZZT
OH! AND YOU CAN TALK NOW. IT'S FINE.
PWAAAAH!
BEEP BEEP
HUH? CLARA-RIN!
PSSHK

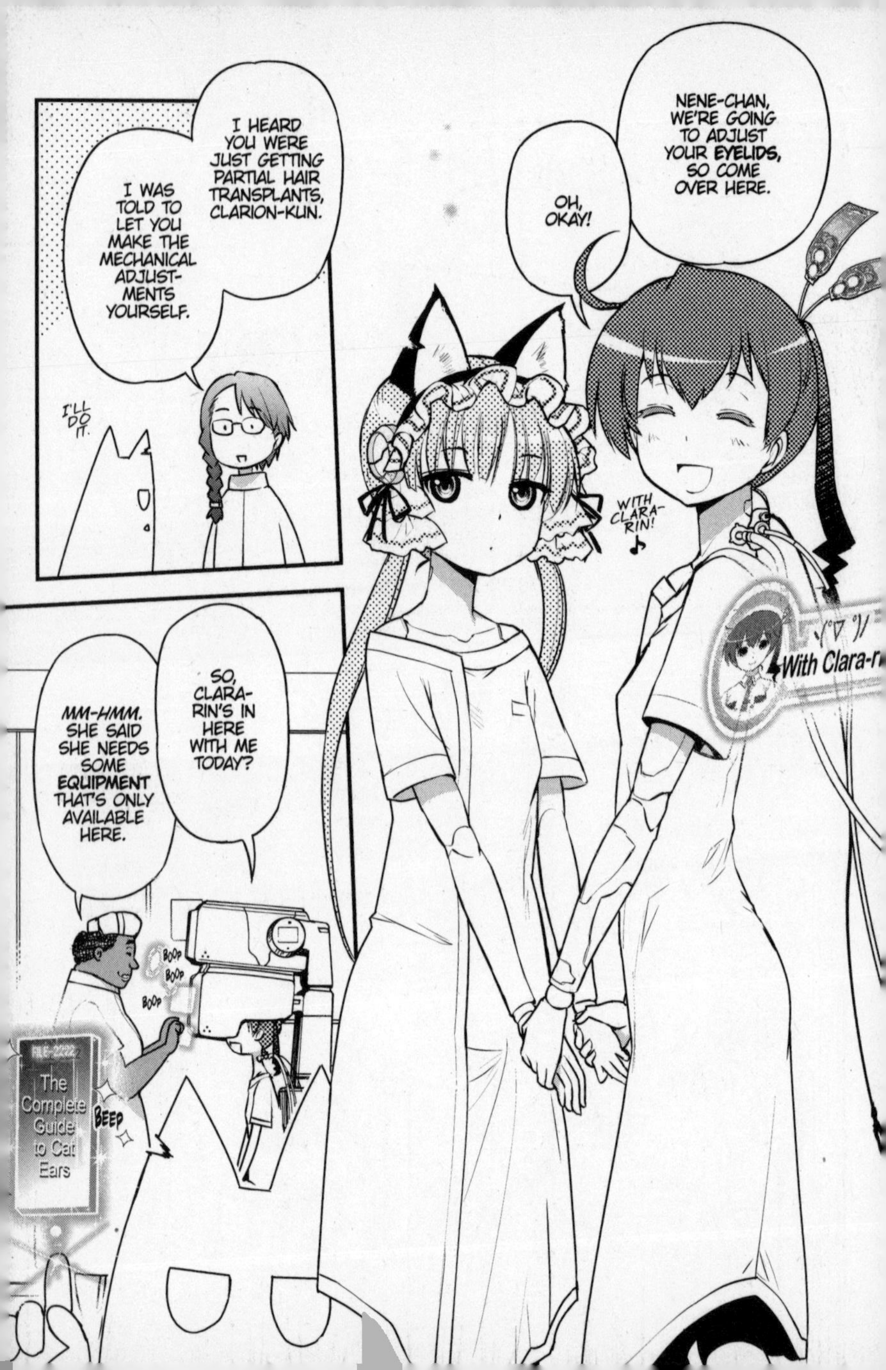
NENE-CHAN, WE'RE GOING TO ADJUST YOUR EYELIDS, SO COME OVER HERE.
OH, OKAY!
WITH CLARA-RIN! ♪
With Clara-r
I HEARD YOU WERE JUST GETTING PARTIAL HAIR TRANSPLANTS, CLARION-KUN.
I WAS TOLD TO LET YOU MAKE THE MECHANICAL ADJUST-MENTS YOURSELF.
I'LL DO IT.
SO, CLARA-RIN'S IN HERE WITH ME TODAY?
MM-HMM. SHE SAID SHE NEEDS SOME EQUIPMENT THAT'S ONLY AVAILABLE HERE.
BOOP
BOOP
BOOP
BEEP
FILE-2222
The Complete Guide to Cat Ears

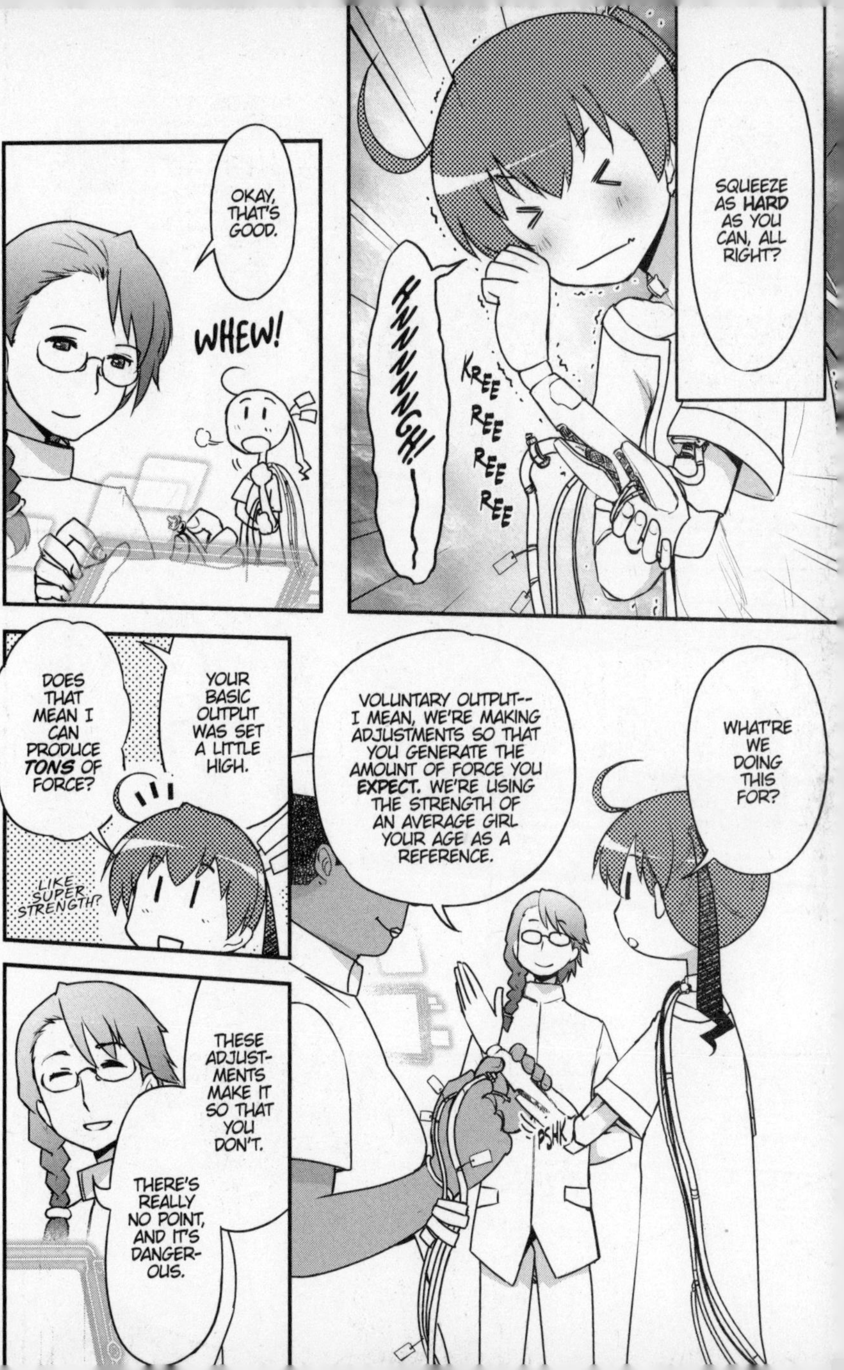
SQUEEZE AS HARD AS YOU CAN, ALL RIGHT?
HNNNNNGH!--
KREE REE REE REE
OKAY, THAT'S GOOD.
WHEW!
WHAT'RE WE DOING THIS FOR?
VOLUNTARY OUTPUT-- I MEAN, WE'RE MAKING ADJUSTMENTS SO THAT YOU GENERATE THE AMOUNT OF FORCE YOU EXPECT. WE'RE USING THE STRENGTH OF AN AVERAGE GIRL YOUR AGE AS A REFERENCE.
PSHK
YOUR BASIC OUTPUT WAS SET A LITTLE HIGH.
DOES THAT MEAN I CAN PRODUCE TONS OF FORCE?
LIKE SUPER STRENGTH?
THESE ADJUSTMENTS MAKE IT SO THAT YOU DON'T.
THERE'S REALLY NO POINT, AND IT'S DANGEROUS.

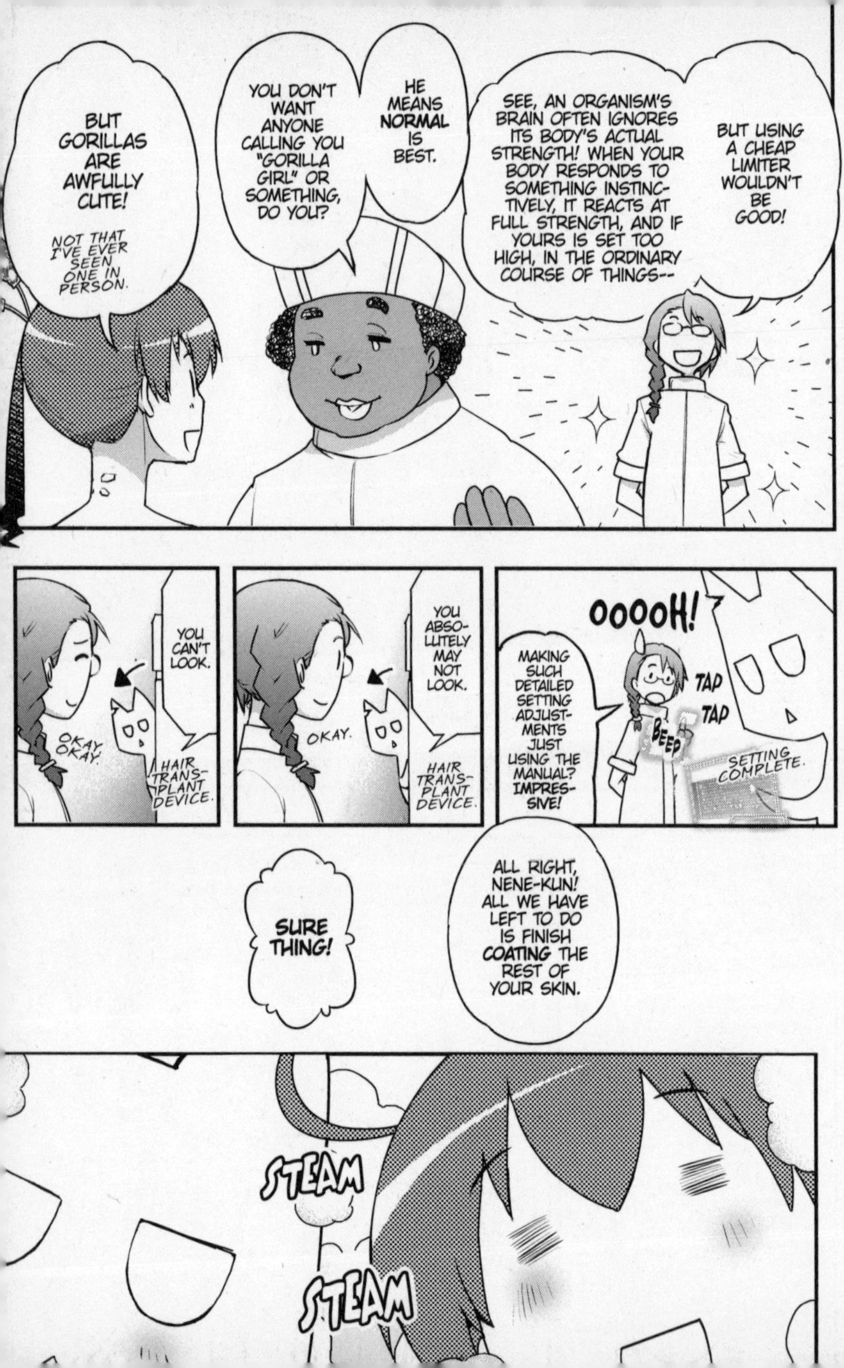
BUT USING A CHEAP LIMITER WOULDN'T BE GOOD!
SEE, AN ORGANISM'S BRAIN OFTEN IGNORES ITS BODY'S ACTUAL STRENGTH! WHEN YOUR BODY RESPONDS TO SOMETHING INSTINCTIVELY, IT REACTS AT FULL STRENGTH, AND IF YOURS IS SET TOO HIGH, IN THE ORDINARY COURSE OF THINGS--
HE MEANS NORMAL IS BEST.
YOU DON'T WANT ANYONE CALLING YOU "GORILLA GIRL" OR SOMETHING, DO YOU?
BUT GORILLAS ARE AWFULLY CUTE!
NOT THAT I'VE EVER SEEN ONE IN PERSON.
OOOOH!
MAKING SUCH DETAILED SETTING ADJUSTMENTS JUST USING THE MANUAL? IMPRESSIVE!
TAP TAP
BEEP
SETTING COMPLETE.
YOU ABSOLUTELY MAY NOT LOOK.
OKAY.
HAIR TRANSPLANT DEVICE.
YOU CAN'T LOOK.
OKAY OKAY.
HAIR TRANSPLANT DEVICE.
ALL RIGHT, NENE-KUN! ALL WE HAVE LEFT TO DO IS FINISH COATING THE REST OF YOUR SKIN.
SURE THING!
STEAM
STEAM

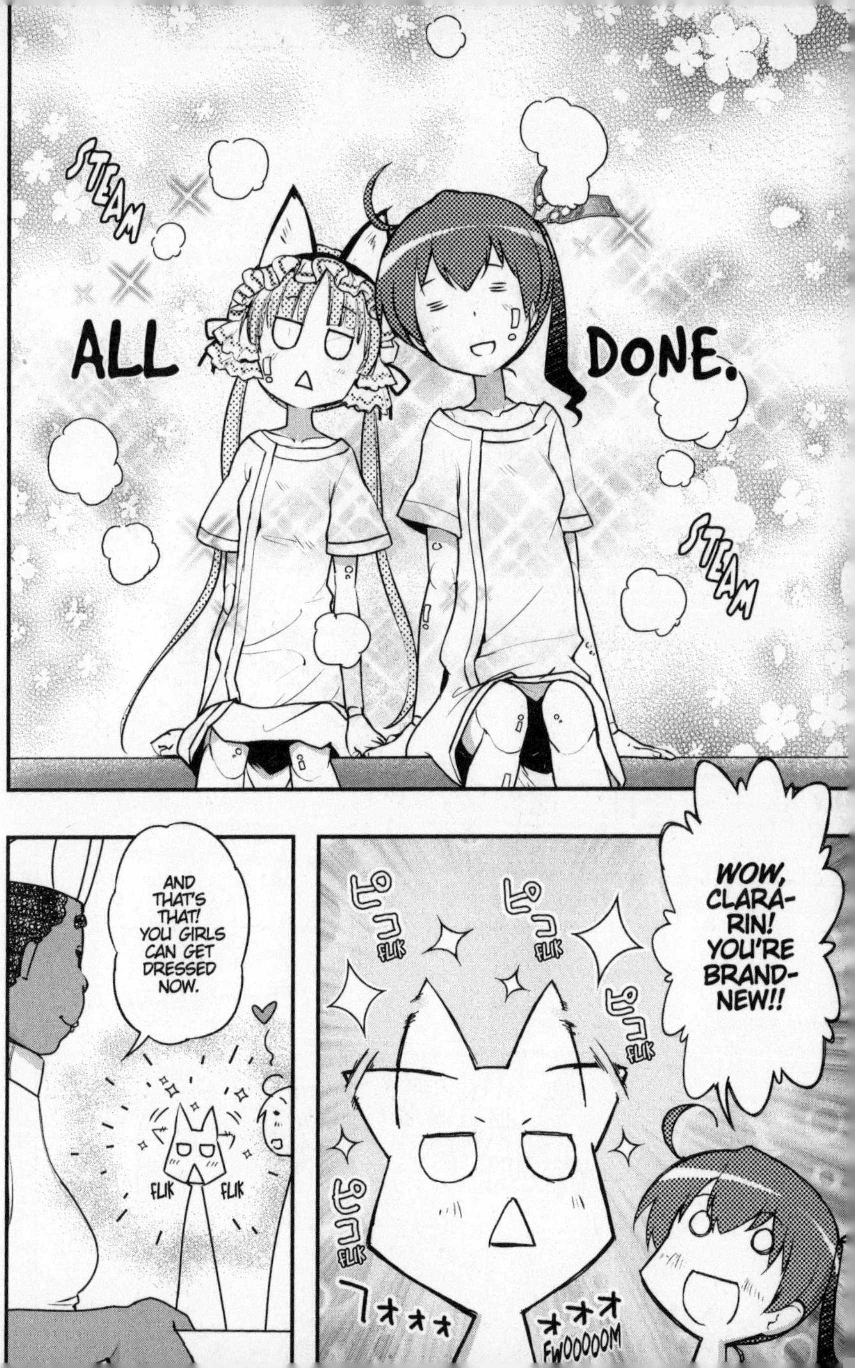
STEAM
STEAM
ALL DONE.
WOW, CLARA-RIN! YOU'RE BRAND-NEW!!
ピコ FLIK
ピコ FLIK
ピコ FLIK
ピコ FLIK
フォォォォォ FWOOOOOM
AND THAT'S THAT! YOU GIRLS CAN GET DRESSED NOW.
FLIK FLIK

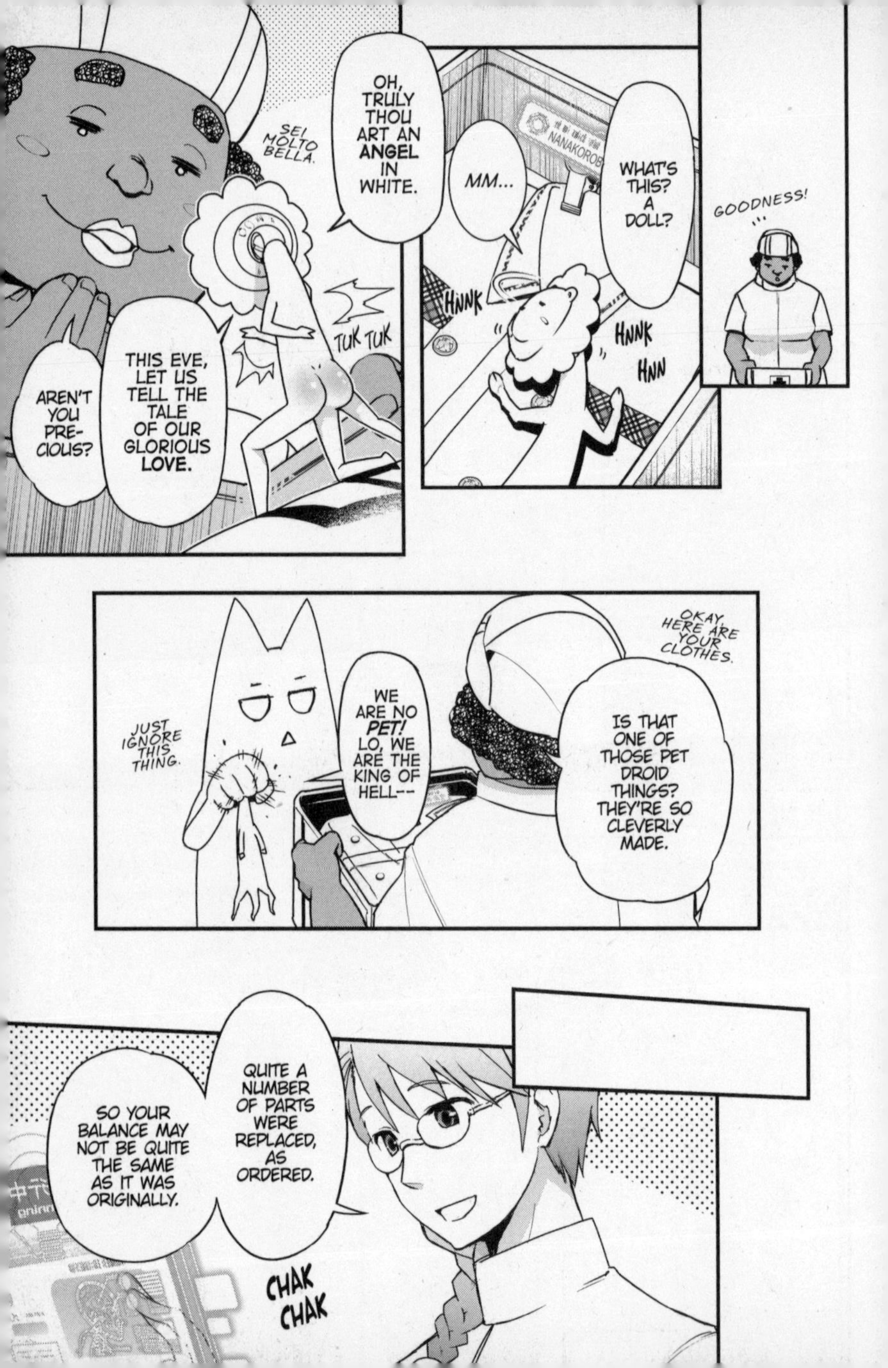
GOODNESS!
...
WHAT'S THIS? A DOLL?
MM...
HNNK
HNNK
HNN
OH, TRULY THOU ART AN ANGEL IN WHITE.
SEI MOLTO BELLA.
TUK TUK
THIS EVE, LET US TELL THE TALE OF OUR GLORIOUS LOVE.
AREN'T YOU PRE-CIOUS?
OKAY, HERE ARE YOUR CLOTHES.
IS THAT ONE OF THOSE PET DROID THINGS? THEY'RE SO CLEVERLY MADE.
WE ARE NO PET! LO, WE ARE THE KING OF HELL--
JUST IGNORE THIS THING.
QUITE A NUMBER OF PARTS WERE REPLACED, AS ORDERED.
SO YOUR BALANCE MAY NOT BE QUITE THE SAME AS IT WAS ORIGINALLY.
CHAK CHAK

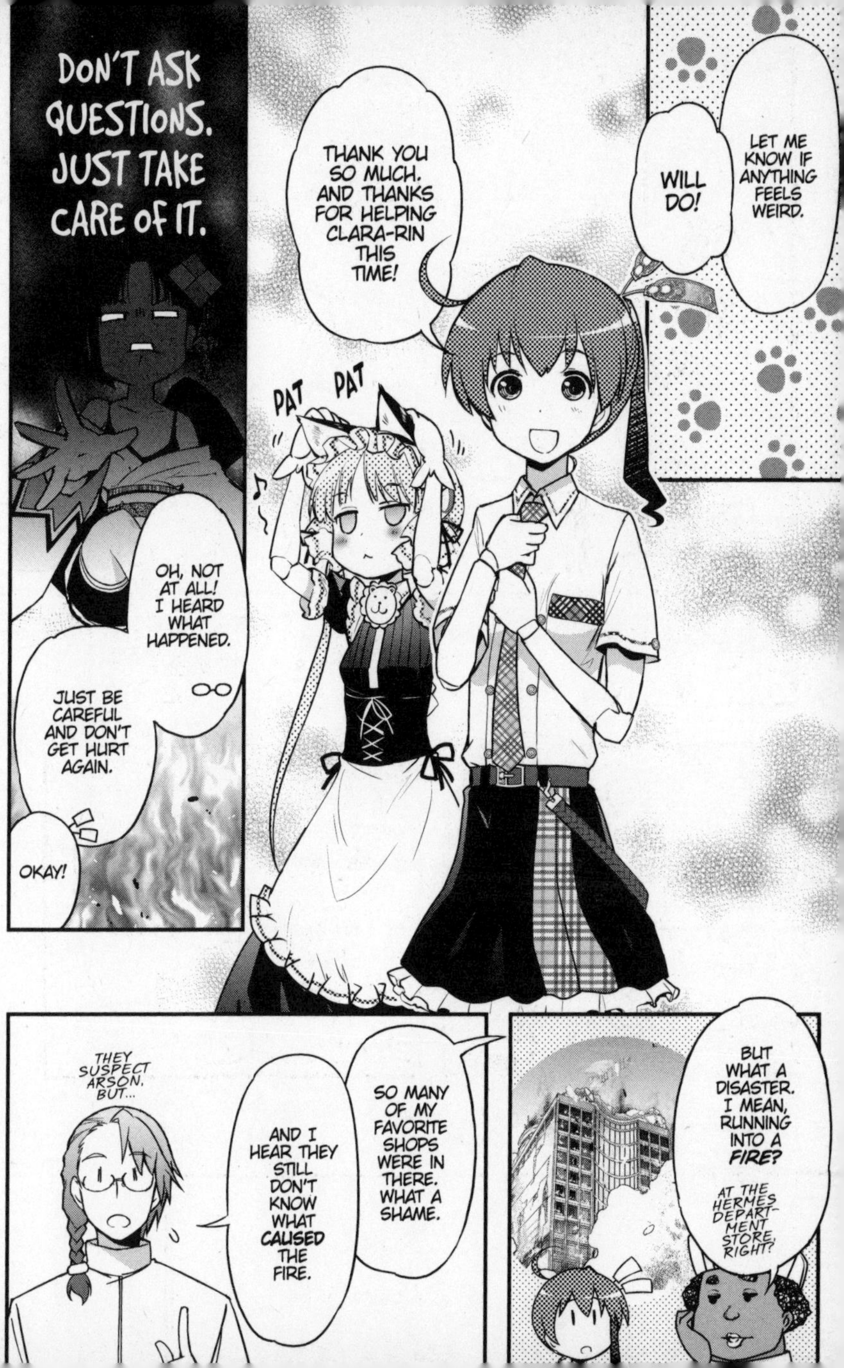
LET ME KNOW IF ANYTHING FEELS WEIRD.
WILL DO!
THANK YOU SO MUCH. AND THANKS FOR HELPING CLARA-RIN THIS TIME!
PAT PAT
DON'T ASK QUESTIONS. JUST TAKE CARE OF IT.
OH, NOT AT ALL! I HEARD WHAT HAPPENED.
JUST BE CAREFUL AND DON'T GET HURT AGAIN.
OKAY!
BUT WHAT A DISASTER. I MEAN, RUNNING INTO A *FIRE?*
AT THE HERMES DEPARTMENT STORE, RIGHT?
SO MANY OF MY FAVORITE SHOPS WERE IN THERE. WHAT A SHAME.
AND I HEAR THEY STILL DON'T KNOW WHAT **CAUSED** THE FIRE.
THEY SUSPECT ARSON, BUT...

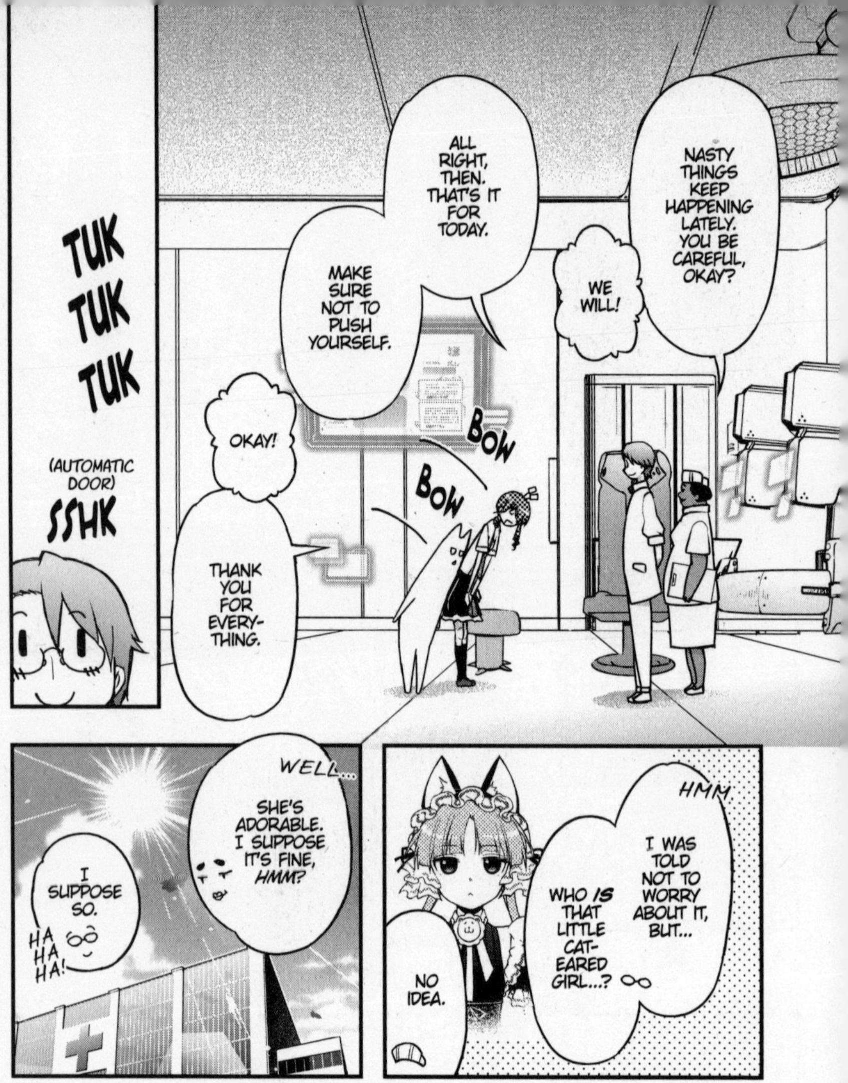
NASTY THINGS KEEP HAPPENING LATELY. YOU BE CAREFUL, OKAY?
WE WILL!
ALL RIGHT, THEN. THAT'S IT FOR TODAY.
MAKE SURE NOT TO PUSH YOURSELF.
BOW
BOW
OKAY!
THANK YOU FOR EVERYTHING.
TUK TUK TUK
(AUTOMATIC DOOR) SSHK
HMM.
I WAS TOLD NOT TO WORRY ABOUT IT, BUT...
WHO *IS* THAT LITTLE CAT-EARED GIRL...?
NO IDEA.
WELL...
SHE'S ADORABLE. I SUPPOSE IT'S FINE, *HMM?*
I SUPPOSE SO.
HA HA HA!

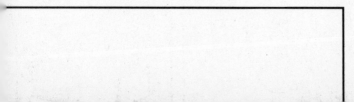

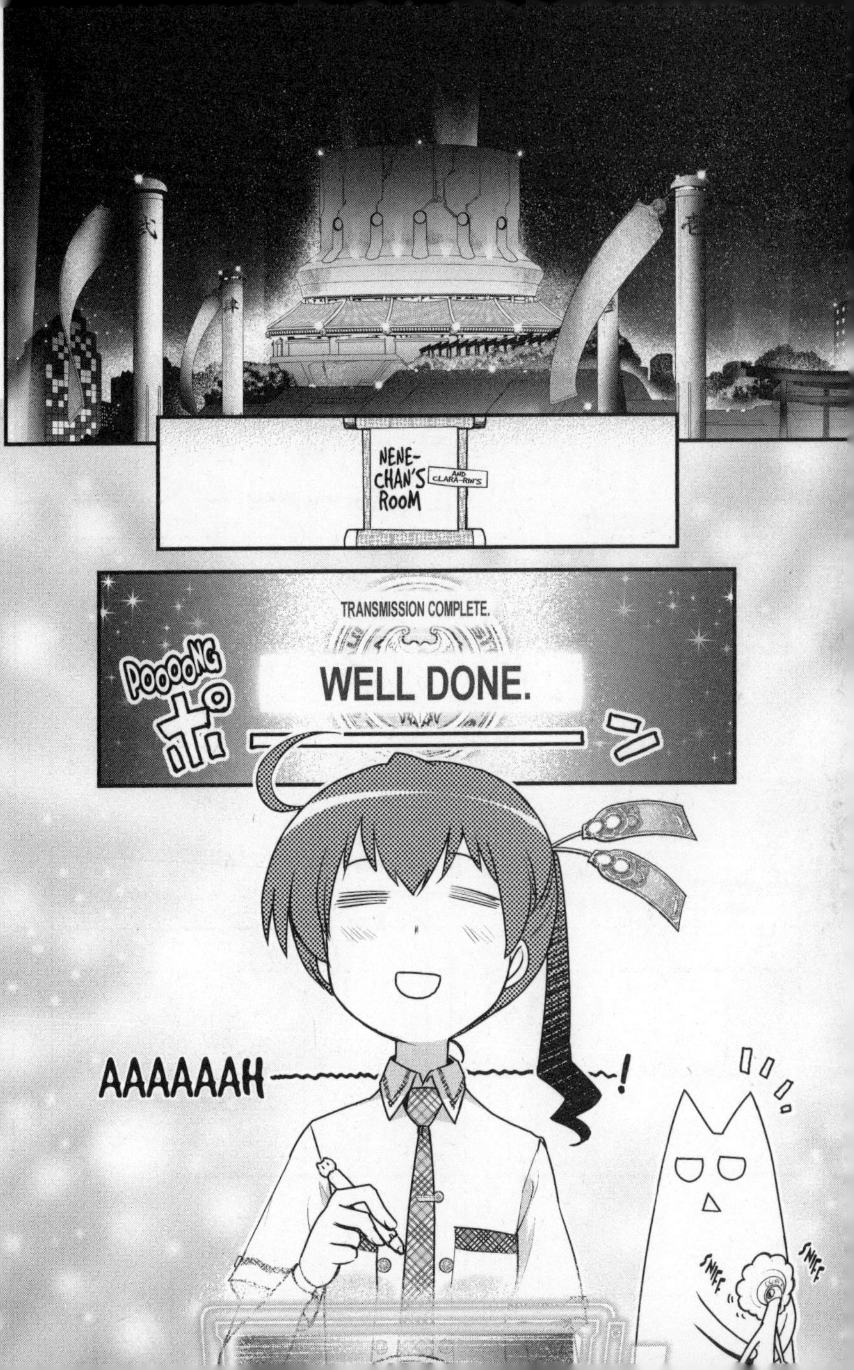
NENE-CHAN'S AND CLARA-RIN'S ROOM
TRANSMISSION COMPLETE.
WELL DONE.
POOOONG
AAAAAAH—!
SNIFF
SNIFF

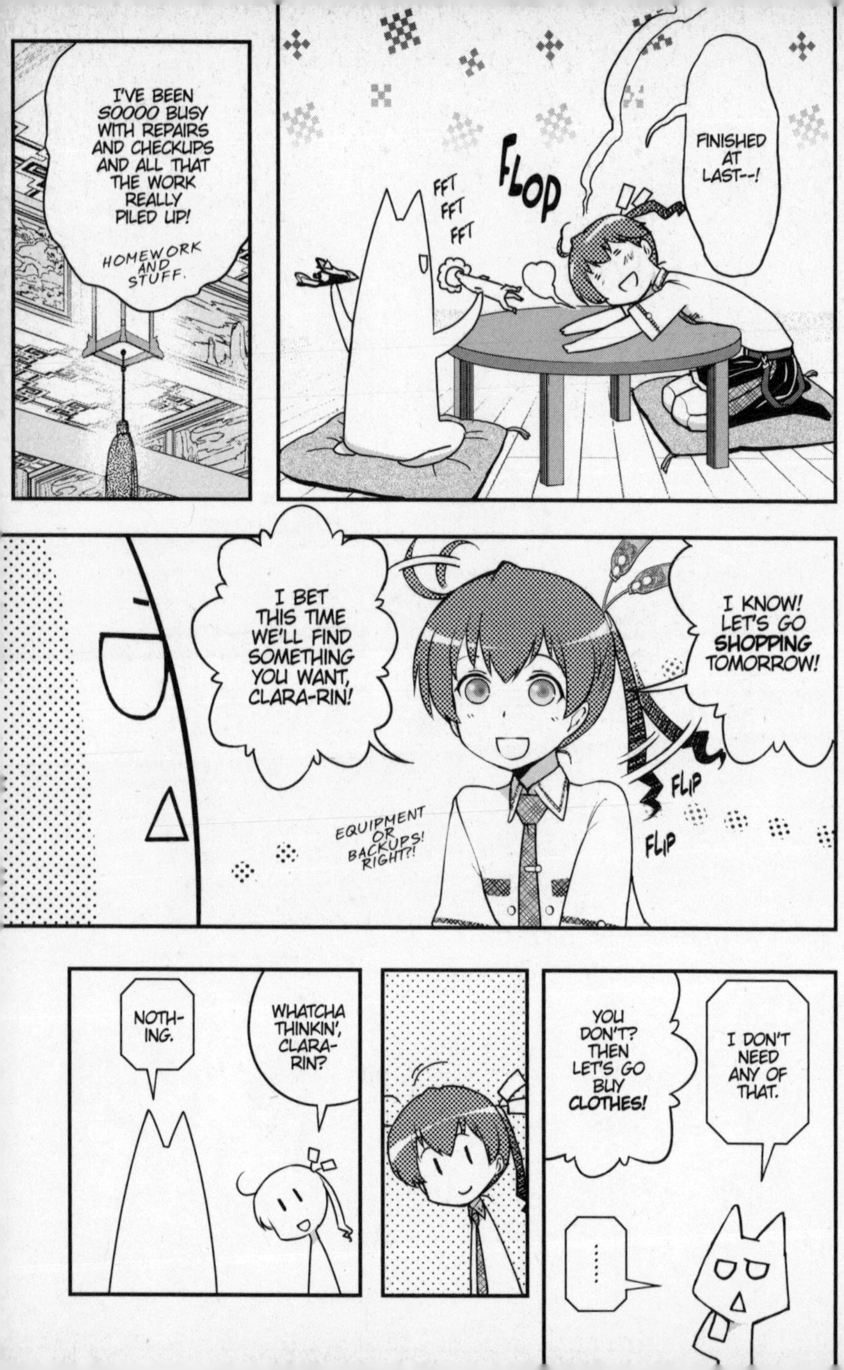
FINISHED AT LAST--!
FLOP
FFT FFT FFT
I'VE BEEN SOOOO BUSY WITH REPAIRS AND CHECKUPS AND ALL THAT THE WORK REALLY PILED UP!
HOMEWORK AND STUFF.
I KNOW! LET'S GO SHOPPING TOMORROW!
FLIP
FLIP
I BET THIS TIME WE'LL FIND SOMETHING YOU WANT, CLARA-RIN!
EQUIPMENT OR BACKUPS! RIGHT?!
I DON'T NEED ANY OF THAT.
YOU DON'T? THEN LET'S GO BUY CLOTHES!
......
WHATCHA THINKIN', CLARA-RIN?
NOTH-ING.

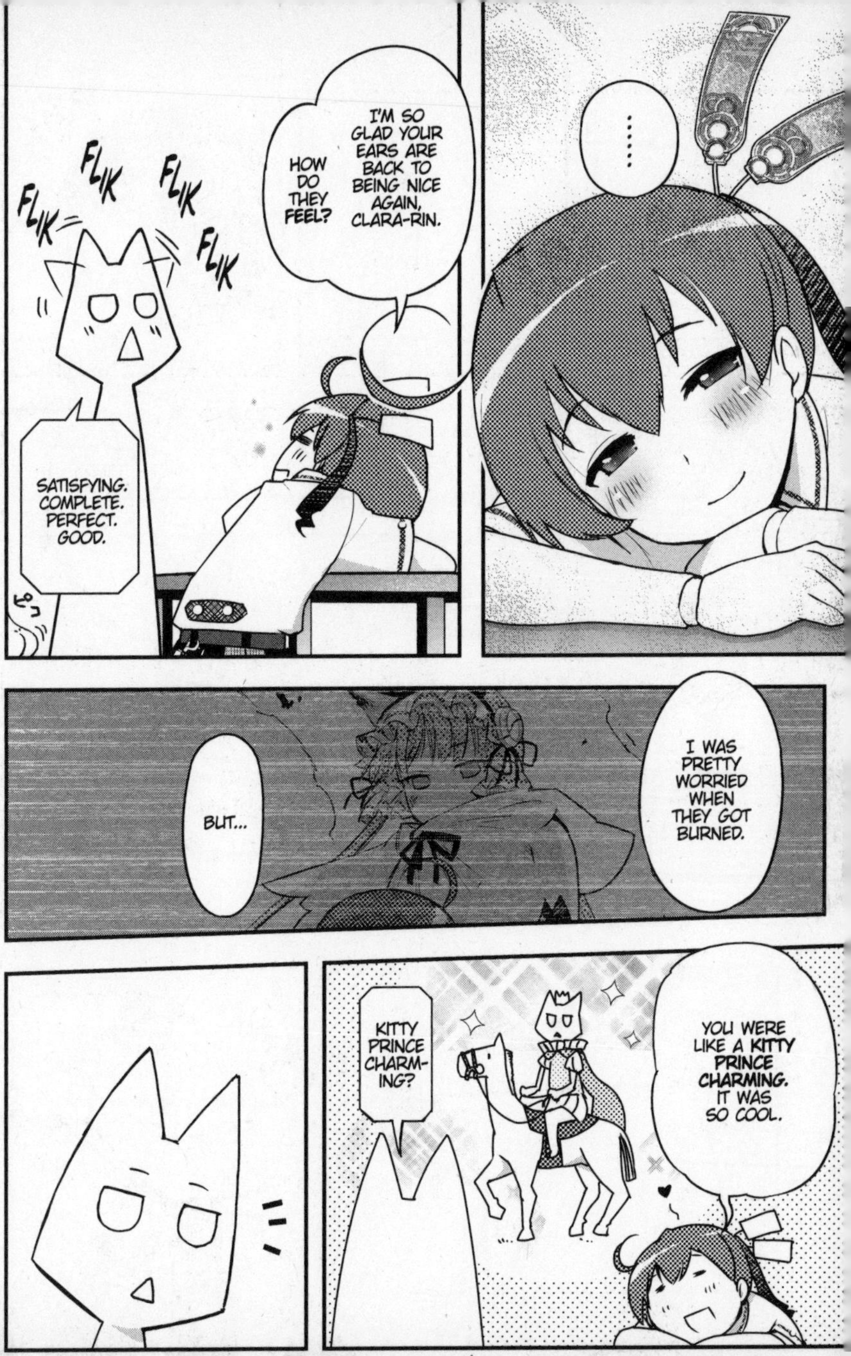
......
I'M SO GLAD YOUR EARS ARE BACK TO BEING NICE AGAIN, CLARA-RIN.
HOW DO THEY FEEL?
FLIK
FLIK
FLIK
FLIK
SATISFYING. COMPLETE. PERFECT. GOOD.
I WAS PRETTY WORRIED WHEN THEY GOT BURNED.
BUT...
YOU WERE LIKE A **KITTY PRINCE CHARMING.** IT WAS SO COOL.
KITTY PRINCE CHARM-ING?

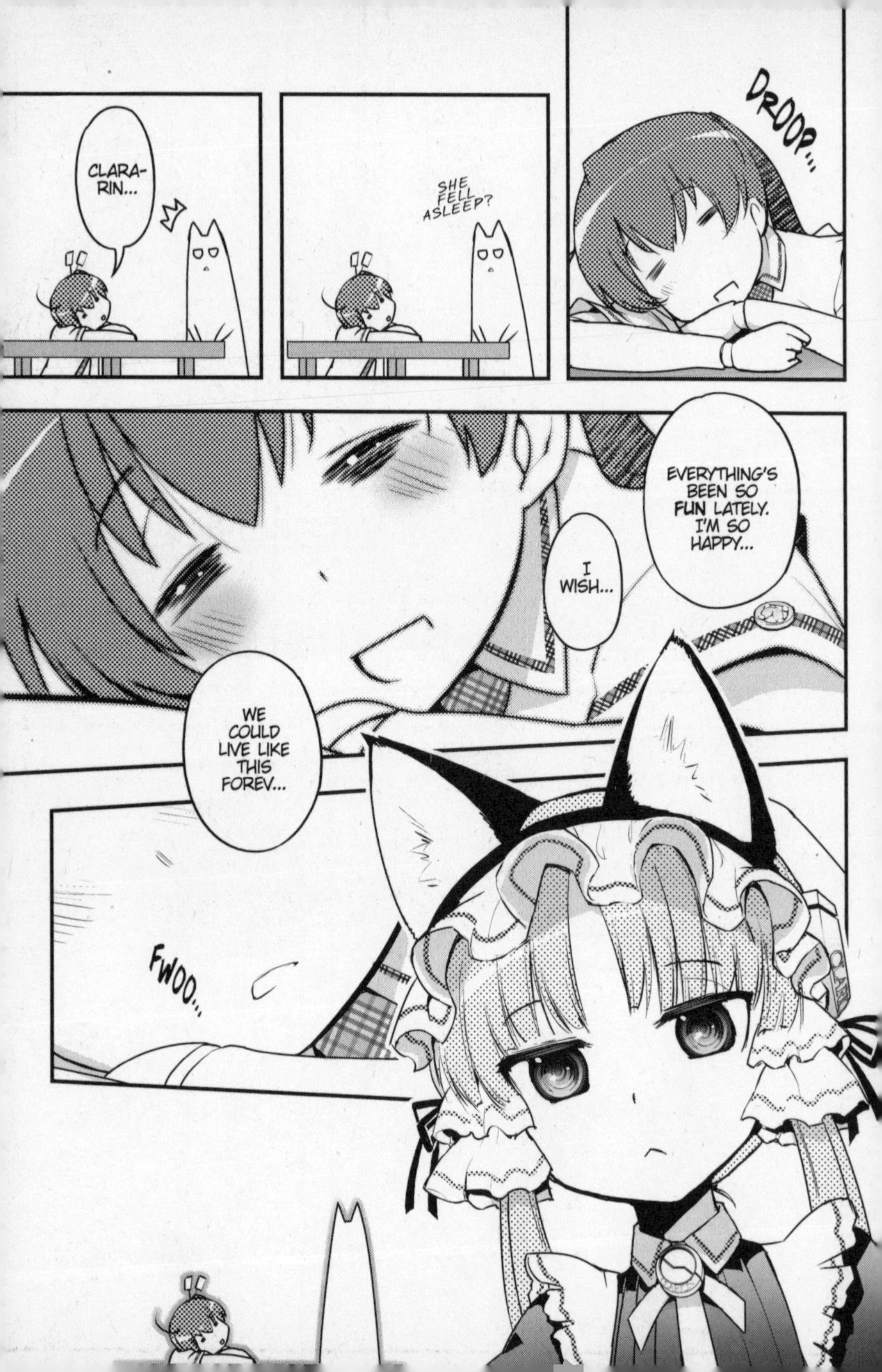
DROOP...
SHE FELL ASLEEP?
CLARA-RIN...
EVERYTHING'S BEEN SO FUN LATELY. I'M SO HAPPY...
I WISH...
WE COULD LIVE LIKE THIS FOREV...
FWOO...

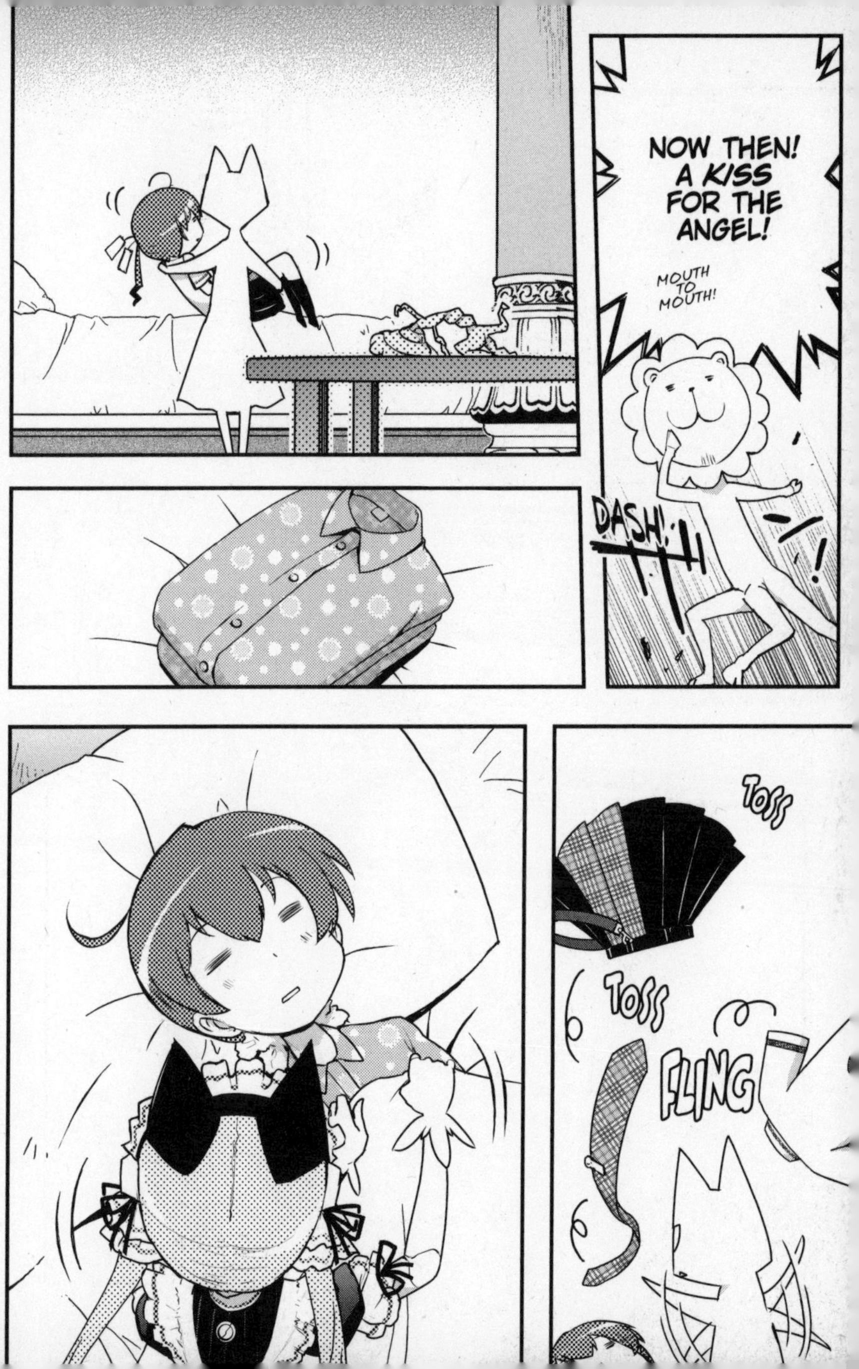
NOW THEN! A KISS FOR THE ANGEL!
MOUTH TO MOUTH!
DASH!
TOSS
TOSS
FLING

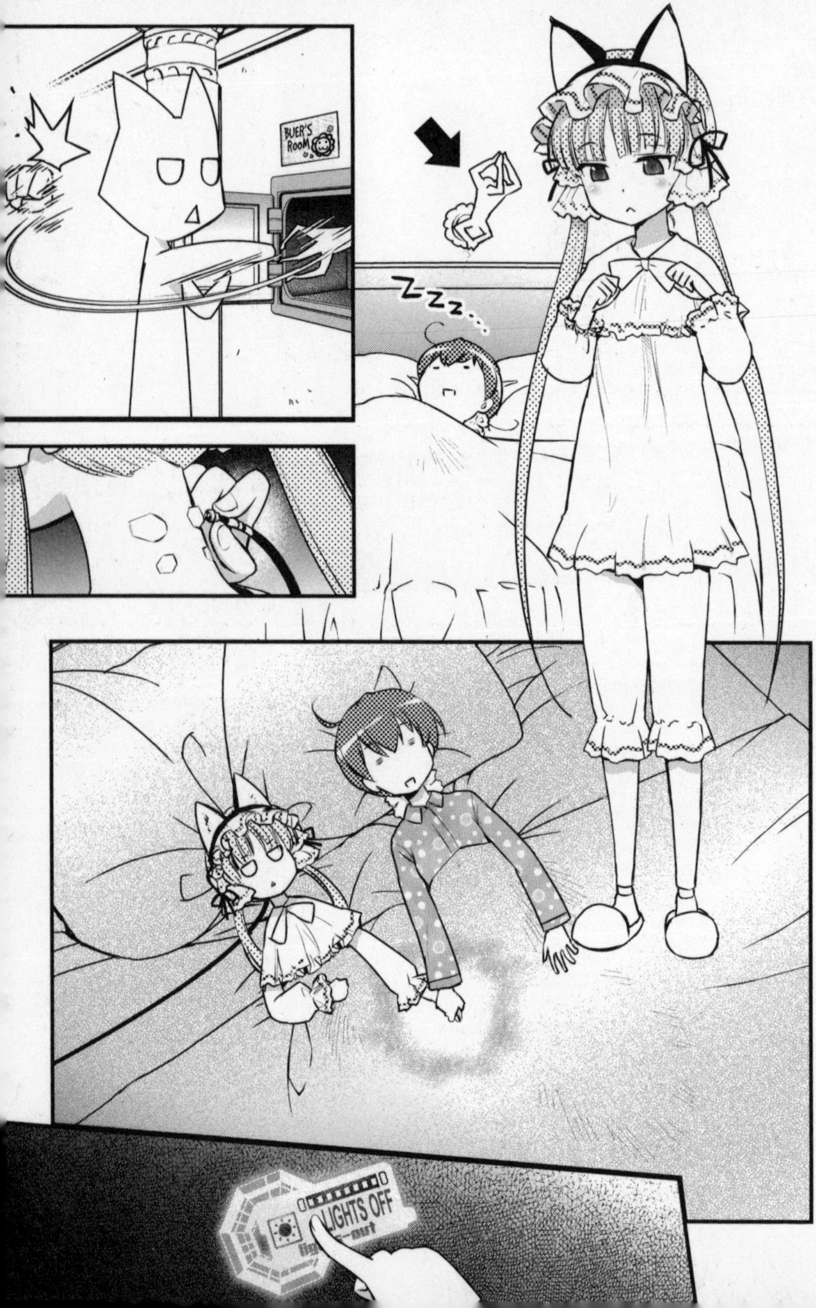
Zzz...
BUER'S ROOM
LIGHTS OFF

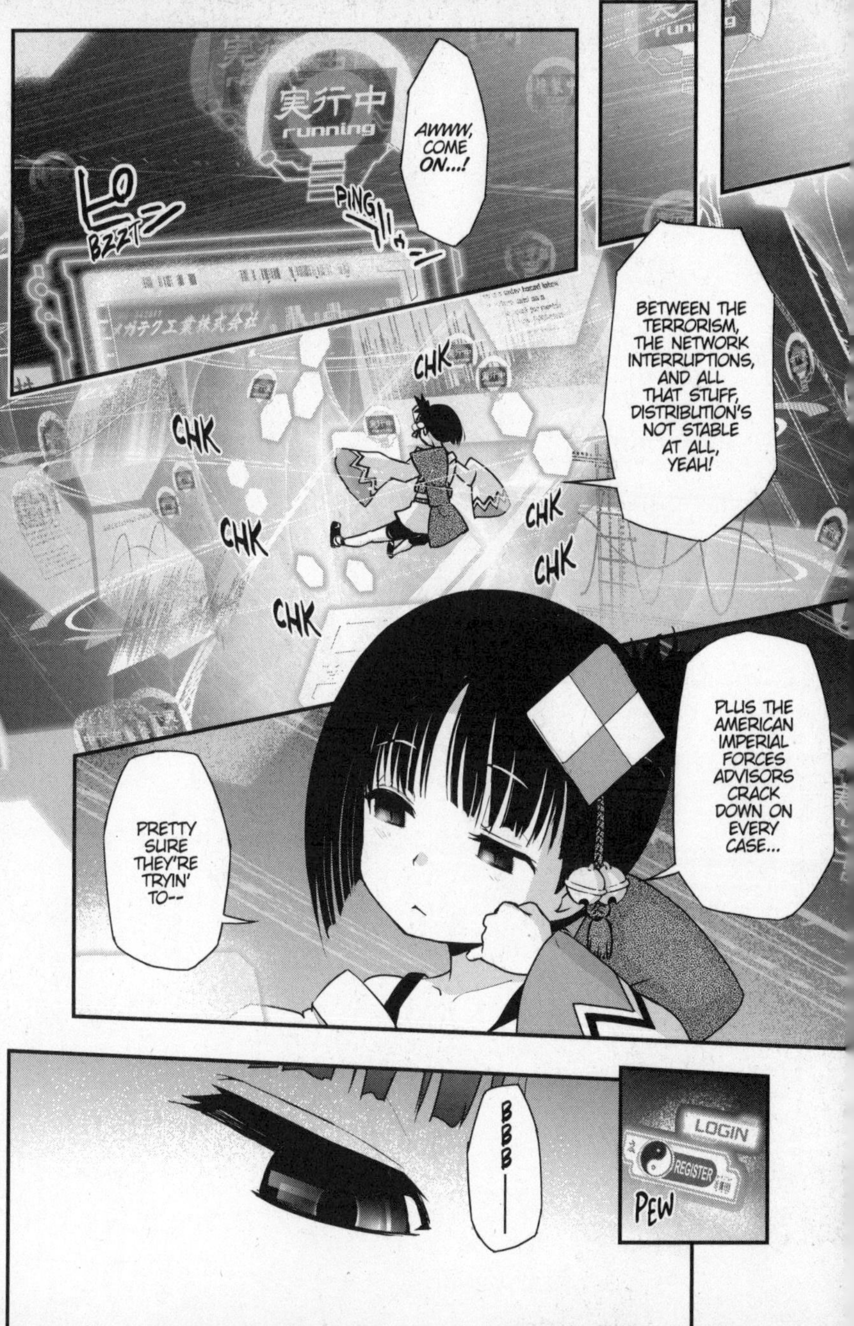
実行中
running
AWWW, COME ON...!
PING
BZZT
BETWEEN THE TERRORISM, THE NETWORK INTERRUPTIONS, AND ALL THAT STUFF, DISTRIBUTION'S NOT STABLE AT ALL, YEAH!
CHK
CHK
CHK
CHK
CHK
CHK
PLUS THE AMERICAN IMPERIAL FORCES ADVISORS CRACK DOWN ON EVERY CASE...
PRETTY SURE THEY'RE TRYIN' TO--
LOGIN
REGISTER
PEW
BBB—

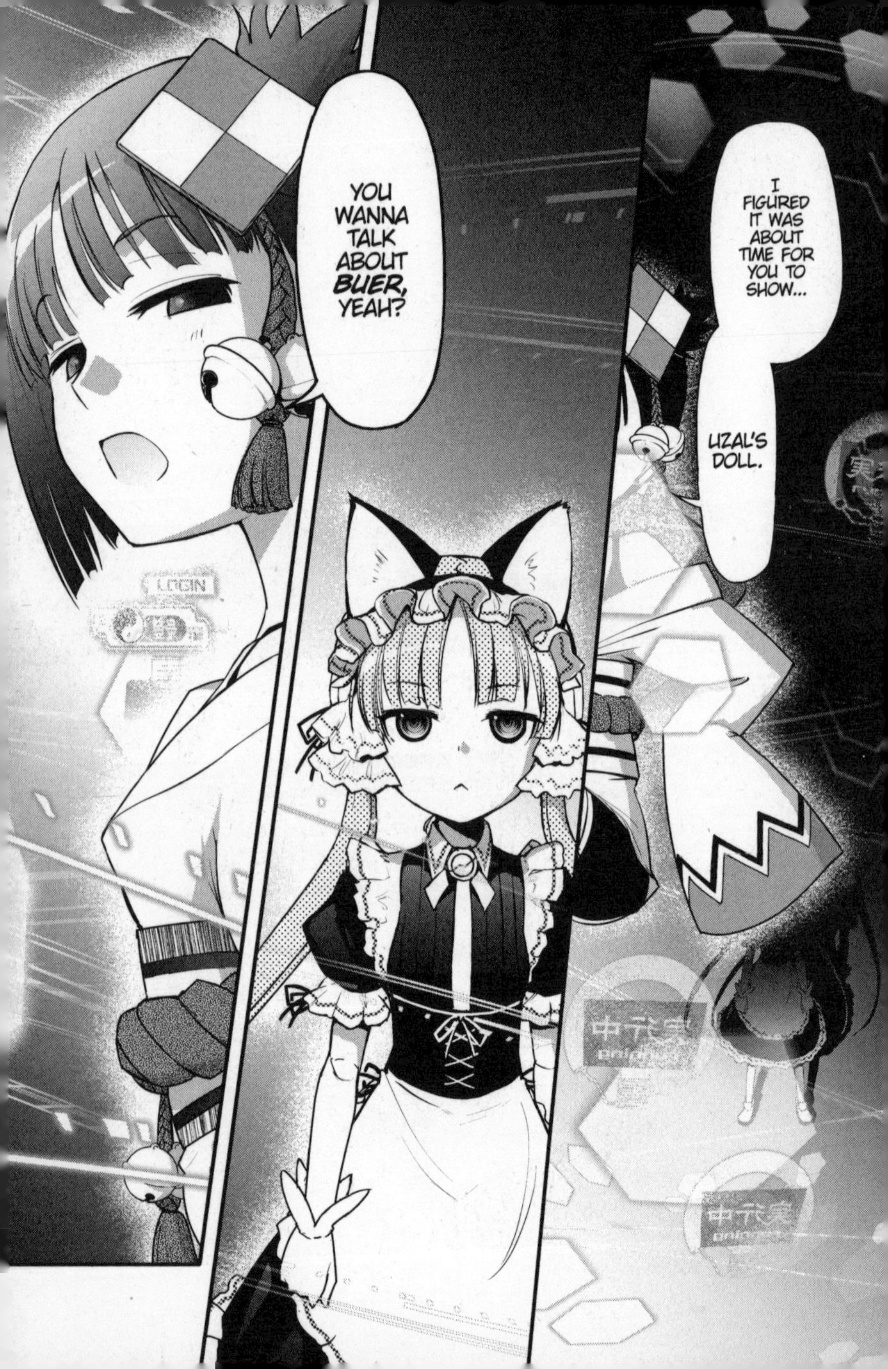
I FIGURED IT WAS ABOUT TIME FOR YOU TO SHOW...
UZAL'S DOLL.
YOU WANNA TALK ABOUT BUER, YEAH?
LOGIN

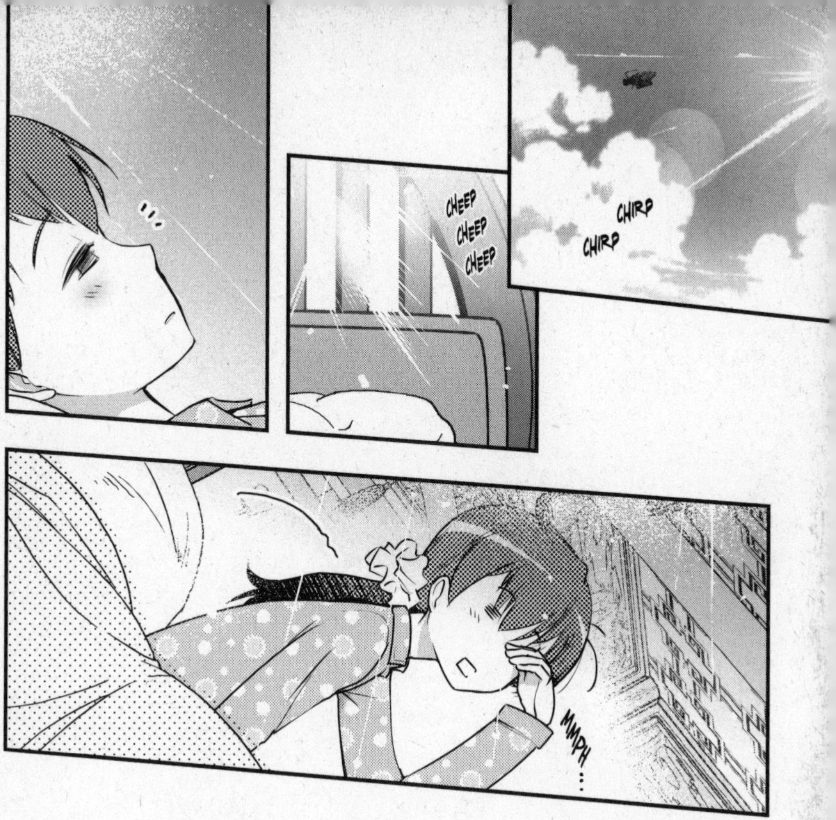
CHIRP
CHIRP
CHEEP
CHEEP
CHEEP
...
MMPH...
MORNING...
CLARA-RIN.
DON'T WORRY.

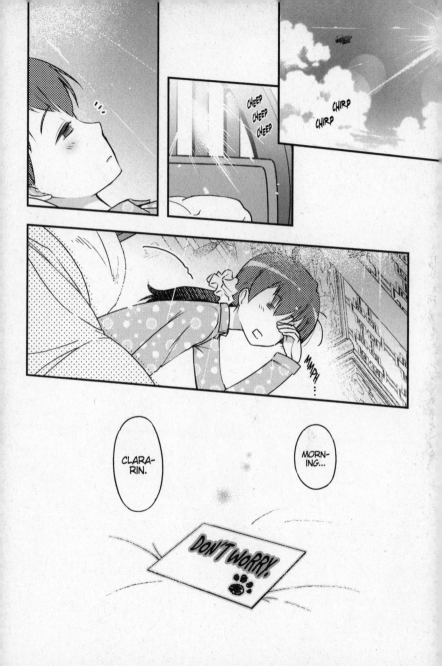

GHOST URN

GHOST URN

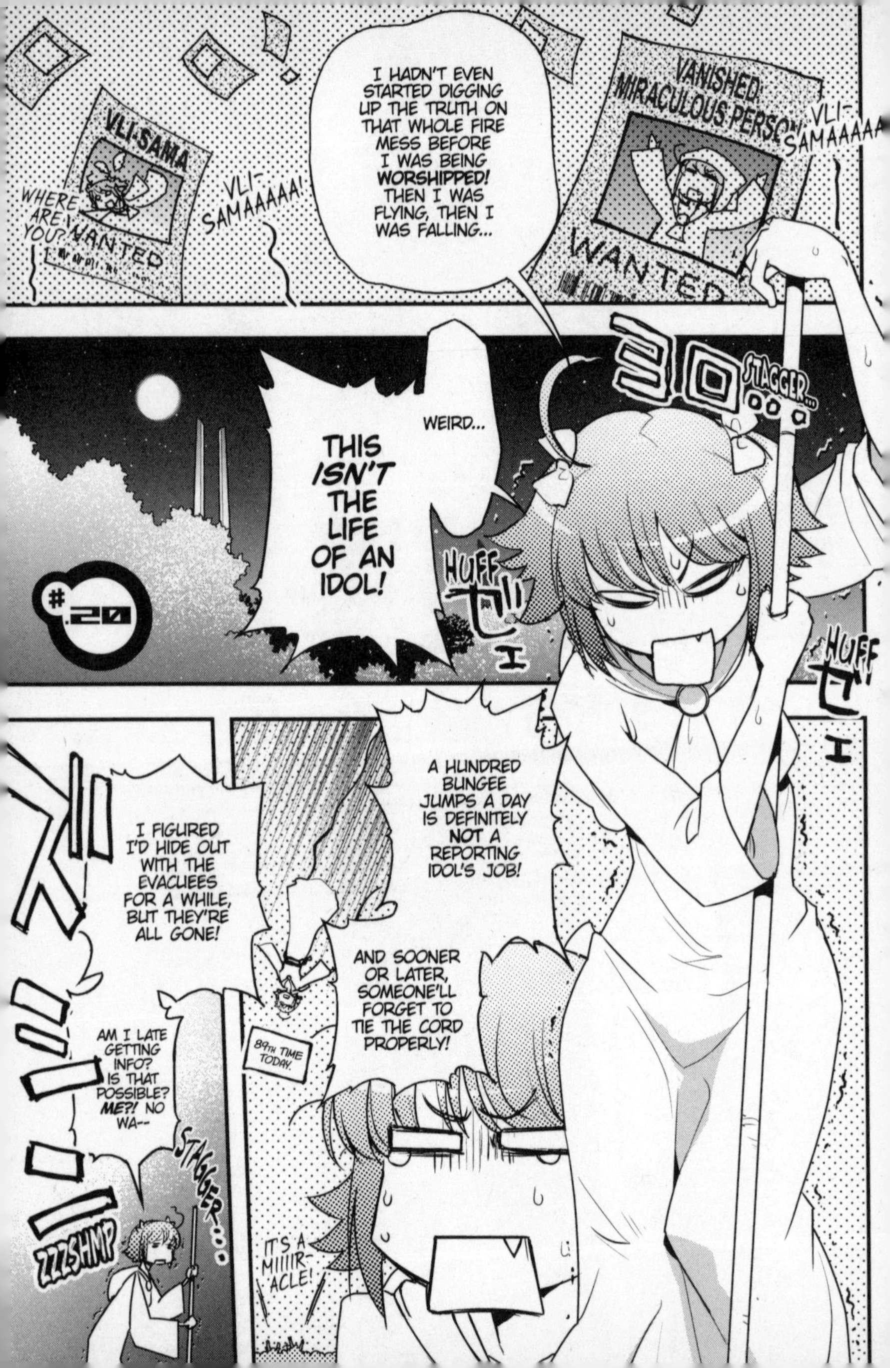
VLI-SAMAAAAA!
VANISHED: MIRACULOUS PERSON
WANTED
I HADN'T EVEN STARTED DIGGING UP THE TRUTH ON THAT WHOLE FIRE MESS BEFORE I WAS BEING **WORSHIPPED!** THEN I WAS FLYING, THEN I WAS FALLING...
VLI-SAMAAAAA!
VLI-SAMA
WANTED
WHERE ARE YOU?!
STAGGER...
HUFF
HUFF
WEIRD...
THIS *ISN'T* THE LIFE OF AN IDOL!
#.20
A HUNDRED BUNGEE JUMPS A DAY IS DEFINITELY **NOT** A REPORTING IDOL'S JOB!
AND SOONER OR LATER, SOMEONE'LL FORGET TO TIE THE CORD PROPERLY!
IT'S A MIIIIR-ACLE!
89TH TIME TODAY.
I FIGURED I'D HIDE OUT WITH THE EVACUEES FOR A WHILE, BUT THEY'RE ALL GONE!
AM I LATE GETTING INFO? IS THAT POSSIBLE? ***ME?!*** NO WA--
STAGGER...
ZZZSHMP

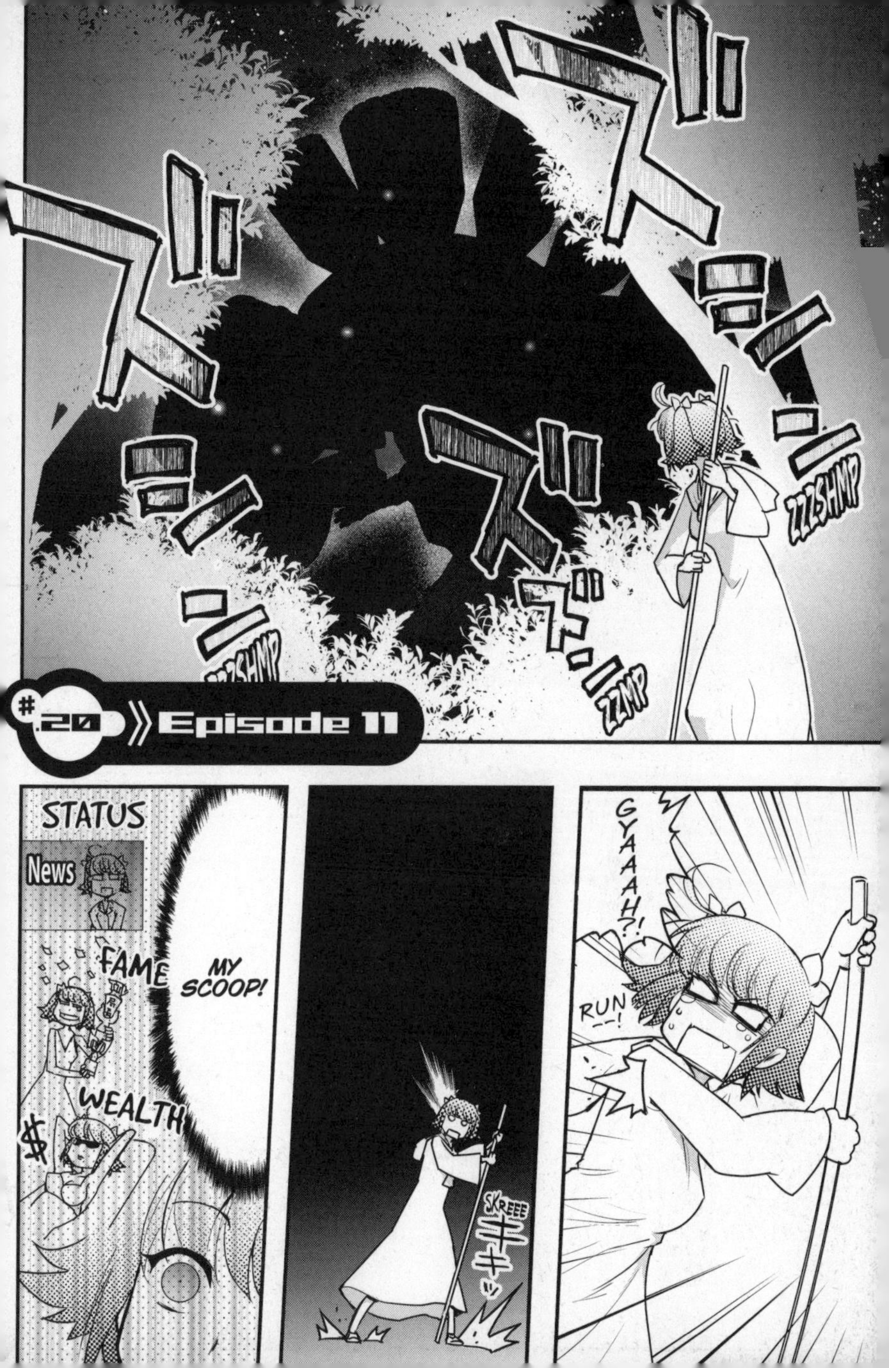
ZZZSHMP
ZZMP
ZZZSHMP
#.20 Episode 11
GYAAAH?!
RUN--!
SKREEE
キキッ
STATUS
News
FAME
MY SCOOP!
WEALTH
$

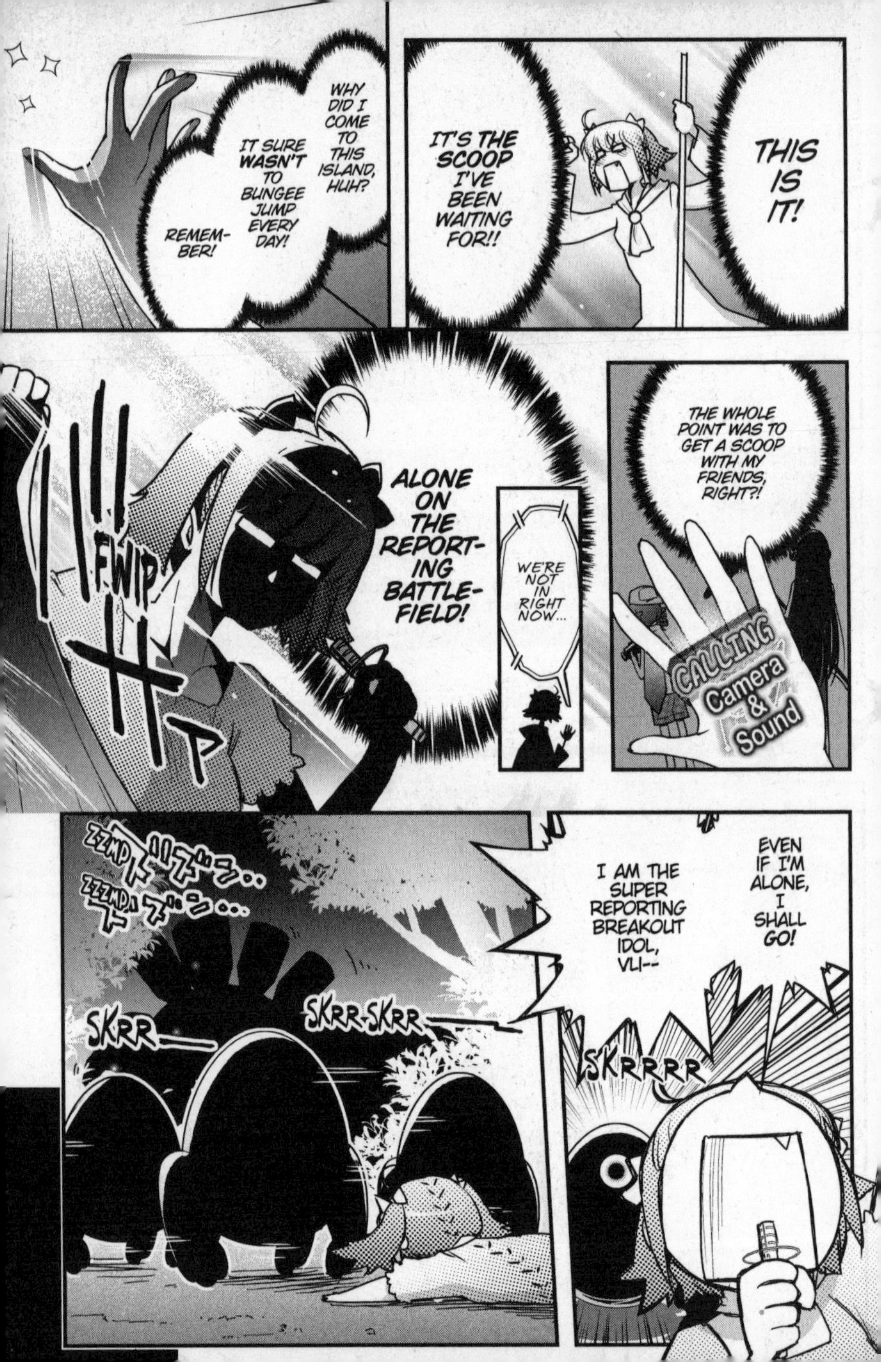
THIS IS IT!
IT'S THE SCOOP I'VE BEEN WAITING FOR!!
WHY DID I COME TO THIS ISLAND, HUH?
IT SURE WASN'T TO BUNGEE JUMP EVERY DAY!
REMEMBER!
THE WHOLE POINT WAS TO GET A SCOOP WITH MY FRIENDS, RIGHT?!
CALLING Camera & Sound
WE'RE NOT IN RIGHT NOW...
ALONE ON THE REPORTING BATTLEFIELD!
FWIP
EVEN IF I'M ALONE, I SHALL GO!
I AM THE SUPER REPORTING BREAKOUT IDOL, VLI--
SKRRRR
ZZMP
ZZZMP
SKRR SKRR
SKRR

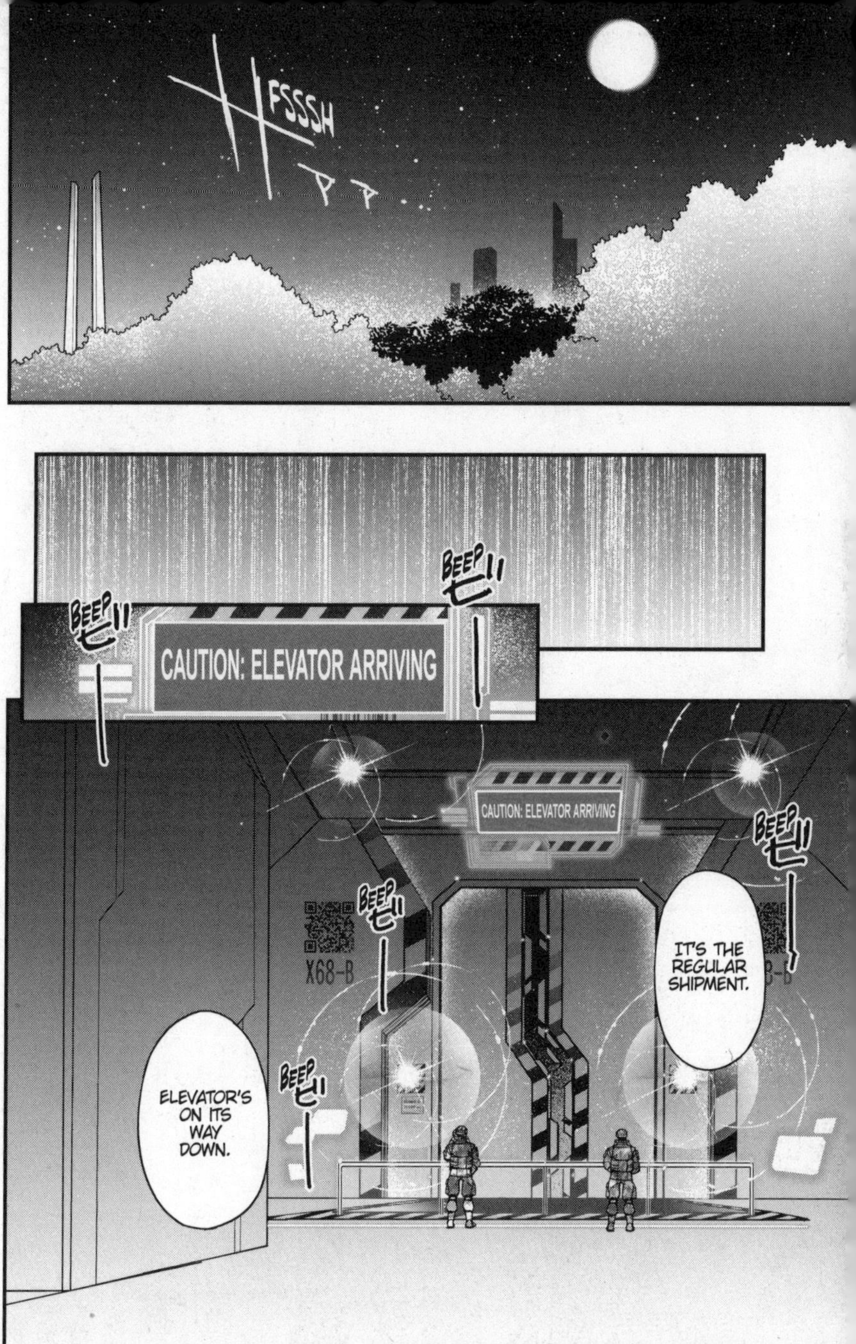

FSSSH
BEEP
BEEP
CAUTION: ELEVATOR ARRIVING
CAUTION: ELEVATOR ARRIVING
BEEP
IT'S THE REGULAR SHIPMENT.
X68-B
BEEP
BEEP
ELEVATOR'S ON ITS WAY DOWN.

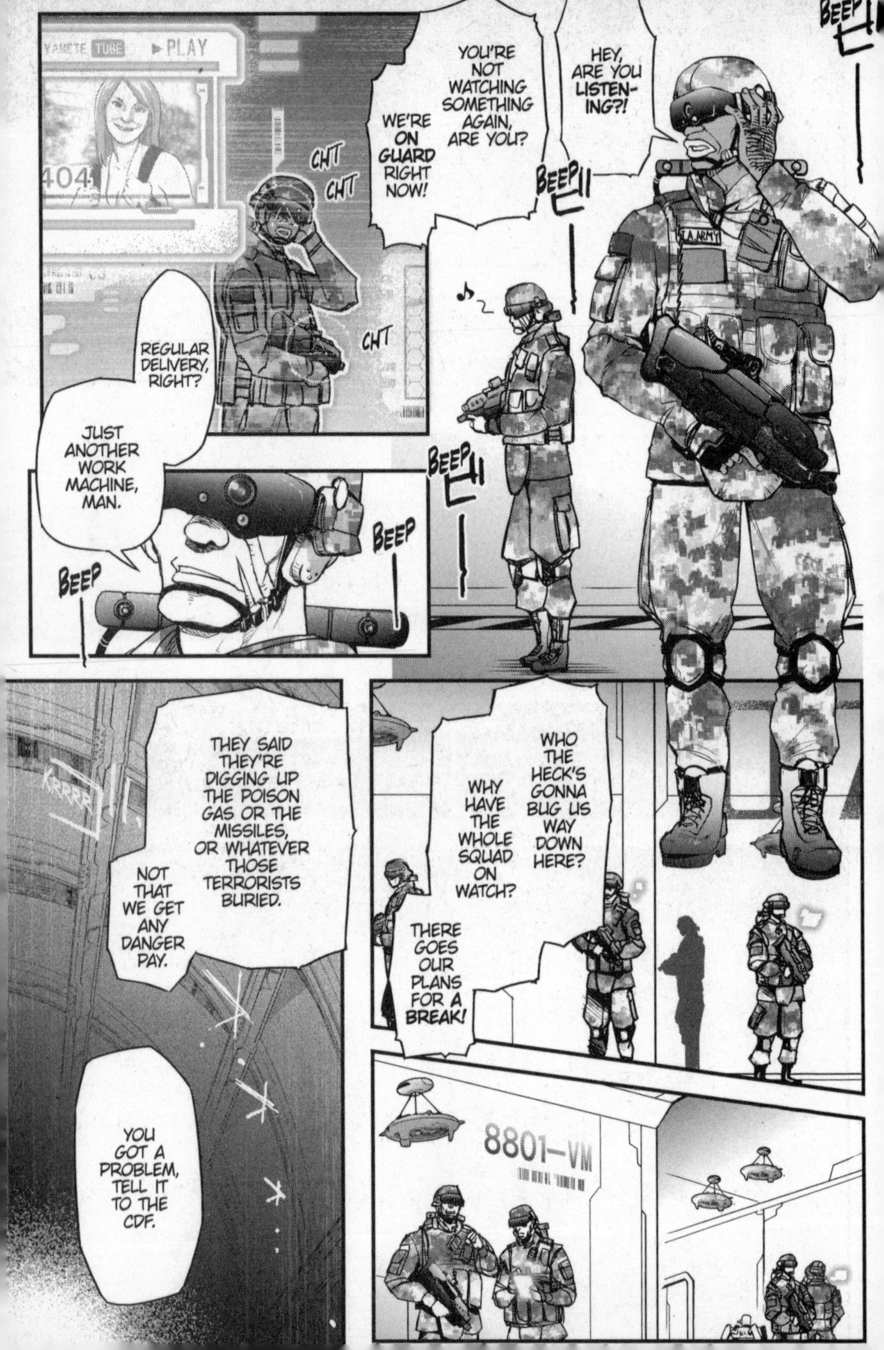
BEEP
HEY, ARE YOU LISTENING?!
YOU'RE NOT WATCHING SOMETHING AGAIN, ARE YOU?
WE'RE ON GUARD RIGHT NOW!
BEEP
BEEP
YAMETE TUBE ▶PLAY
404
CHT
CHT
CHT
REGULAR DELIVERY, RIGHT?
JUST ANOTHER WORK MACHINE, MAN.
BEEP
BEEP
WHO THE HECK'S GONNA BUG US WAY DOWN HERE?
WHY HAVE THE WHOLE SQUAD ON WATCH?
THERE GOES OUR PLANS FOR A BREAK!
8801-VM
KRRRR
THEY SAID THEY'RE DIGGING UP THE POISON GAS OR THE MISSILES, OR WHATEVER THOSE TERRORISTS BURIED.
NOT THAT WE GET ANY DANGER PAY.
YOU GOT A PROBLEM, TELL IT TO THE CDF.

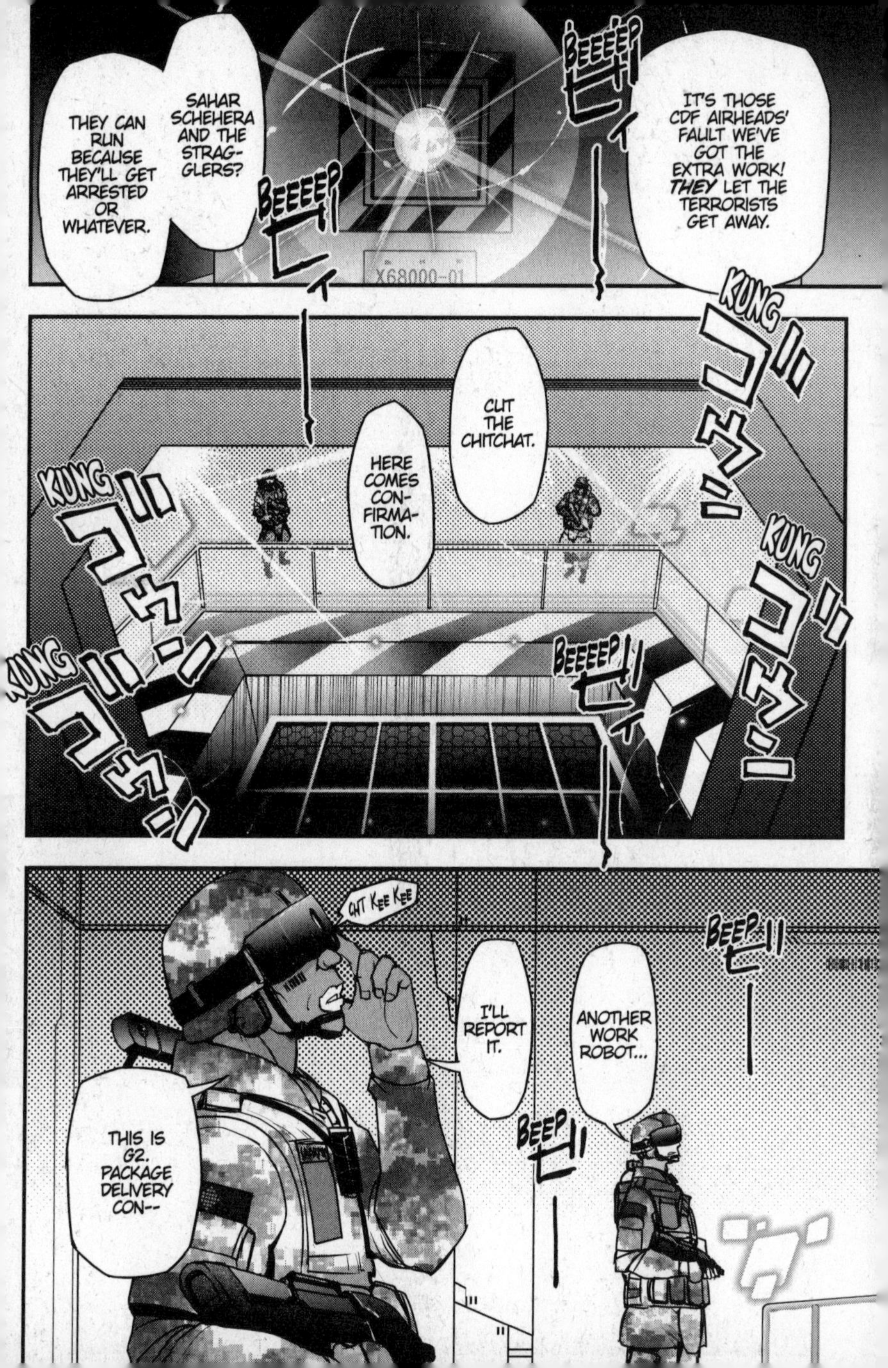

BEEEEP
IT'S THOSE CDF AIRHEADS' FAULT WE'VE GOT THE EXTRA WORK! *THEY* LET THE TERRORISTS GET AWAY.
SAHAR SCHEHERA AND THE STRAG-GLERS?
BEEEEP
THEY CAN RUN BECAUSE THEY'LL GET ARRESTED OR WHATEVER.
X68000-01
KUNG
KUNG
CUT THE CHITCHAT.
HERE COMES CON-FIRMA-TION.
BEEEEP
KUNG
KUNG
BEEP
ANOTHER WORK ROBOT...
I'LL REPORT IT.
CHT KEE KEE
BEEP
THIS IS G2. PACKAGE DELIVERY CON--

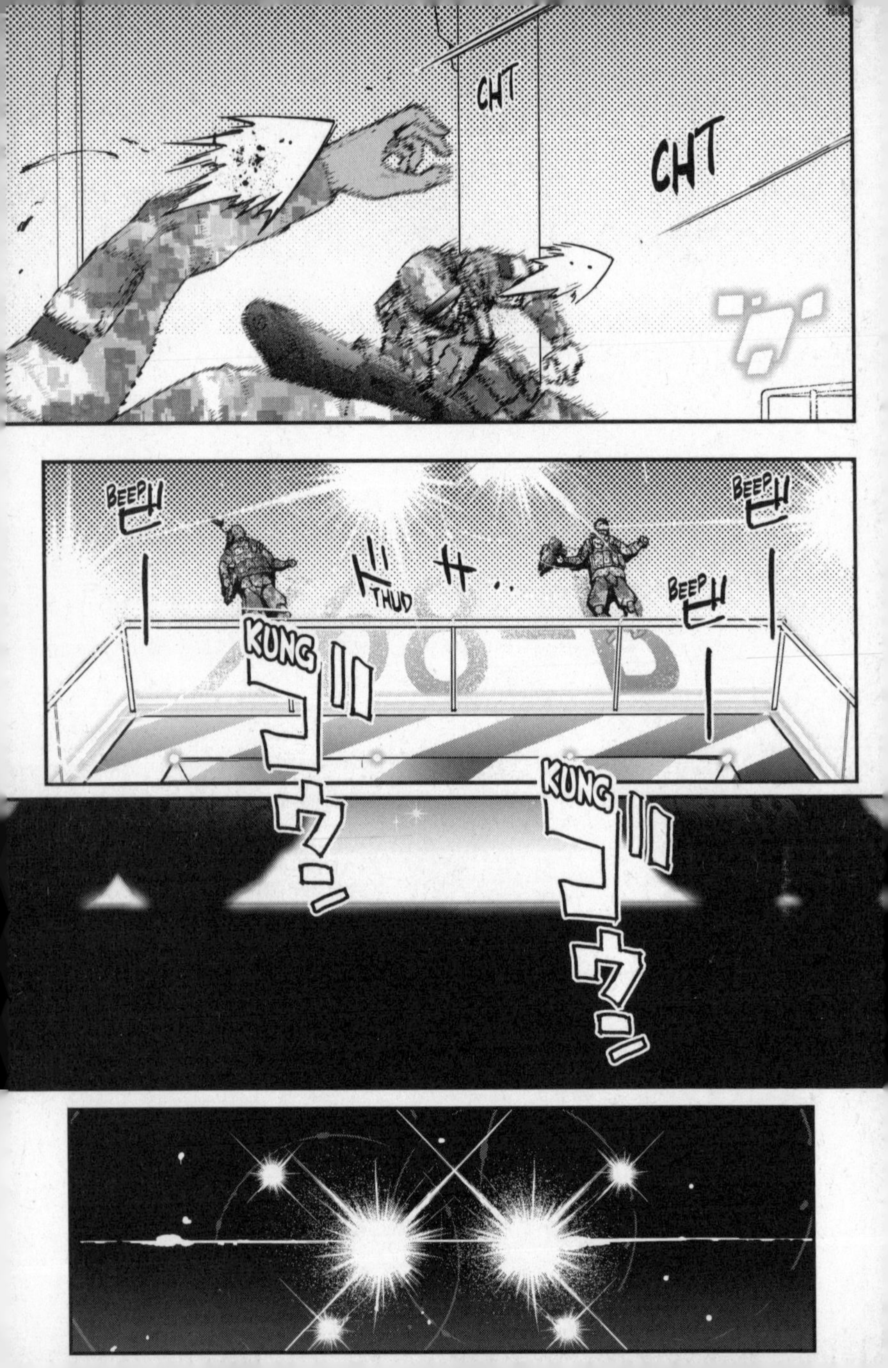

CHT
CHT
BEEP
ビー
BEEP
ビー
ドサ..
THUD
BEEP
ビー
KUNG
ゴウン
KUNG
ゴウン

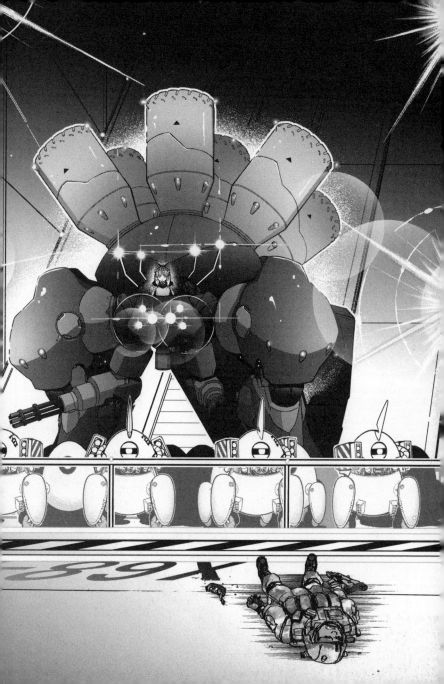

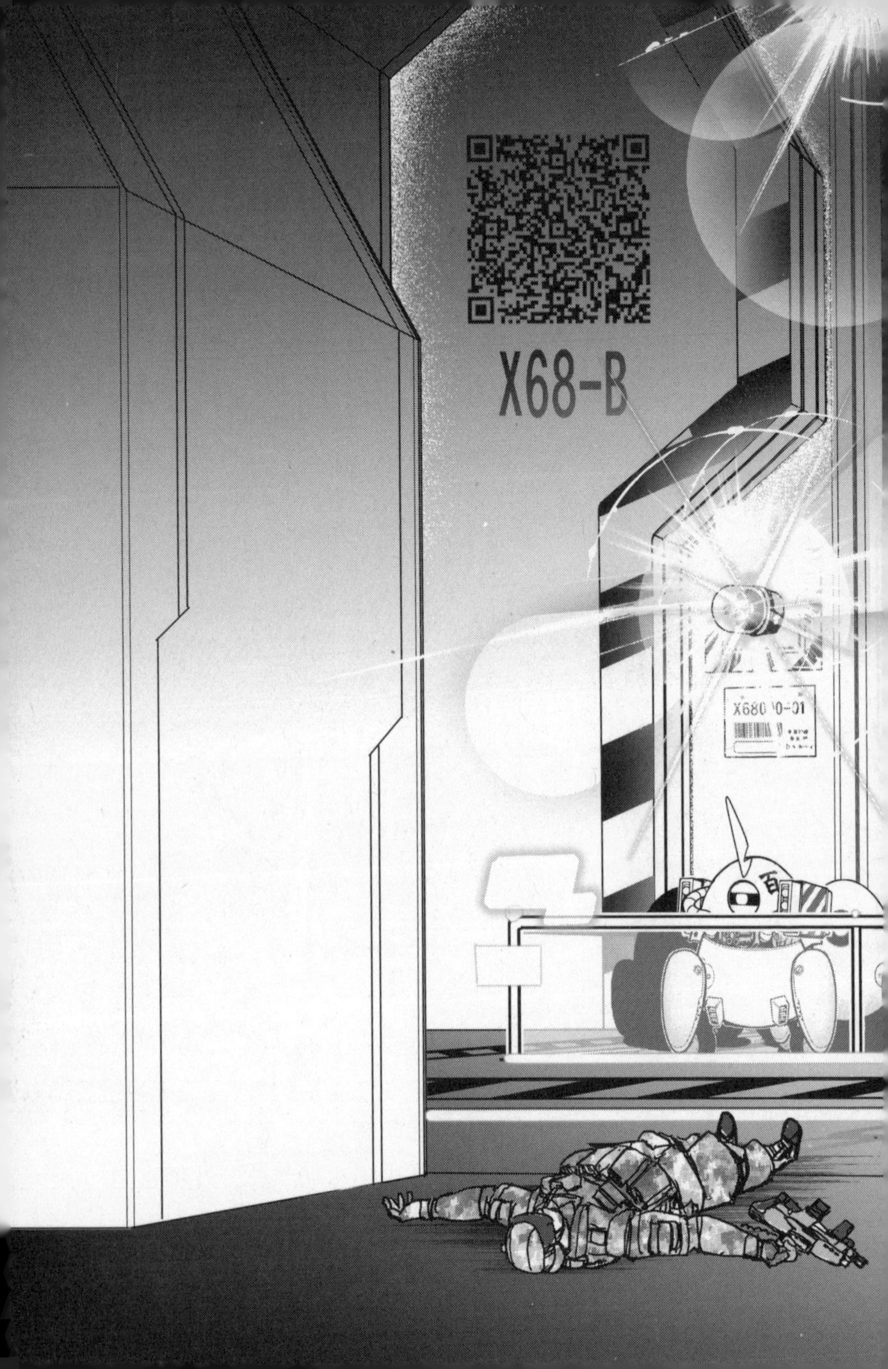
X68-B
百

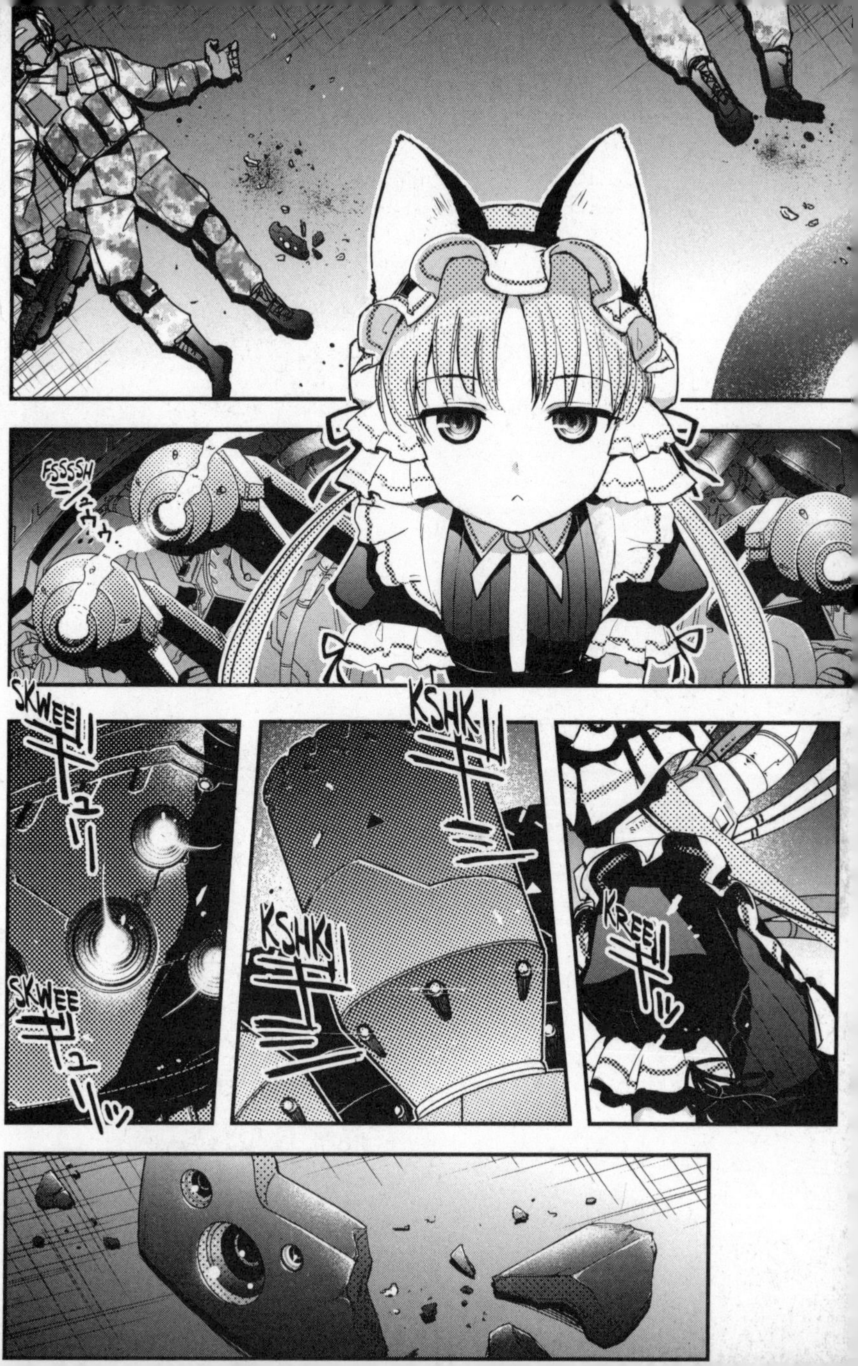
FSSSSH
KREE!!
KSHK!!
KSHK!
SKWEE!!
SKWEE

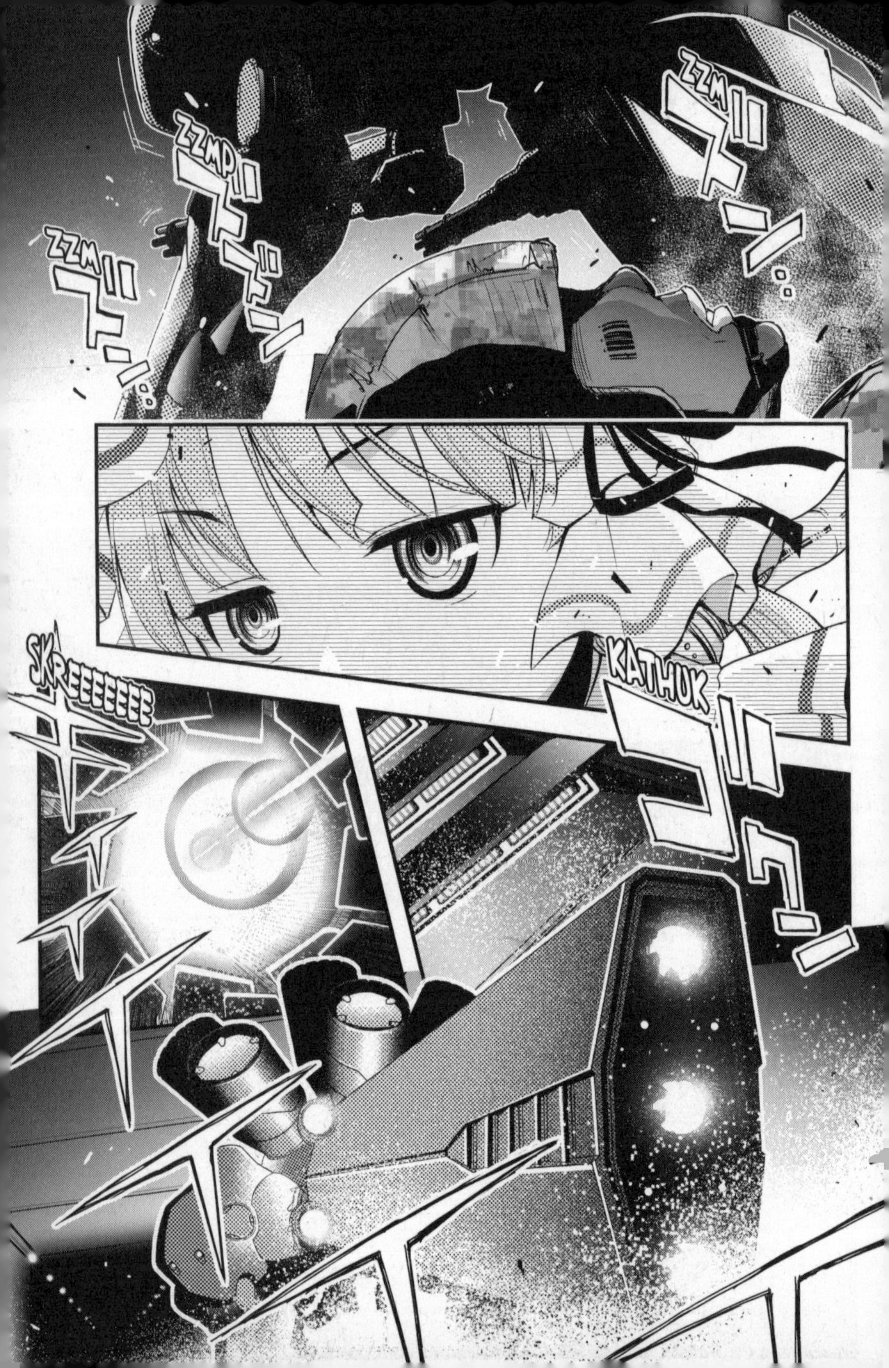
ZZM!!
ZZMP!!
ZZM!!
KATHUK
SKREEEEEEE

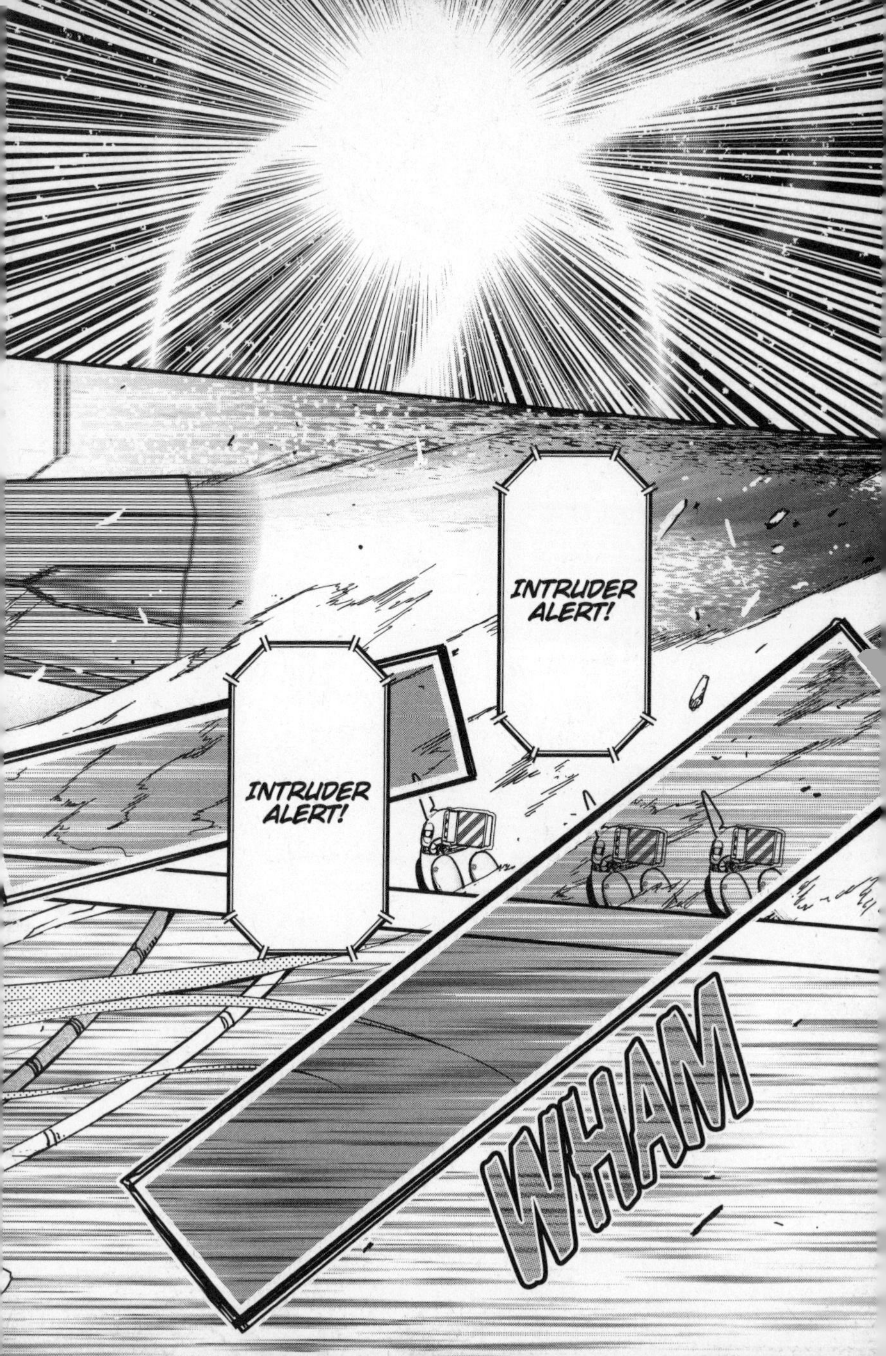
INTRUDER ALERT!
INTRUDER ALERT!
WHAM

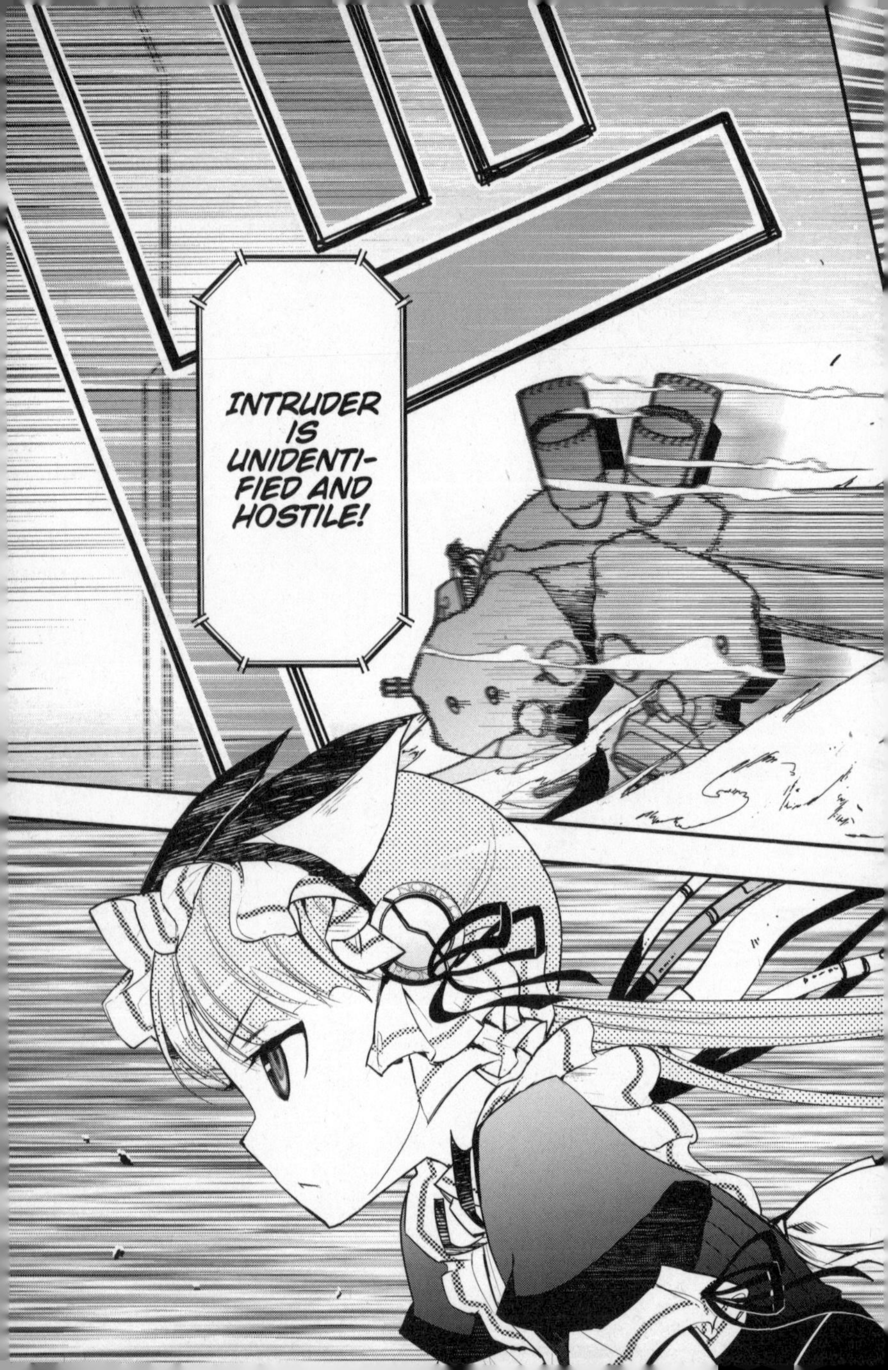
INTRUDER IS UNIDENTI-FIED AND HOSTILE!

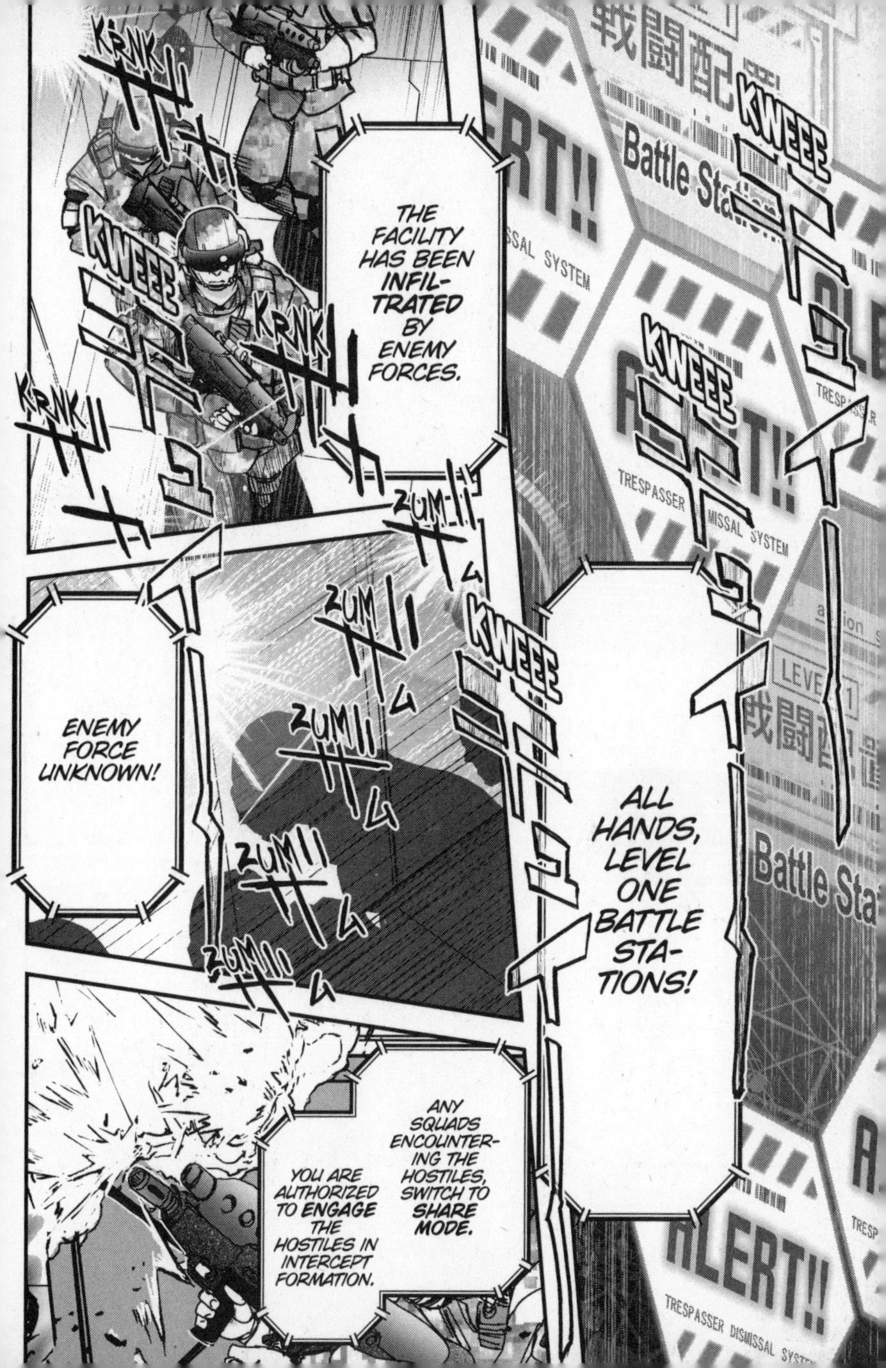

戦闘配
ERT!!
Battle Sta
KWEEE
KWEEE
TRESPASSER
MISSAL SYSTEM
LEVEL
戦闘
Battle Sta
ALL HANDS, LEVEL ONE BATTLE STATIONS!
KWEEE
ALERT!!
TRESPASSER DISMISSAL SYSTE
KRNK!!
KWEEE
KRNK
KRNK!!
THE FACILITY HAS BEEN INFILTRATED BY ENEMY FORCES.
ZUM!!
ZUM!!
ZUM!!
ZUM!!
ZUM!!
ENEMY FORCE UNKNOWN!
ANY SQUADS ENCOUNTERING THE HOSTILES, SWITCH TO SHARE MODE.
YOU ARE AUTHORIZED TO ENGAGE THE HOSTILES IN INTERCEPT FORMATION.

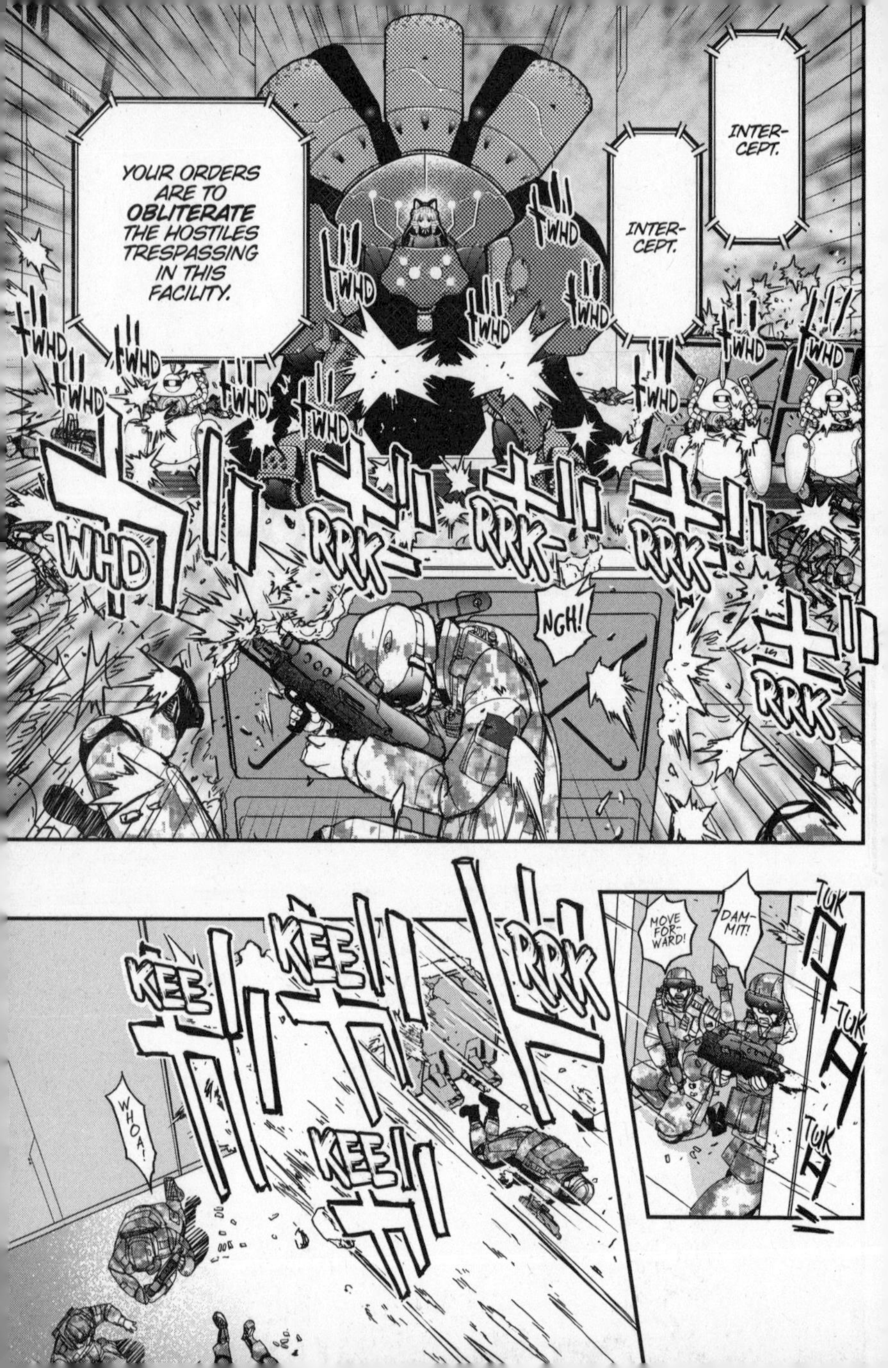

INTER-CEPT.
INTER-CEPT.
YOUR ORDERS ARE TO **OBLITERATE** THE HOSTILES TRESPASSING IN THIS FACILITY.
WHD
WHD
WHD
WHD
WHD
WHD
WHD
WHD
WHD
WHD
WHD
RRK
RRK
RRK
NGH!
RRK
TUK
DAM-MIT!
MOVE FOR-WARD!
TUK
TUK
RRK
KEE
KEE
KEE
WHOA!

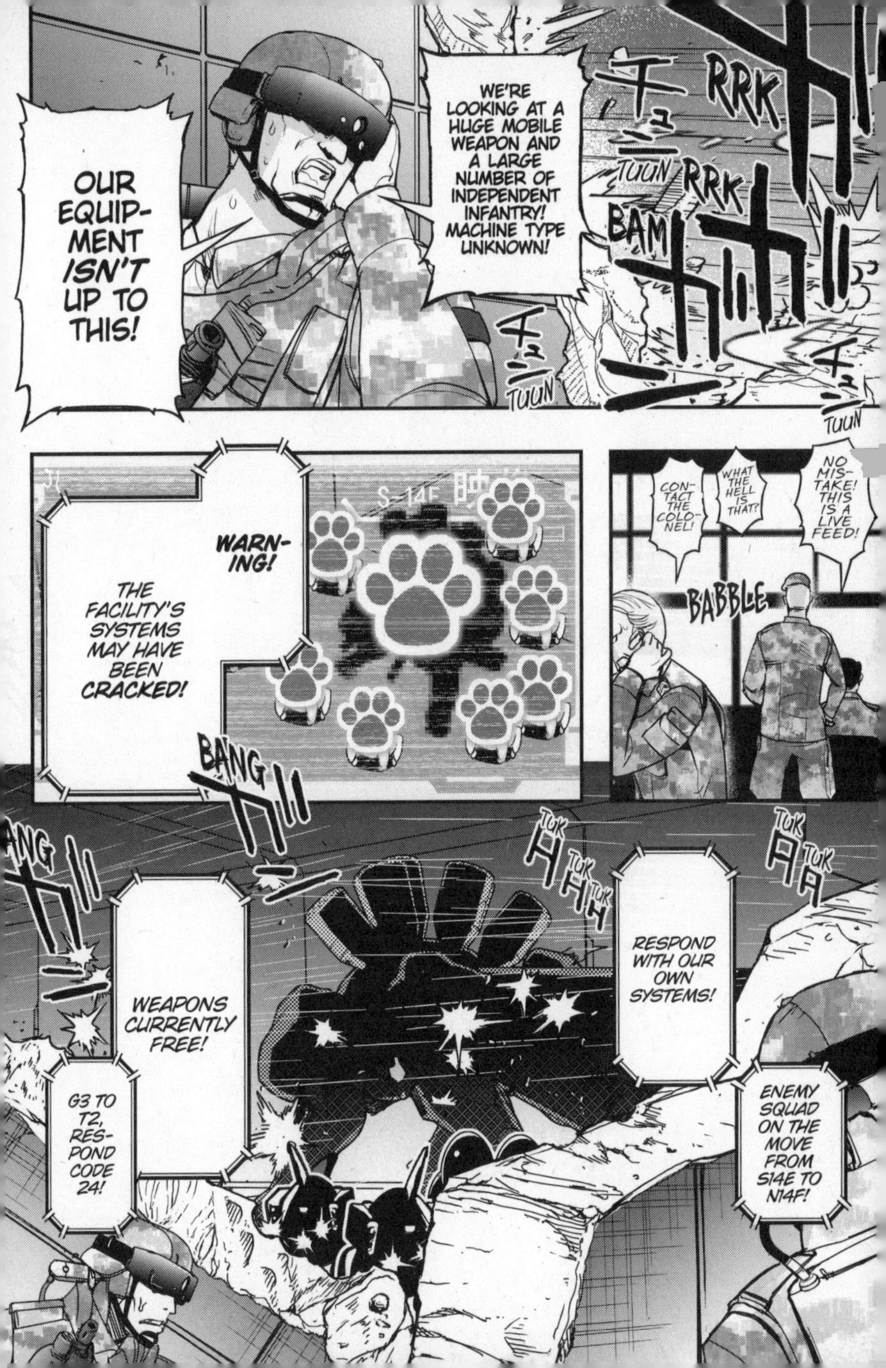
RRK
TUUN
RRK
BAM
TUUN
WE'RE LOOKING AT A HUGE MOBILE WEAPON AND A LARGE NUMBER OF INDEPENDENT INFANTRY! MACHINE TYPE UNKNOWN!
OUR EQUIPMENT ISN'T UP TO THIS!
TUUN
NO MISTAKE! THIS IS A LIVE FEED!
WHAT THE HELL IS THAT?
CONTACT THE COLONEL!
BABBLE
WARNING!
THE FACILITY'S SYSTEMS MAY HAVE BEEN CRACKED!
BANG
TUK TUK
TUK TUK TUK
RESPOND WITH OUR OWN SYSTEMS!
ENEMY SQUAD ON THE MOVE FROM S14E TO N14F!
BANG
WEAPONS CURRENTLY FREE!
G3 TO T2, RESPOND CODE 24!

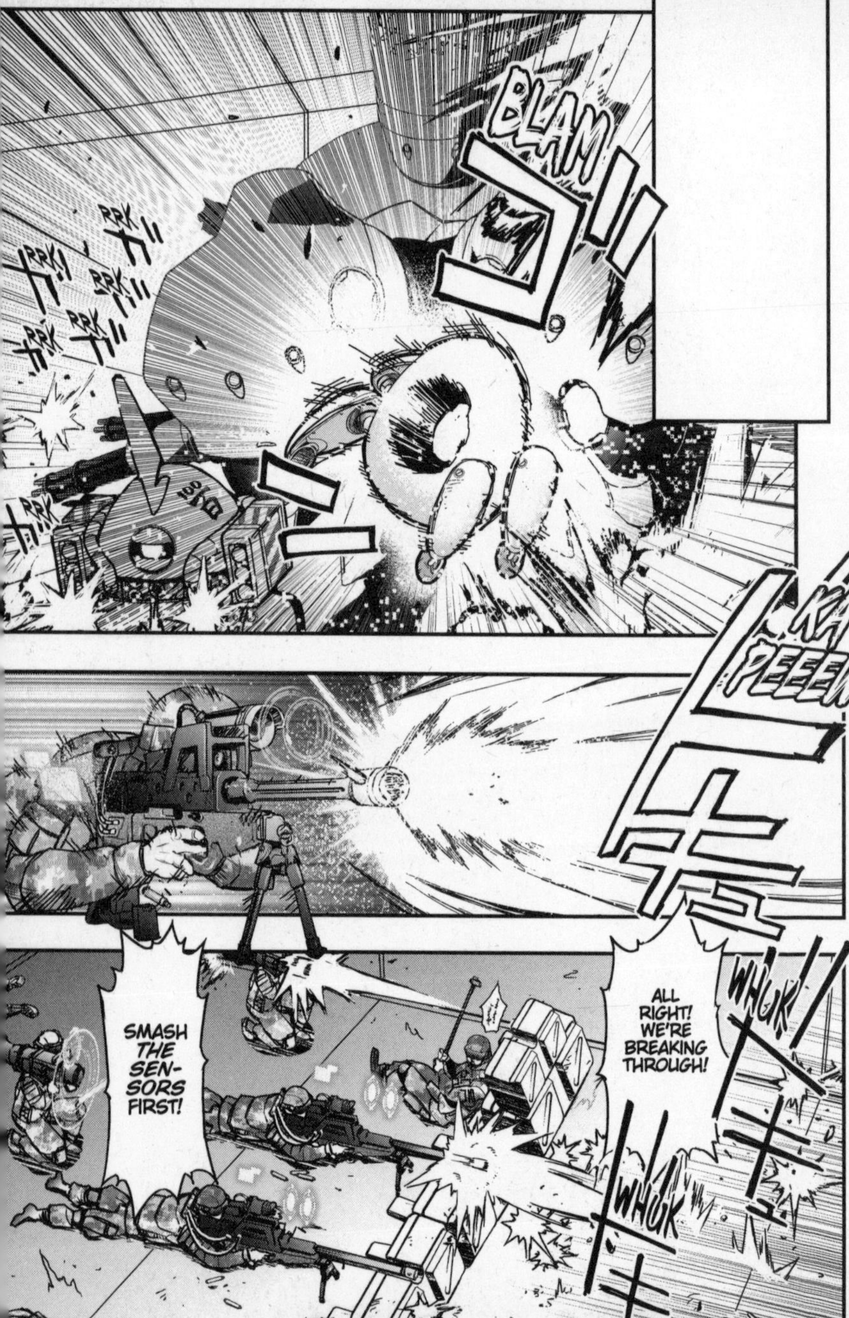
BLAM
RRK
RRK!
RRK
RRK
RRK
RRK
KA-PEEEN
WHUK!
ALL RIGHT! WE'RE BREAKING THROUGH!
WHUK
SMASH THE SEN-SORS FIRST!

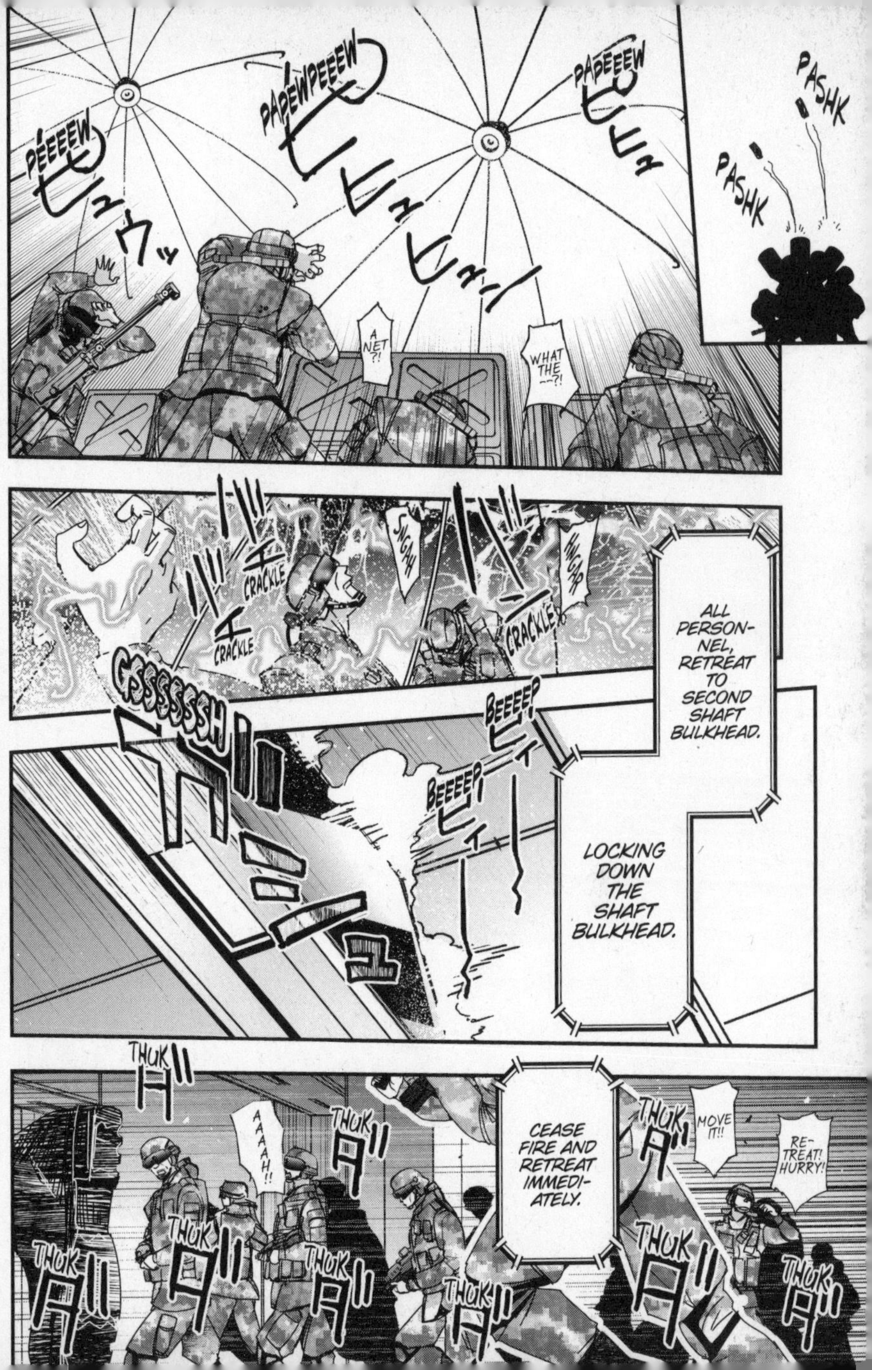
PASHK
PASHK
PAPEEEW
WHAT THE --?!
PAPEWPEEEW
A NET?!
PEEEEW
ALL PERSONNEL, RETREAT TO SECOND SHAFT BULKHEAD.
HNGAH
CRACKLE
SNGAH
CRACKLE
CRACKLE
BEEEEP
BEEEEP
LOCKING DOWN THE SHAFT BULKHEAD.
GRSSSSSSH
RE-TREAT! HURRY!
MOVE IT!!
THUK
CEASE FIRE AND RETREAT IMMEDIATELY.
THUK
AAAAH!!
THUK
THUK
THUK
THUK
THUK
THUK
THUK

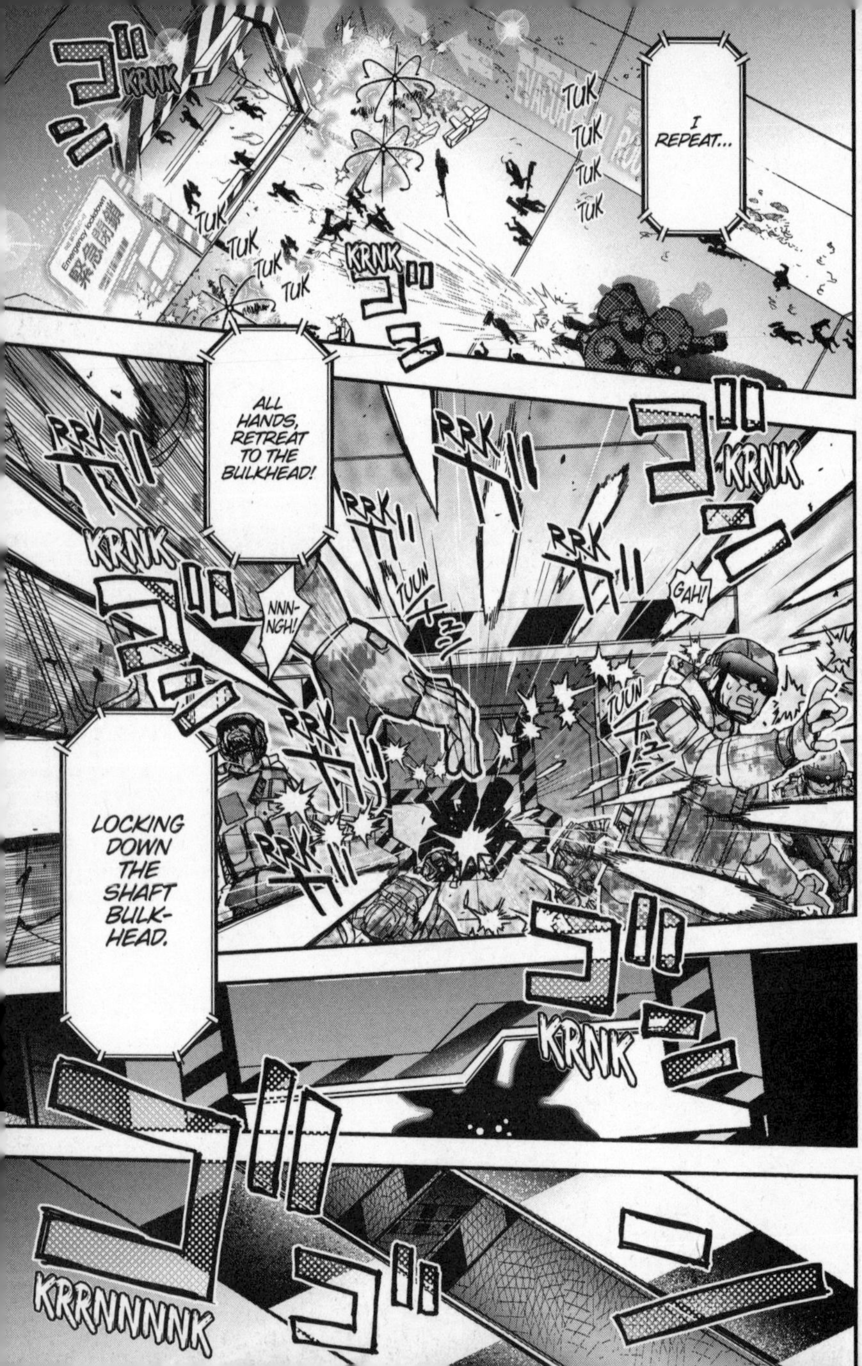
I REPEAT...
TUK
TUK
TUK
TUK
KRNK
Emergency lockdown
緊急閉鎖
TUK
TUK
TUK
TUK
KRNK
ALL HANDS, RETREAT TO THE BULKHEAD!
KRNK
GAH!
RRK
TUUN
RRK
RRK
NNN-NGH!
RRK
KRNK
RRK
RRK
TUUN
LOCKING DOWN THE SHAFT BULKHEAD.
KRNK
KRRNNNNNK

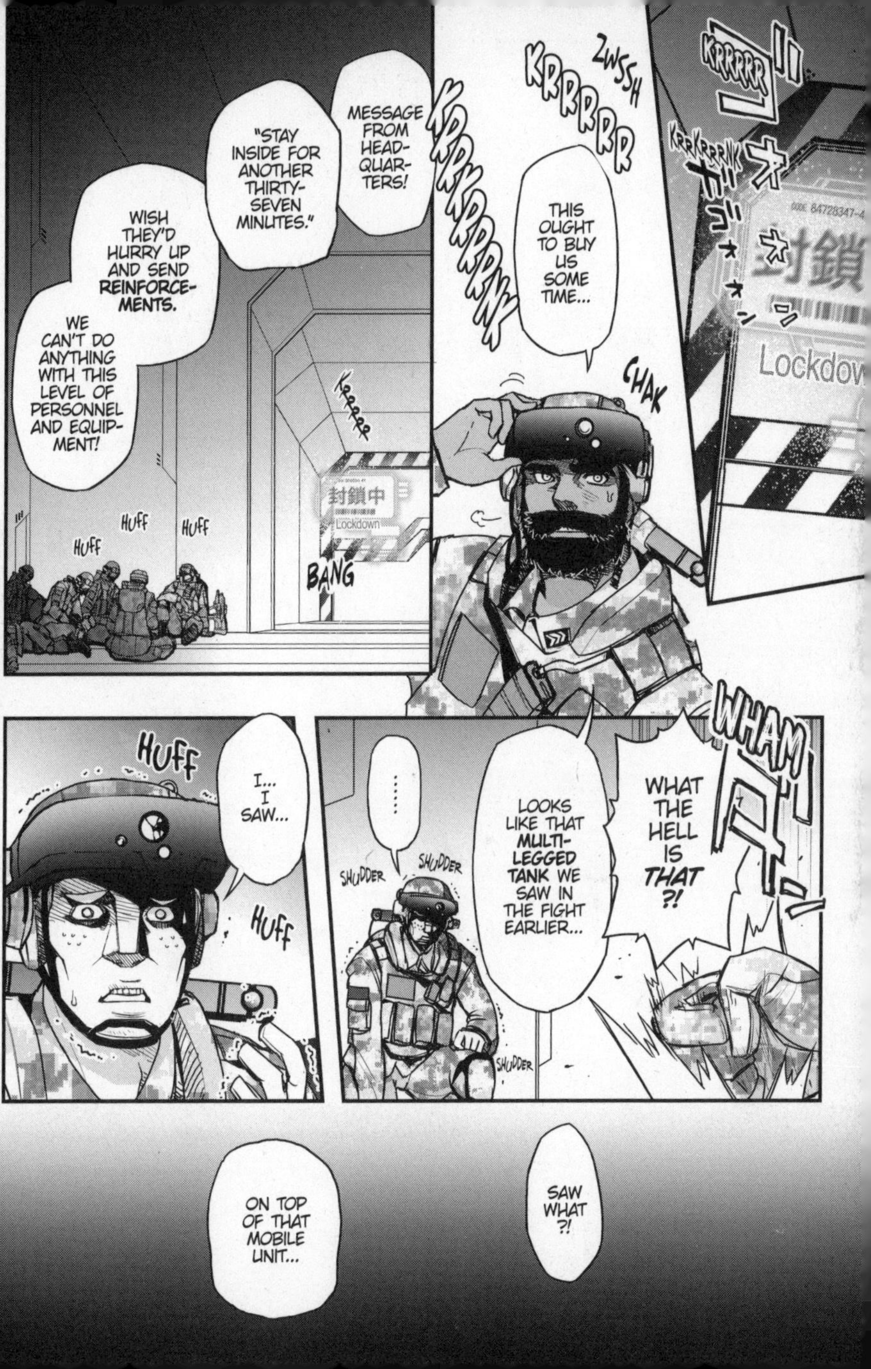
KRRRRR
KRRKRRRNK
封鎖
Lockdow
ZWSSH
KRRRRRR
KRRKRRRRNK
THIS OUGHT TO BUY US SOME TIME...
CHAK
MESSAGE FROM HEAD-QUAR-TERS!
"STAY INSIDE FOR ANOTHER THIRTY-SEVEN MINUTES."
WISH THEY'D HURRY UP AND SEND REINFORCE-MENTS.
WE CAN'T DO ANYTHING WITH THIS LEVEL OF PERSONNEL AND EQUIP-MENT!
封鎖中
Lockdown
HUFF
HUFF
HUFF
BANG
WHAM
WHAT THE HELL IS THAT?!
LOOKS LIKE THAT MULTI-LEGGED TANK WE SAW IN THE FIGHT EARLIER...
......
SHUDDER
SHUDDER
SHUDDER
HUFF
I... I SAW...
HUFF
SAW WHAT?!
ON TOP OF THAT MOBILE UNIT...

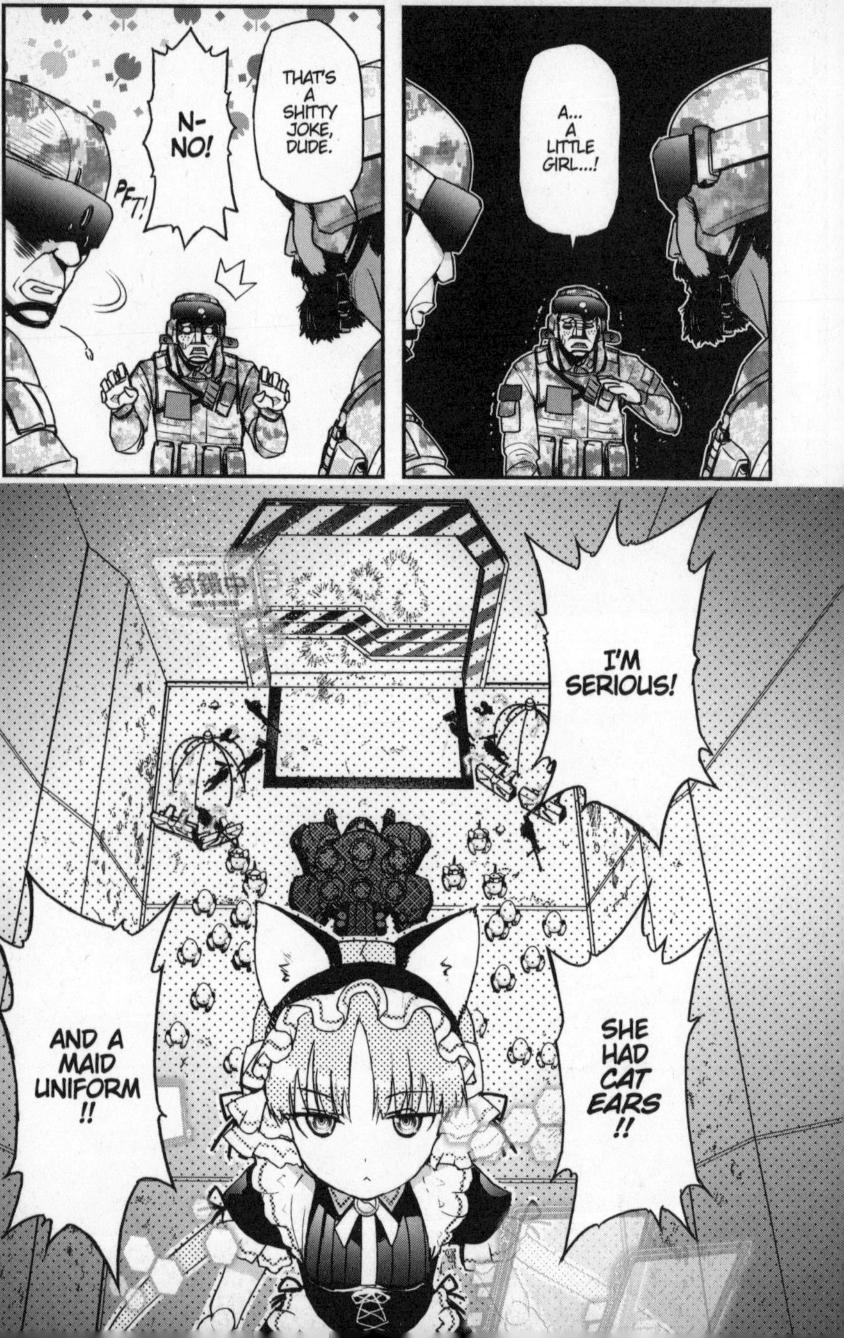
A... A LITTLE GIRL...!
THAT'S A SHITTY JOKE, DUDE.
N-NO!
PFFT!
封鎖中
I'M SERIOUS!
SHE HAD CAT EARS!!
AND A MAID UNIFORM!!

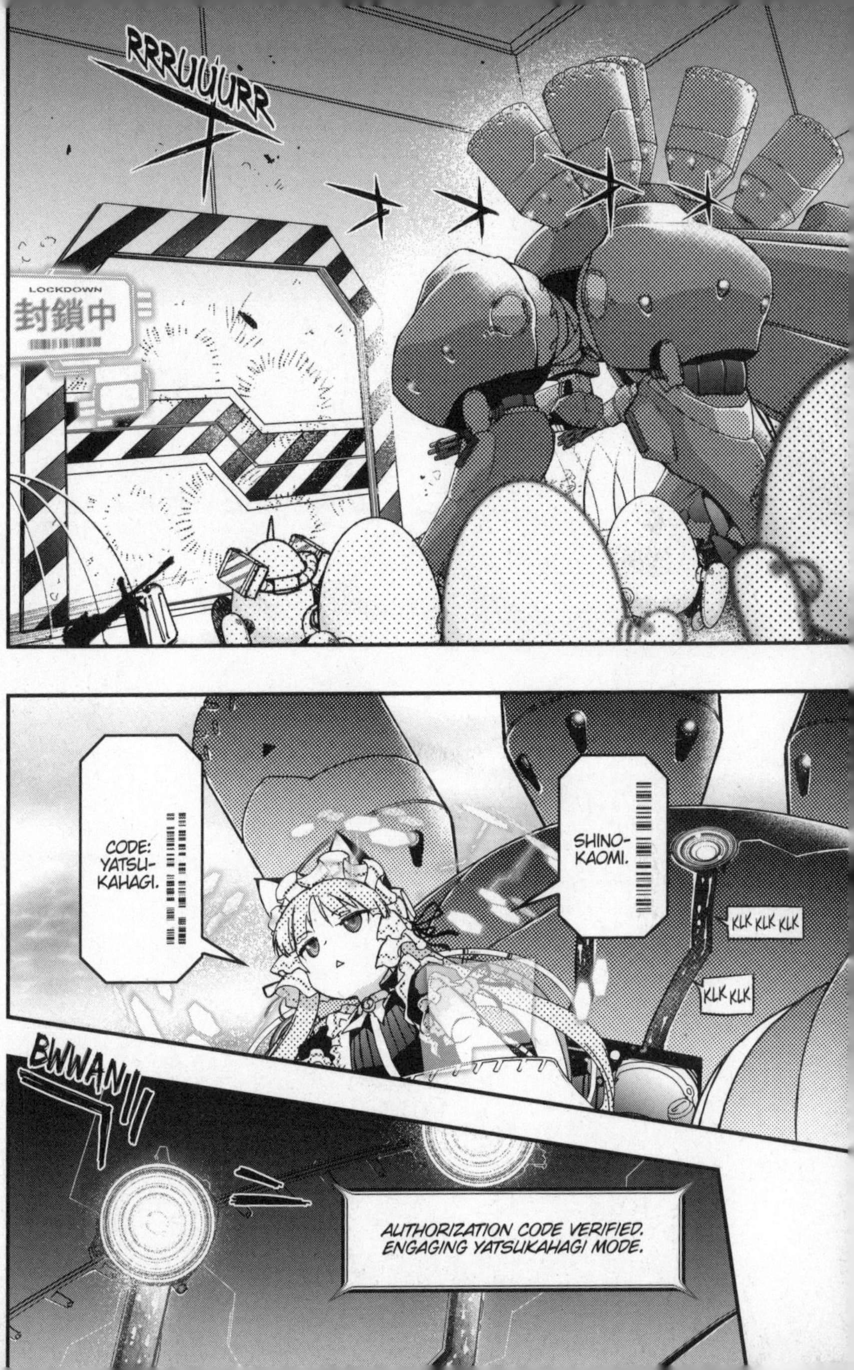
RRRUUURR
LOCKDOWN
封鎖中
SHINO-KAOMI.
KLK KLK KLK
KLK KLK
CODE: YATSUKAHAGI.
BWWAN
AUTHORIZATION CODE VERIFIED. ENGAGING YATSUKAHAGI MODE.

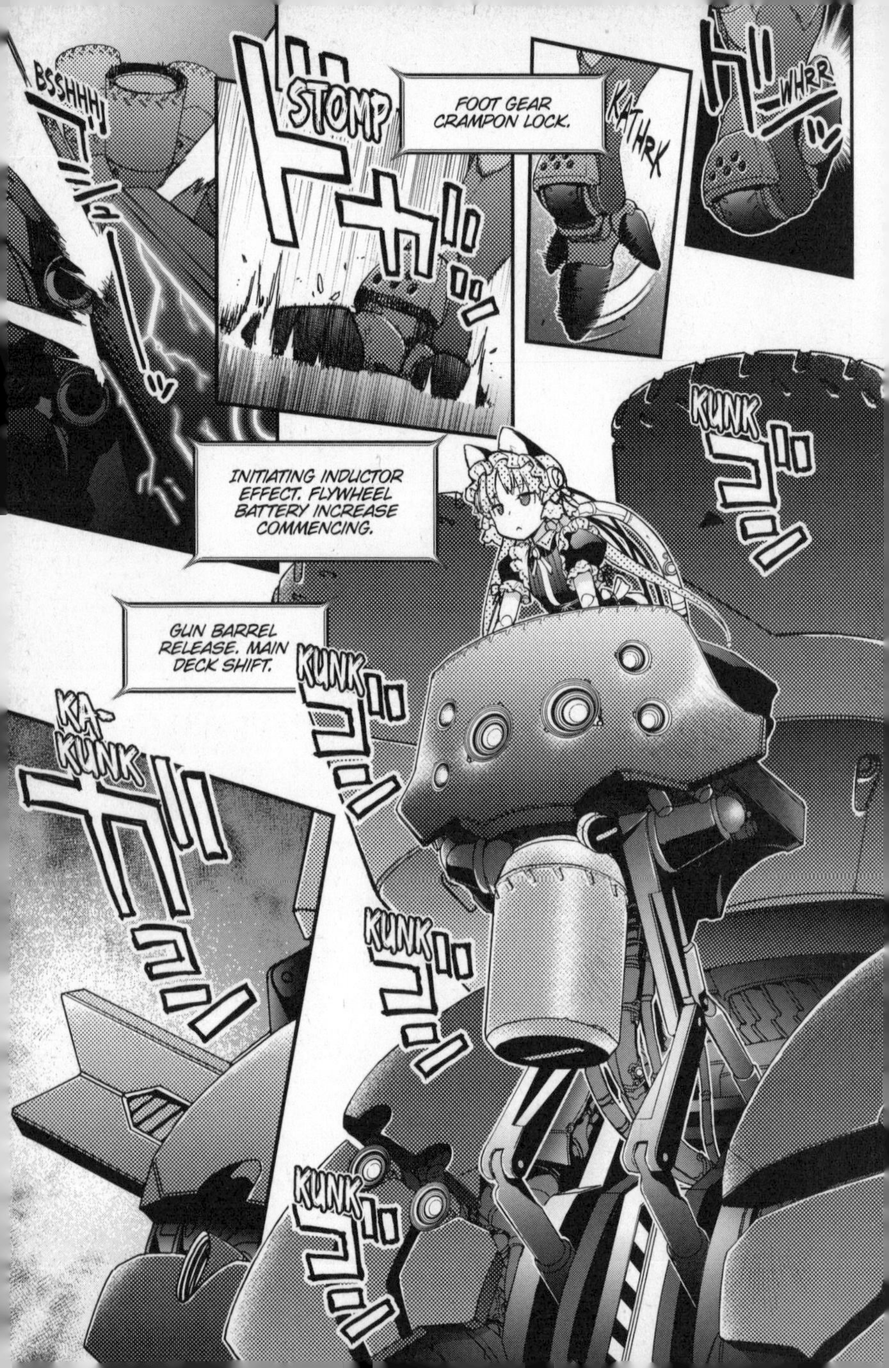

WHRR
KATHRK
FOOT GEAR CRAMPON LOCK.
STOMP
BSSHHH
KUNK
INITIATING INDUCTOR EFFECT. FLYWHEEL BATTERY INCREASE COMMENCING.
GUN BARREL RELEASE. MAIN DECK SHIFT.
KUNK
KA-KUNK
KUNK
KUNK

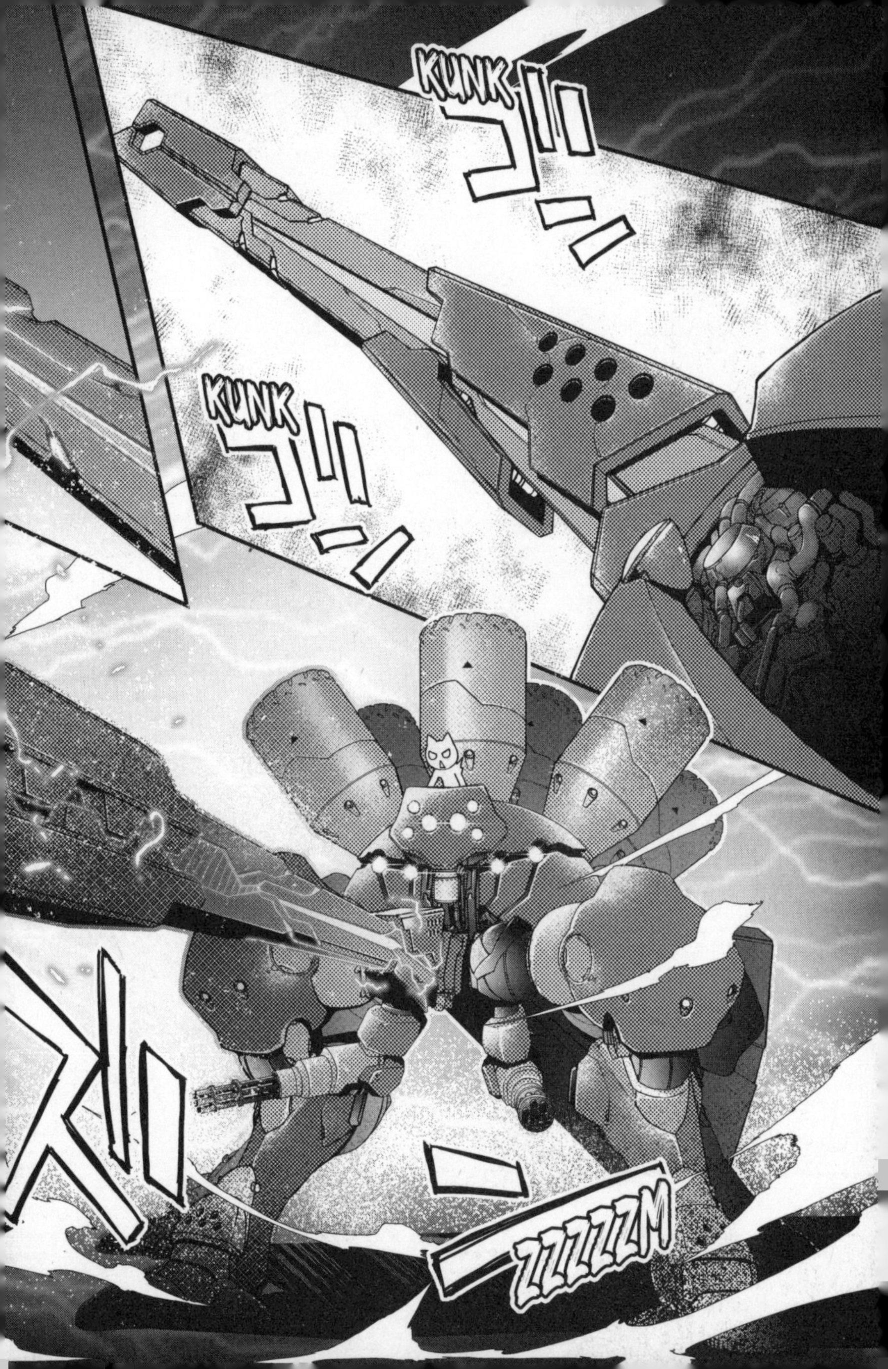
KUNK
KUNK
ZZZZZZM

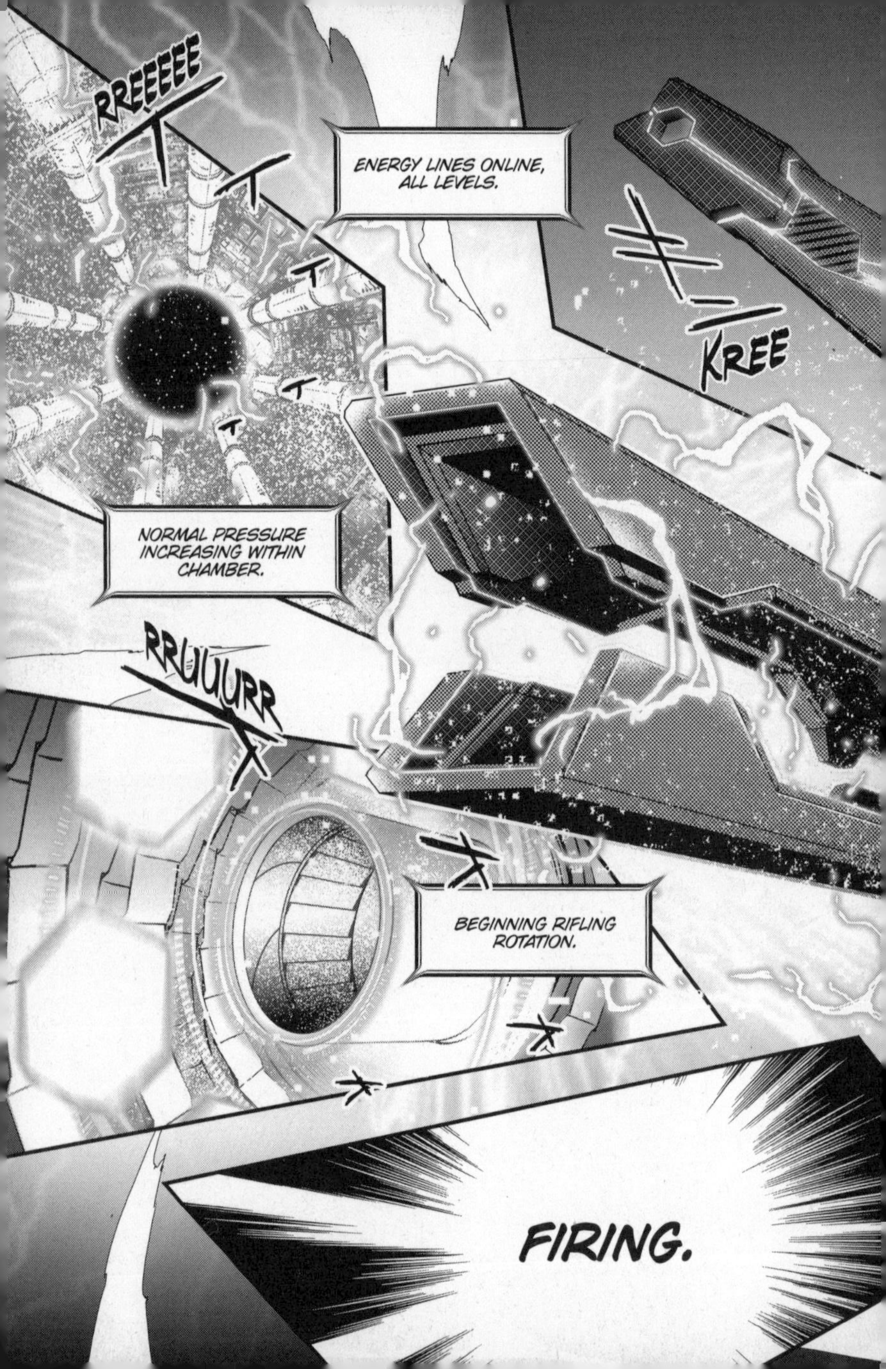
KREE
ENERGY LINES ONLINE, ALL LEVELS.
RREEEEE
NORMAL PRESSURE INCREASING WITHIN CHAMBER.
RRUUURR
BEGINNING RIFLING ROTATION.
FIRING.

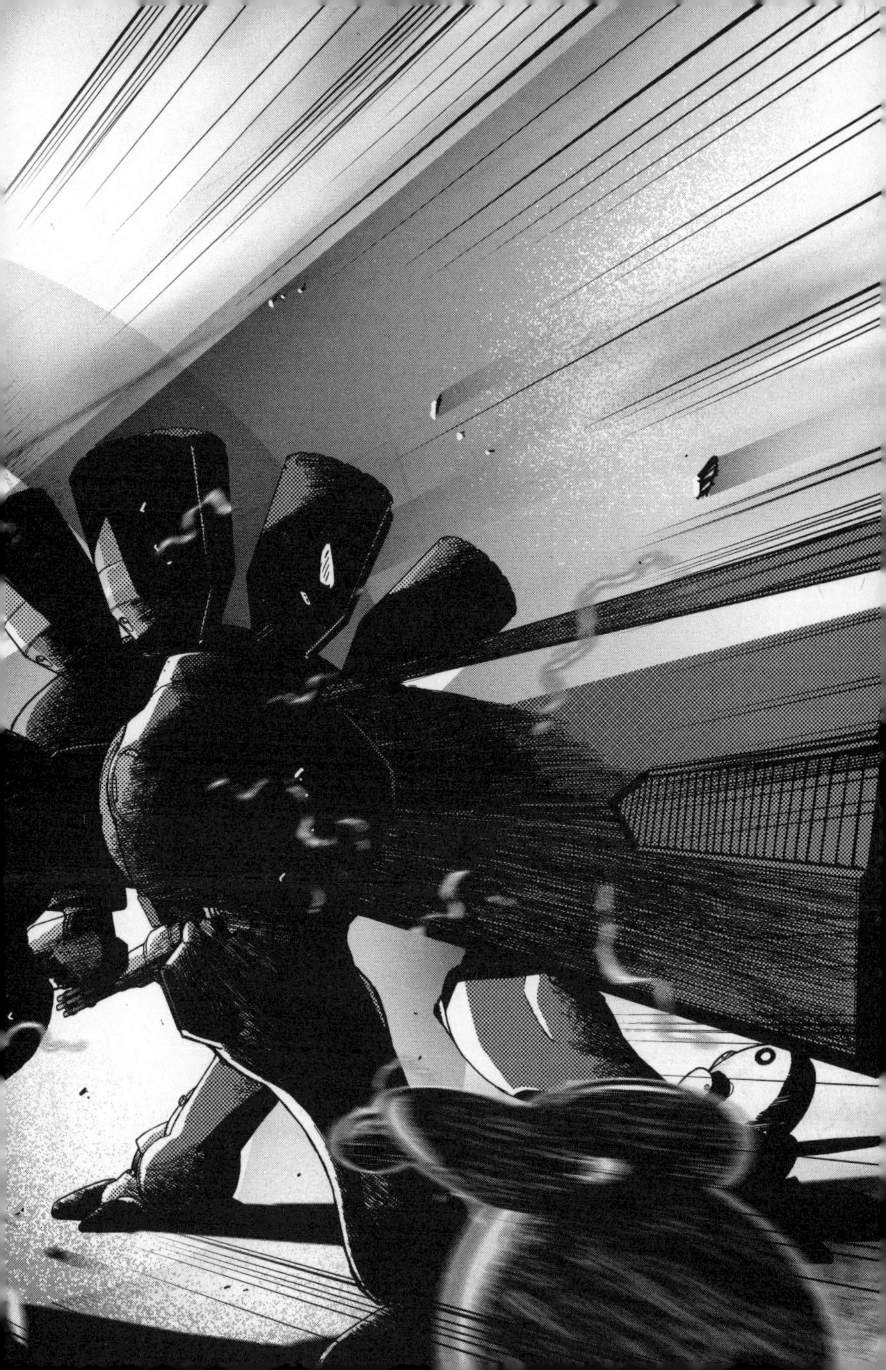

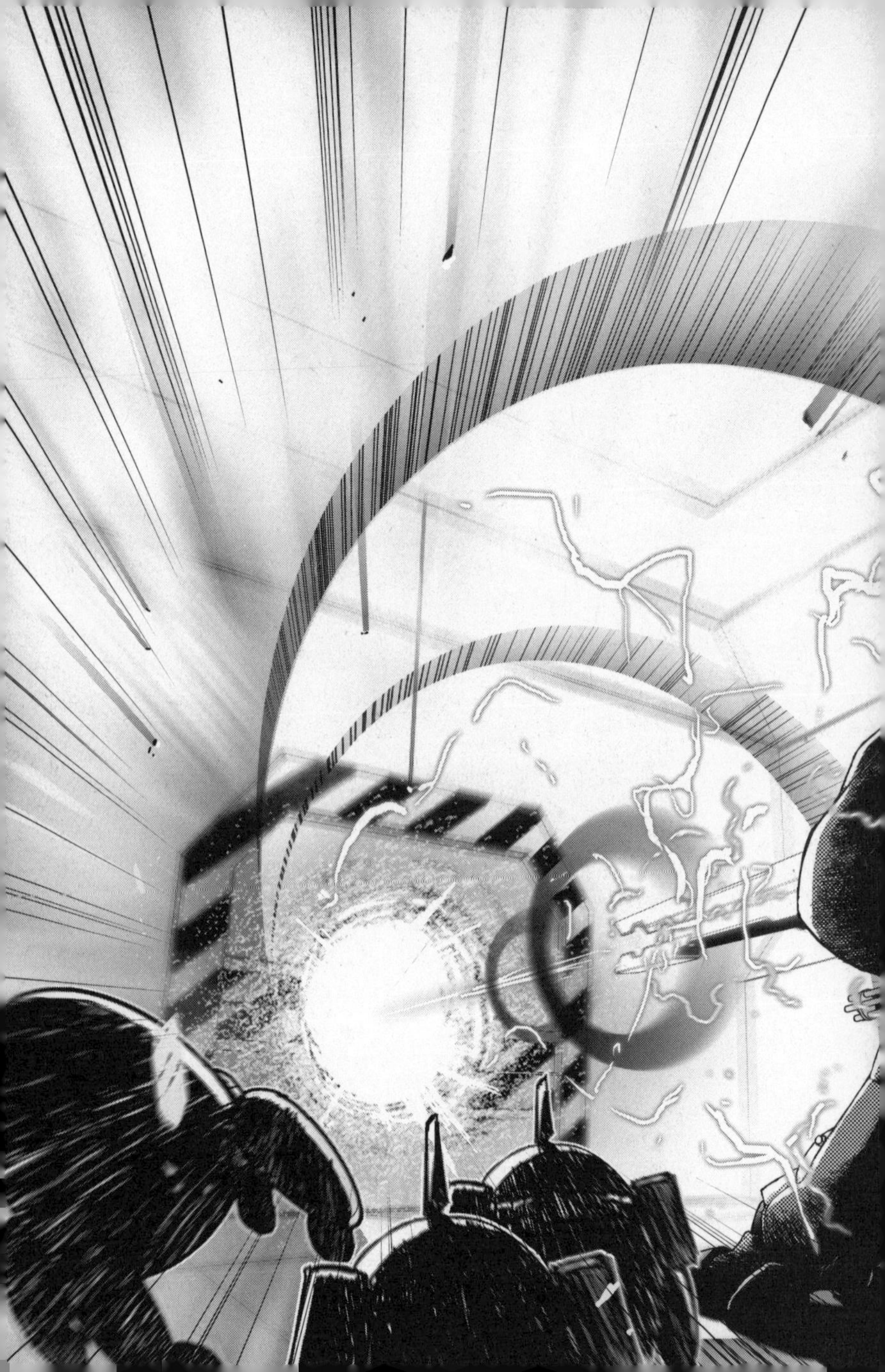

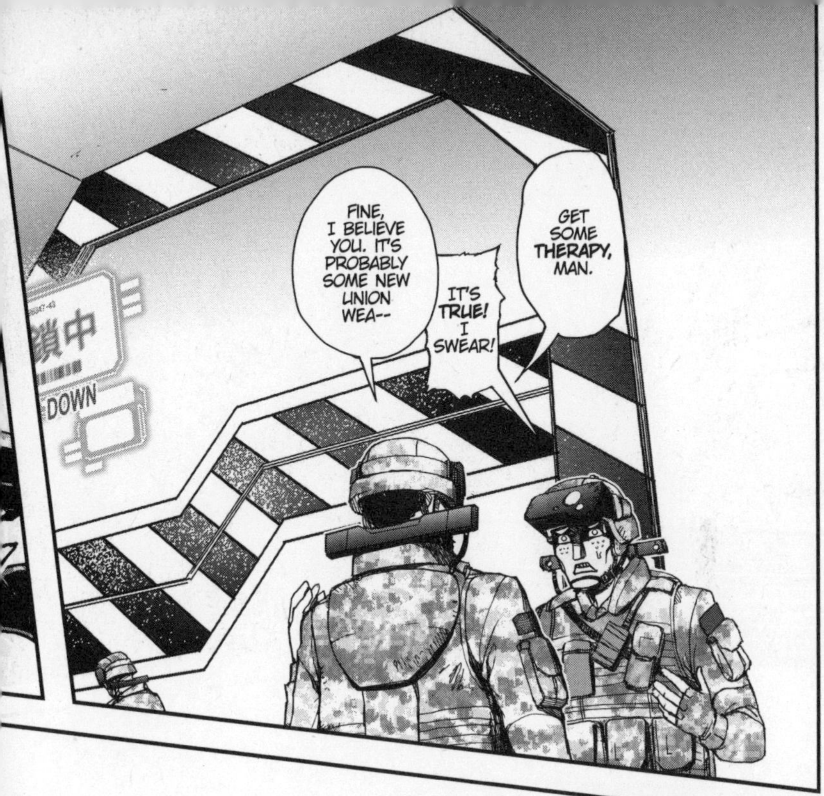
GET SOME THERAPY, MAN.
IT'S TRUE! I SWEAR!
FINE, I BELIEVE YOU. IT'S PROBABLY SOME NEW UNION WEA--
鎖中
DOWN
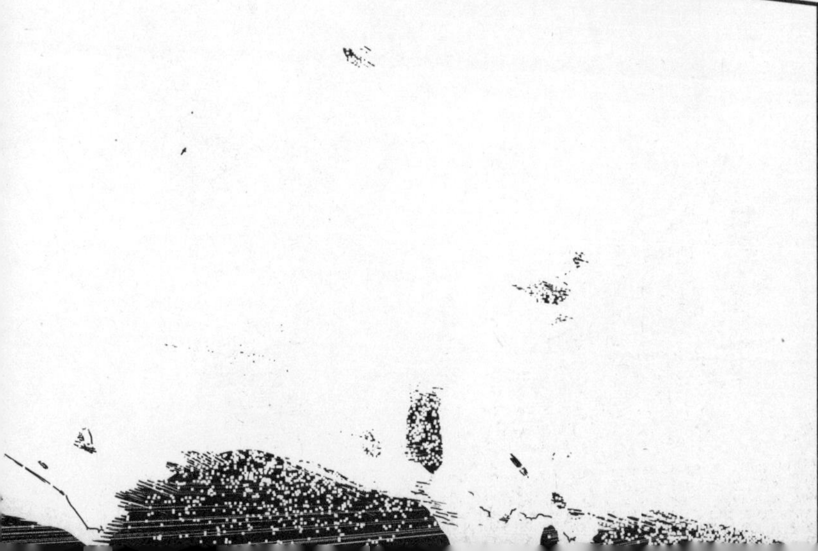

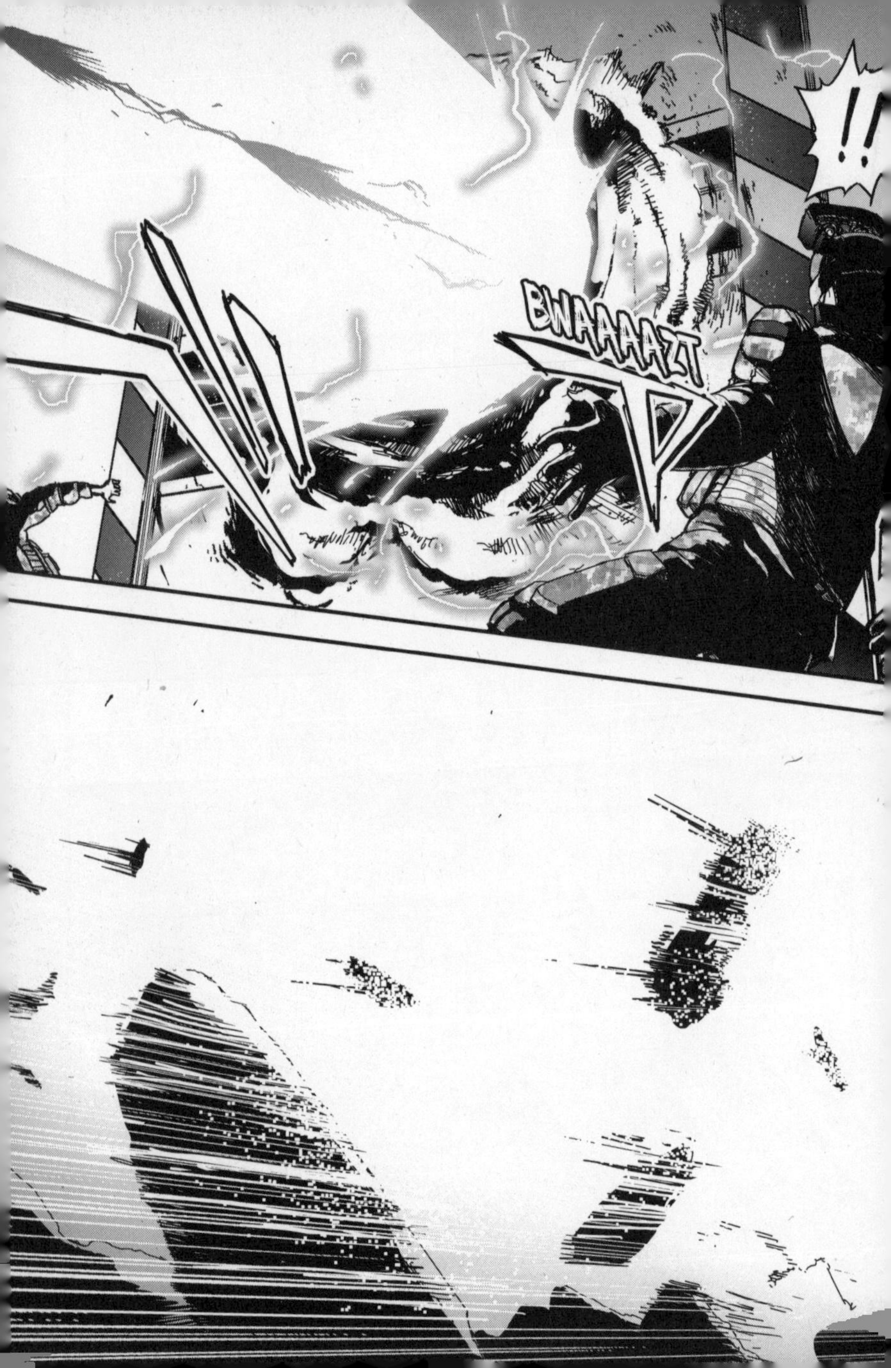
!!
BWAAAAAZT

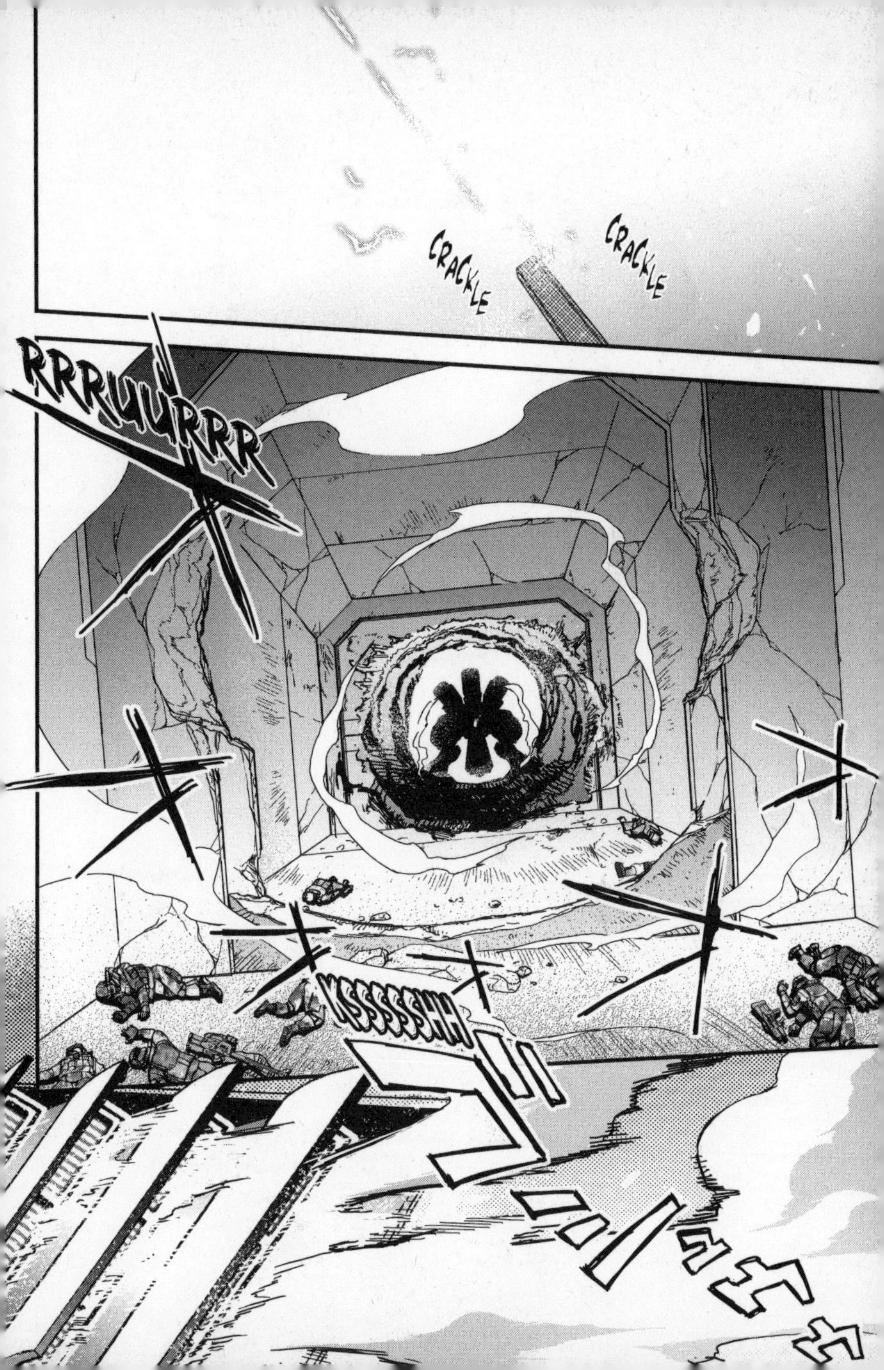
CRACKLE
CRACKLE
RRRUUURRRR
KSSSSSSHH

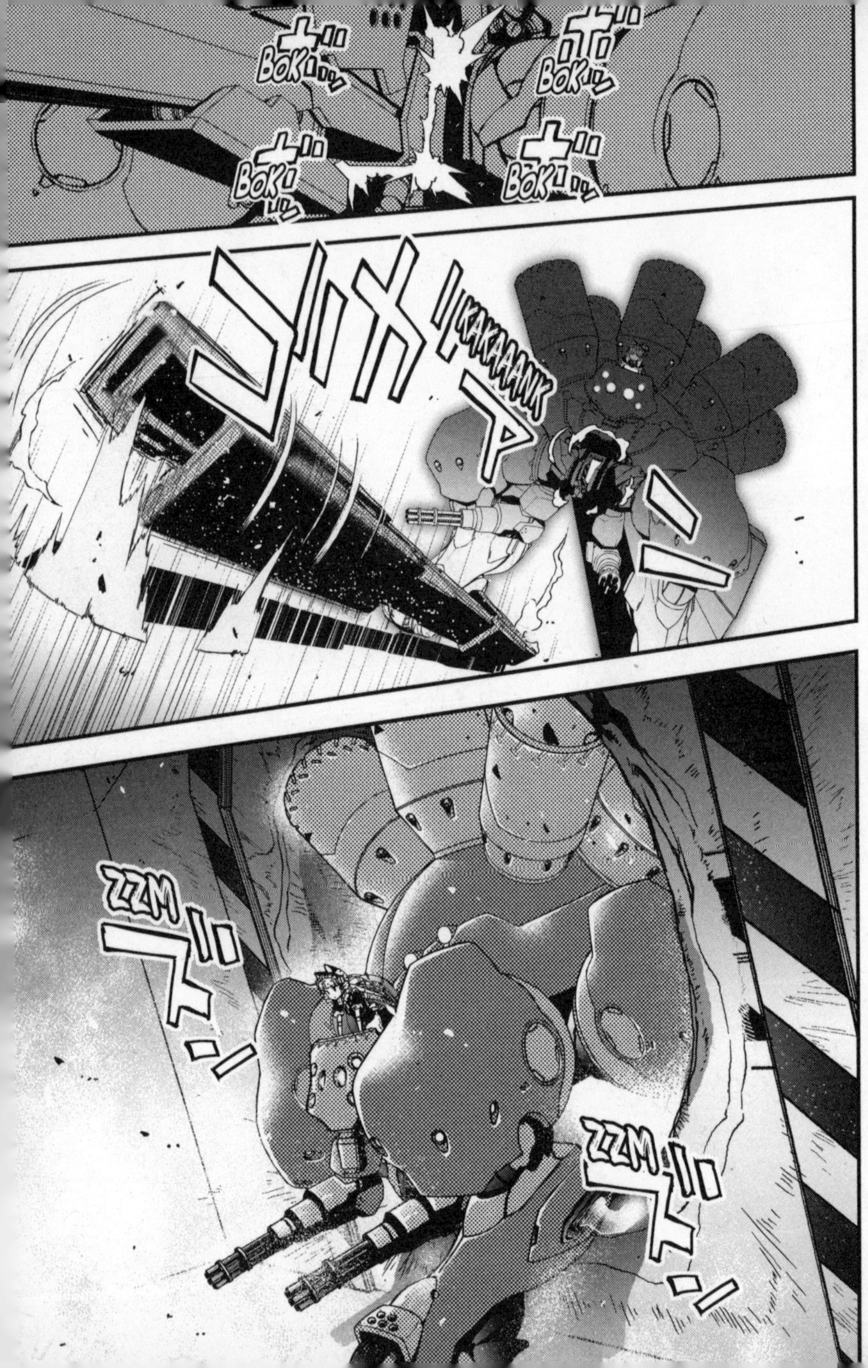
BOK
BOK
BOK
BOK
KAKAAAANK
ZZAM
ZZAM

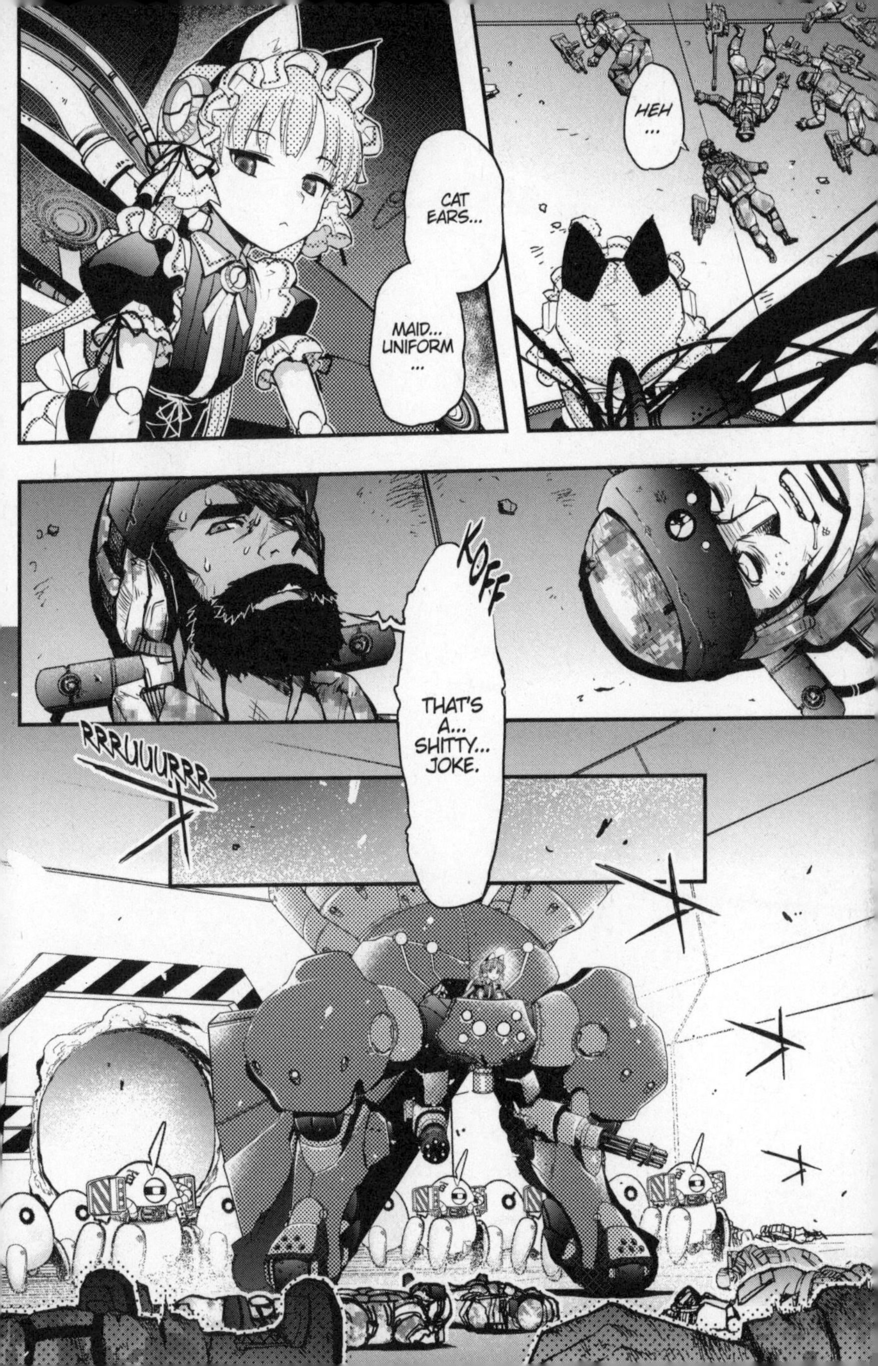
HEH ...
CAT EARS...
MAID... UNIFORM ...
KOFF
THAT'S A... SHITTY... JOKE.
RRRUUUURRR

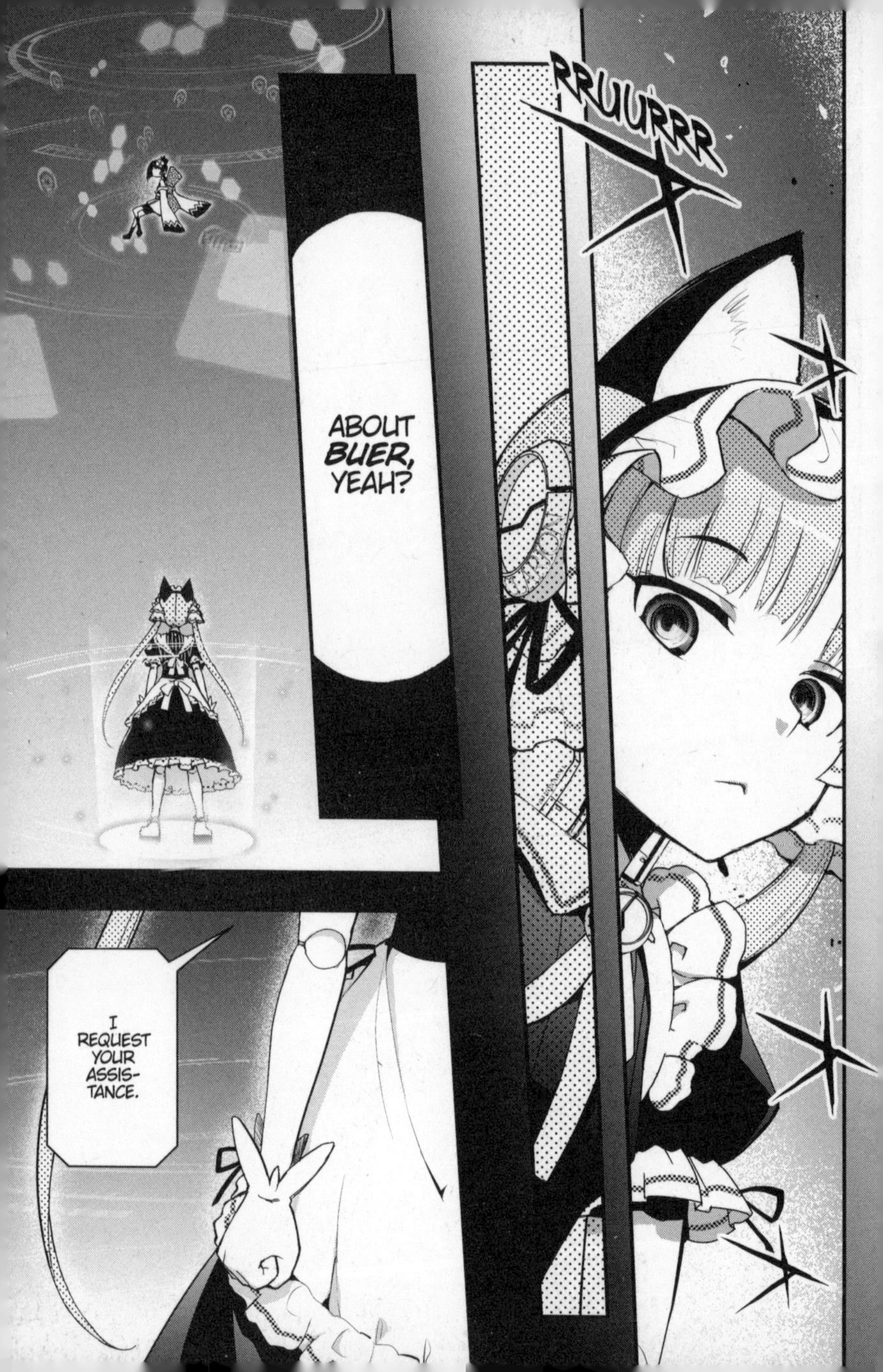
RRUURRR
ABOUT BUER, YEAH?
I REQUEST YOUR ASSIS-TANCE.

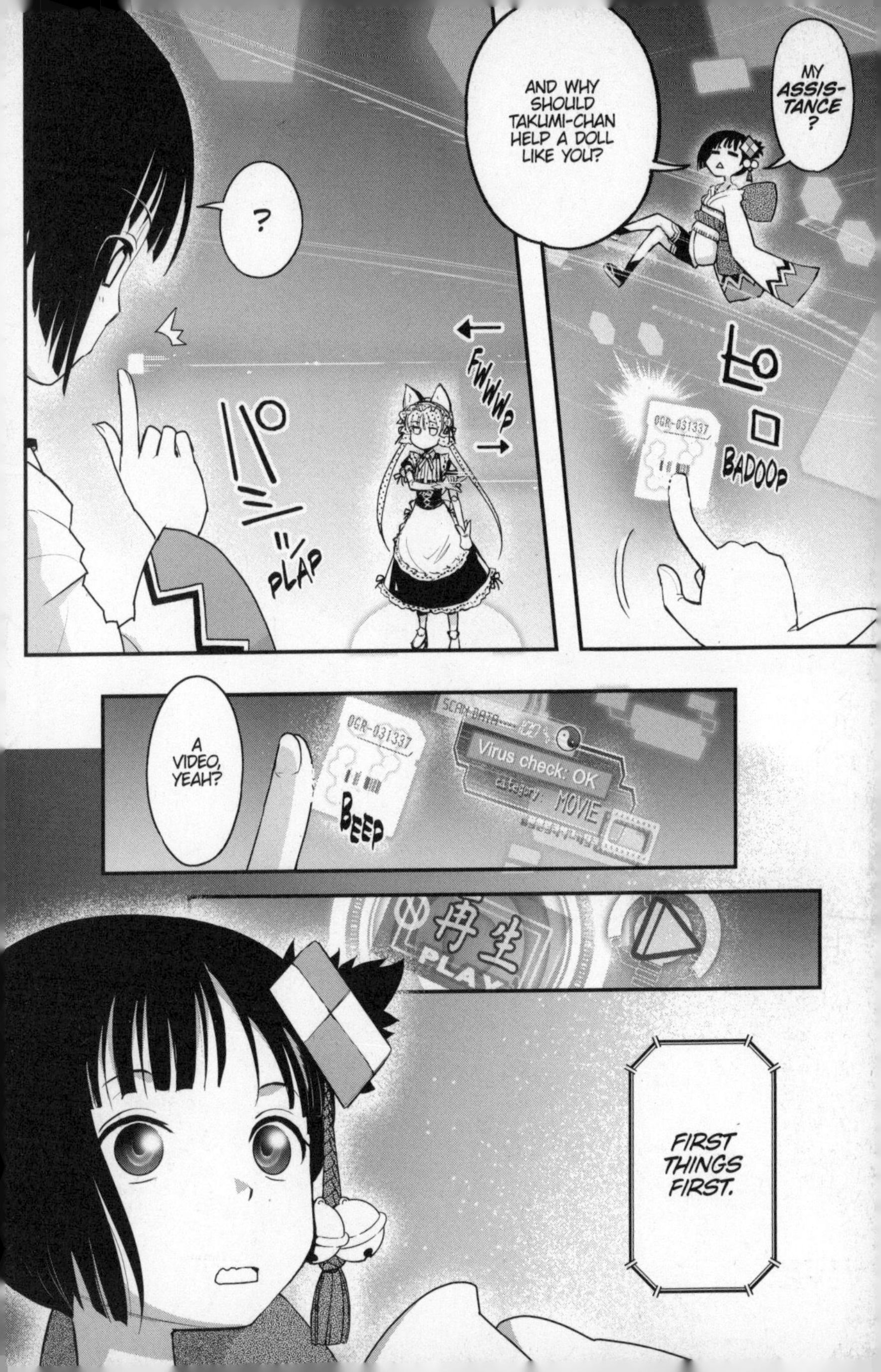
MY ASSISTANCE?
AND WHY SHOULD TAKUMI-CHAN HELP A DOLL LIKE YOU?
OGR-031337
BADOOP
?
FWWWP
PLAP
A VIDEO, YEAH?
OGR-031337
BEEP
SCAN DATA
Virus check: OK
category: MOVIE
再生
PLAY
FIRST THINGS FIRST.

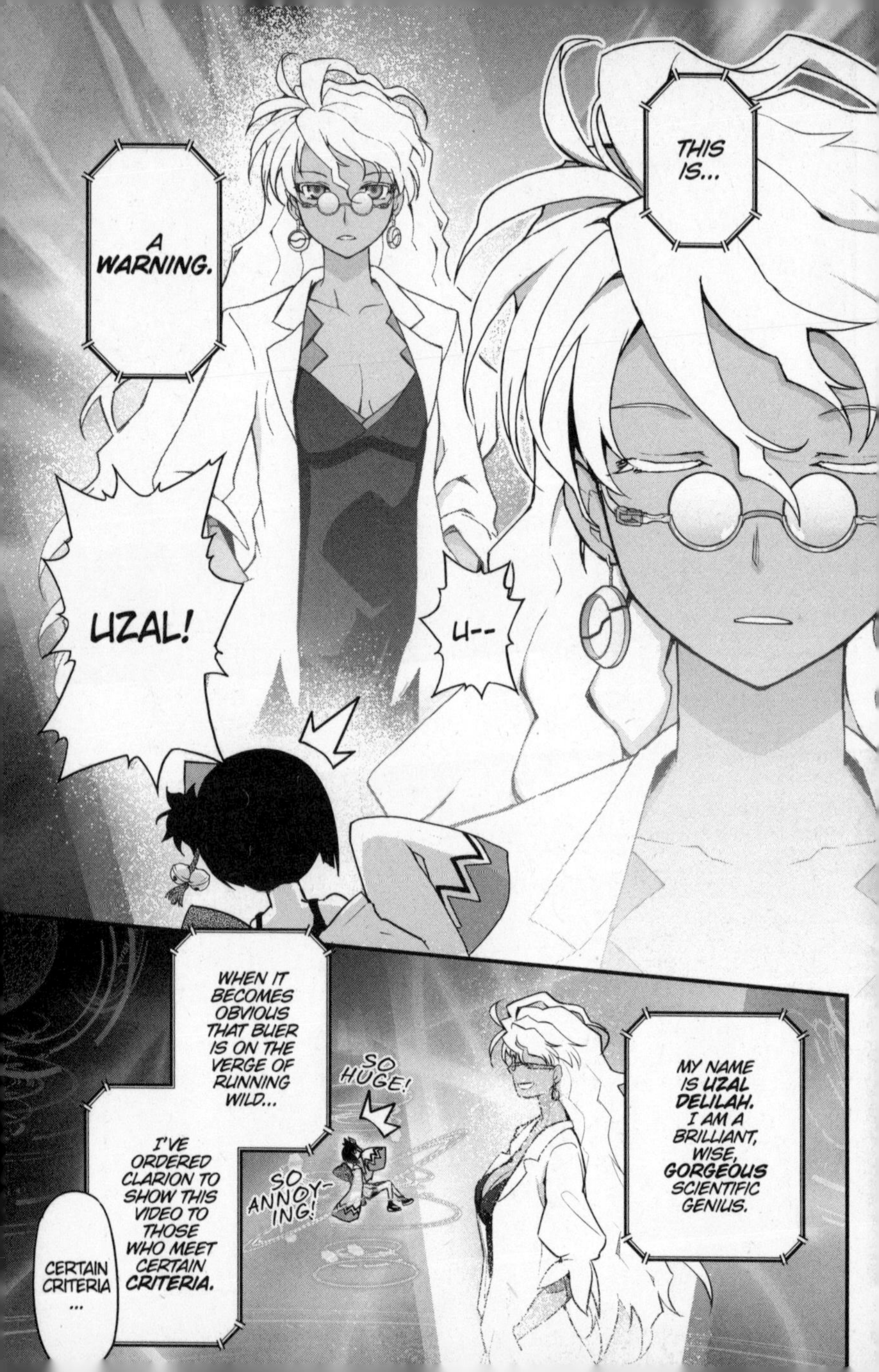
THIS IS...
A WARNING.
U--
UZAL!
MY NAME IS UZAL DELILAH. I AM A BRILLIANT, WISE, GORGEOUS SCIENTIFIC GENIUS.
SO HUGE!
SO ANNOY-ING!
WHEN IT BECOMES OBVIOUS THAT BUER IS ON THE VERGE OF RUNNING WILD...
I'VE ORDERED CLARION TO SHOW THIS VIDEO TO THOSE WHO MEET CERTAIN CRITERIA.
CERTAIN CRITERIA ...

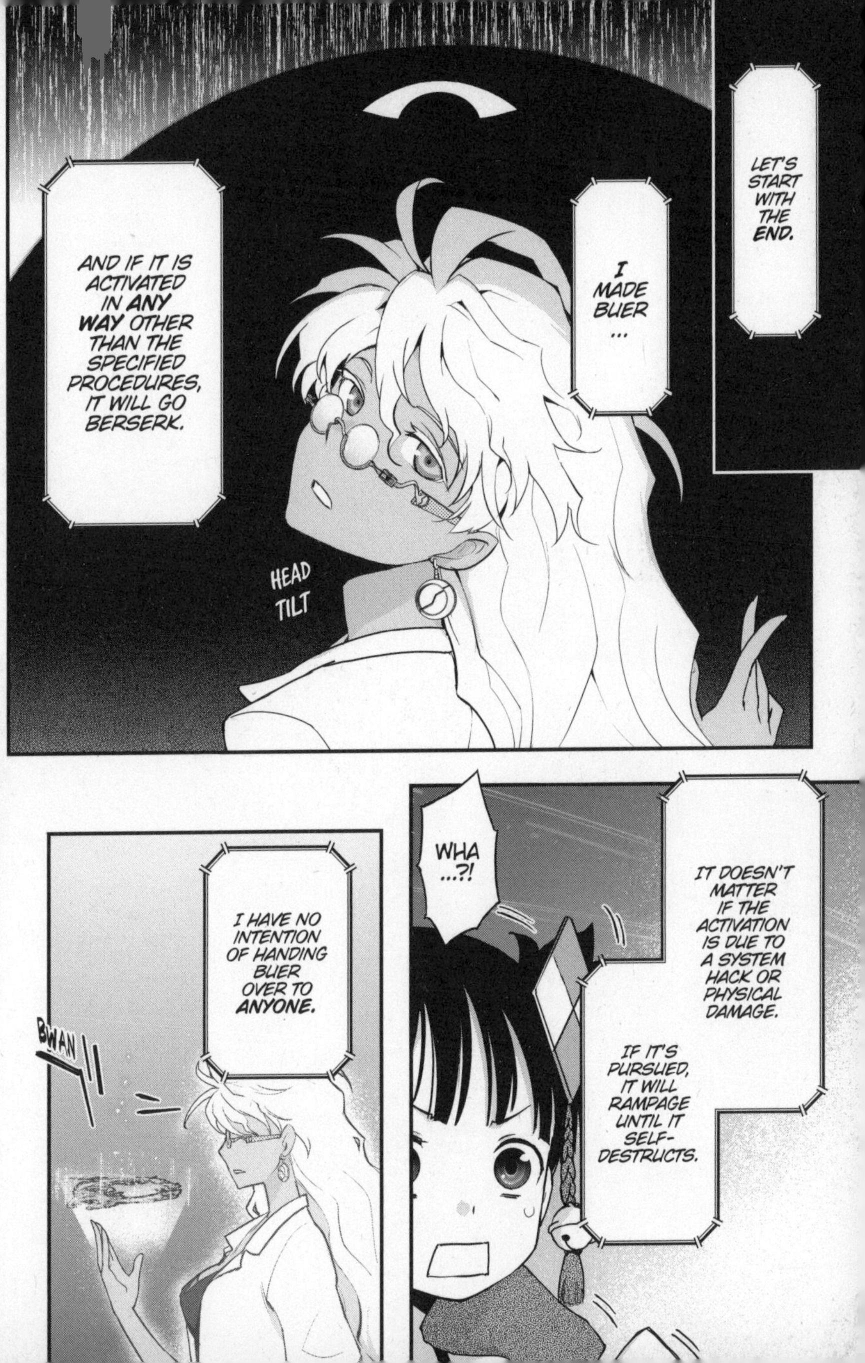
LET'S START WITH THE END.
I MADE BUER ...
AND IF IT IS ACTIVATED IN ANY WAY OTHER THAN THE SPECIFIED PROCEDURES, IT WILL GO BERSERK.
HEAD TILT
WHA ...?!
IT DOESN'T MATTER IF THE ACTIVATION IS DUE TO A SYSTEM HACK OR PHYSICAL DAMAGE.
IF IT'S PURSUED, IT WILL RAMPAGE UNTIL IT SELF-DESTRUCTS.
I HAVE NO INTENTION OF HANDING BUER OVER TO ANYONE.
BWAN

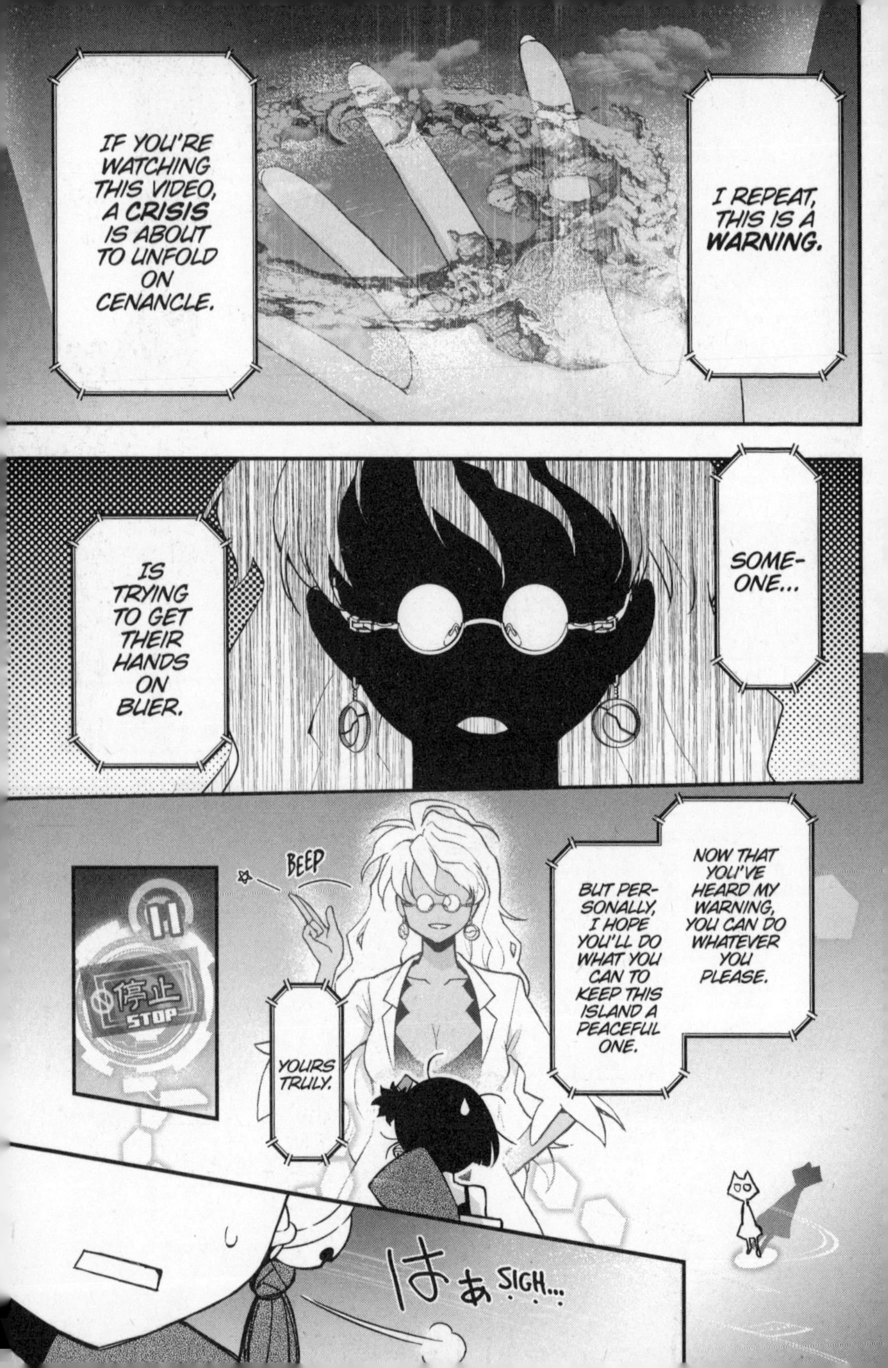
I REPEAT, THIS IS A WARNING.
IF YOU'RE WATCHING THIS VIDEO, A CRISIS IS ABOUT TO UNFOLD ON CENANCLE.
SOME-ONE...
IS TRYING TO GET THEIR HANDS ON BUER.
NOW THAT YOU'VE HEARD MY WARNING, YOU CAN DO WHATEVER YOU PLEASE.
BUT PER-SONALLY, I HOPE YOU'LL DO WHAT YOU CAN TO KEEP THIS ISLAND A PEACEFUL ONE.
BEEP
YOURS TRULY.
停止
STOP
はぁ SIGH...

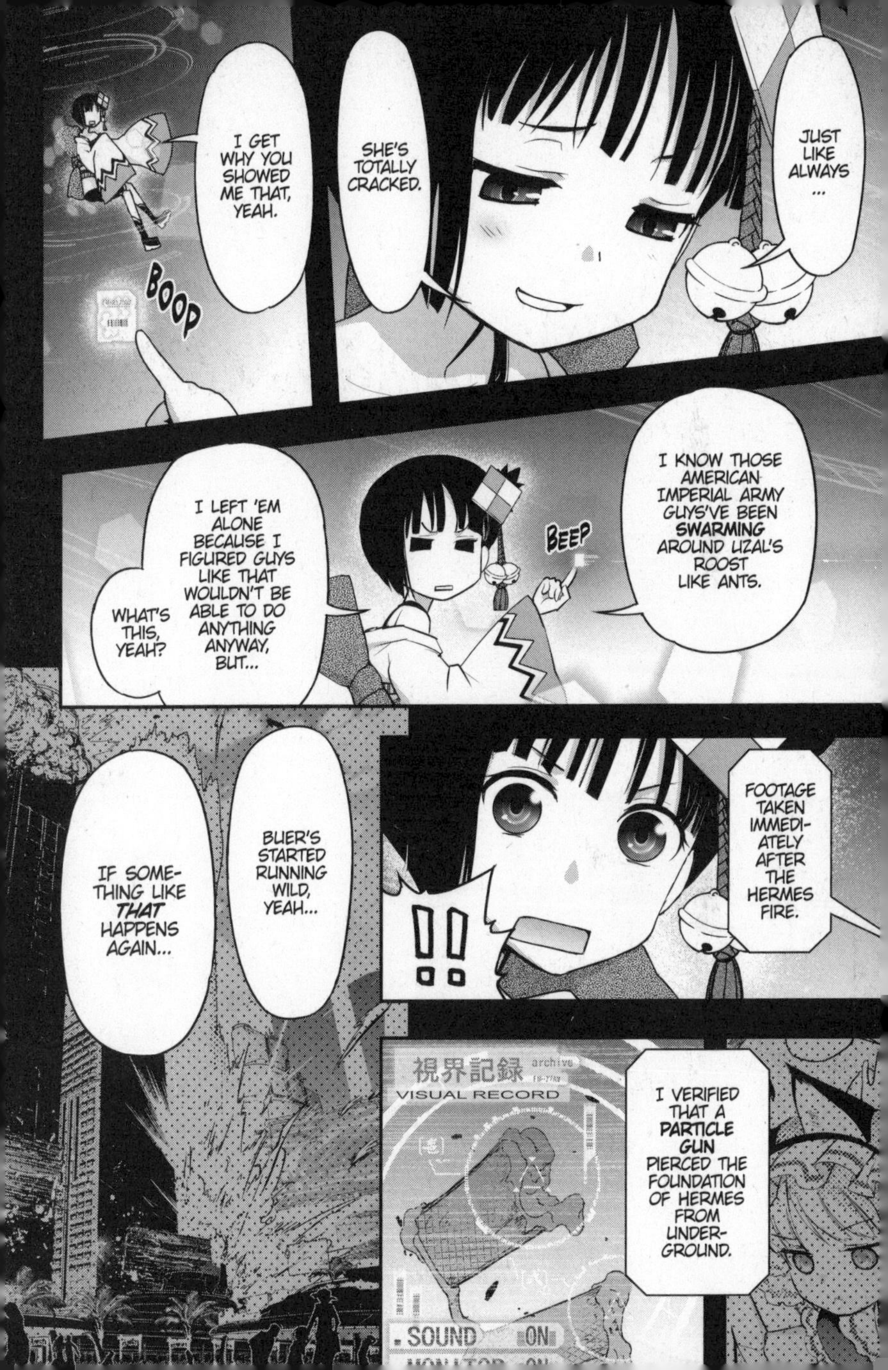

JUST LIKE ALWAYS ...
SHE'S TOTALLY CRACKED.
I GET WHY YOU SHOWED ME THAT, YEAH.
BOOP
I KNOW THOSE AMERICAN IMPERIAL ARMY GUYS'VE BEEN **SWARMING** AROUND UZAL'S ROOST LIKE ANTS.
BEEP
I LEFT 'EM ALONE BECAUSE I FIGURED GUYS LIKE THAT WOULDN'T BE ABLE TO DO ANYTHING ANYWAY, BUT...
WHAT'S THIS, YEAH?
FOOTAGE TAKEN IMMEDI-ATELY AFTER THE HERMES FIRE.
!!
視界記録 archive
VISUAL RECORD
SOUND ON
I VERIFIED THAT A **PARTICLE GUN** PIERCED THE FOUNDATION OF HERMES FROM UNDER-GROUND.
BUER'S STARTED RUNNING WILD, YEAH...
IF SOME-THING LIKE ***THAT*** HAPPENS AGAIN...

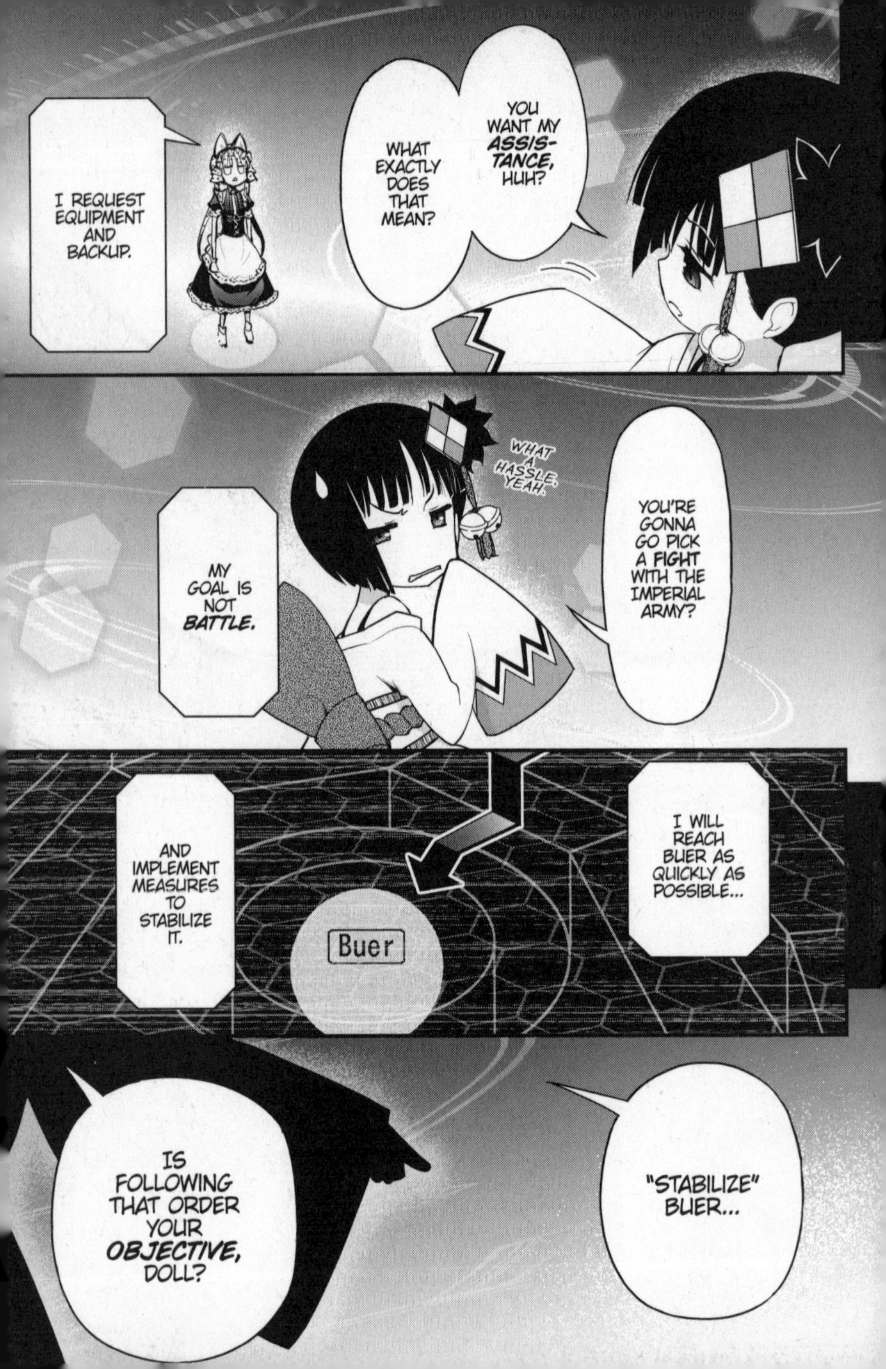
YOU WANT MY ASSISTANCE, HUH?
WHAT EXACTLY DOES THAT MEAN?
I REQUEST EQUIPMENT AND BACKUP.
YOU'RE GONNA GO PICK A FIGHT WITH THE IMPERIAL ARMY?
WHAT A HASSLE, YEAH.
MY GOAL IS NOT BATTLE.
I WILL REACH BUER AS QUICKLY AS POSSIBLE...
Buer
AND IMPLEMENT MEASURES TO STABILIZE IT.
"STABILIZE" BUER...
IS FOLLOWING THAT ORDER YOUR OBJECTIVE, DOLL?

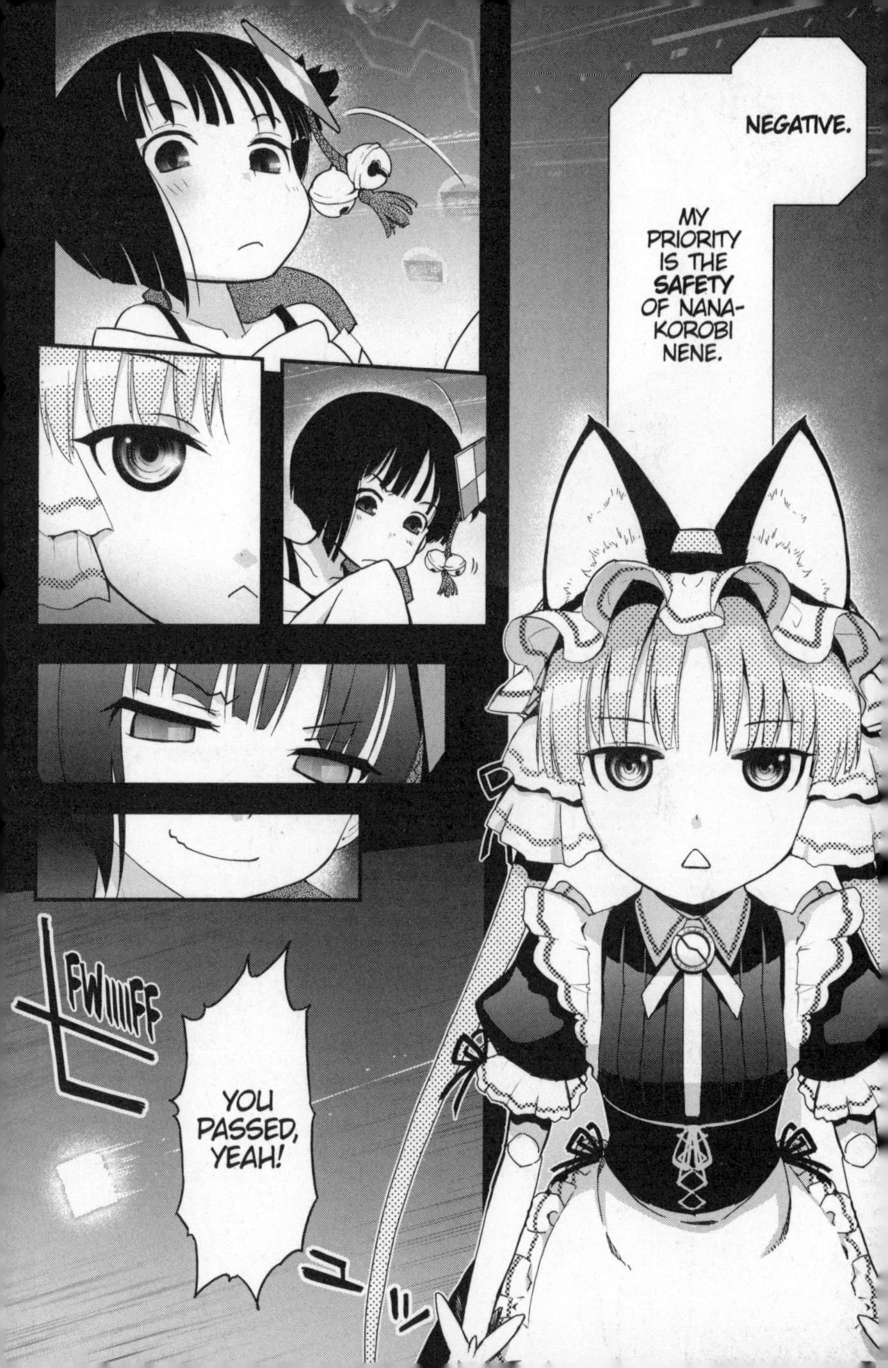
NEGATIVE.
MY PRIORITY IS THE SAFETY OF NANA-KOROBI NENE.
YOU PASSED, YEAH!
FWIIIIFF

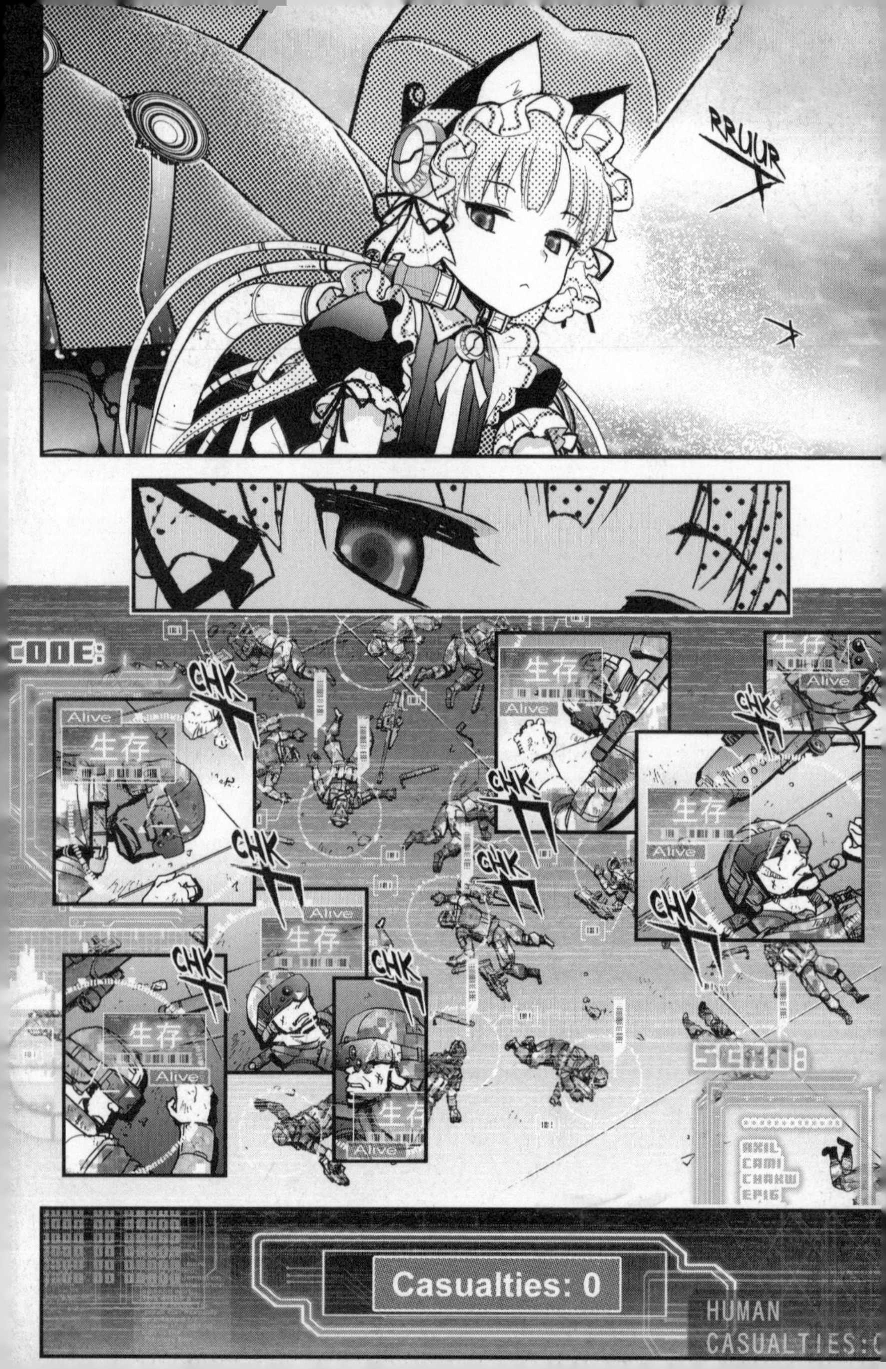

RRUUR
CODE:
生存
Alive
CHK
生存
Alive
CHK
生存
Alive
CHK
CHK
CHK
生存
Alive
CHK
生存
Alive
CHK
生存
Alive
CHK
生存
Alive
Casualties: 0
HUMAN
CASUALTIES:

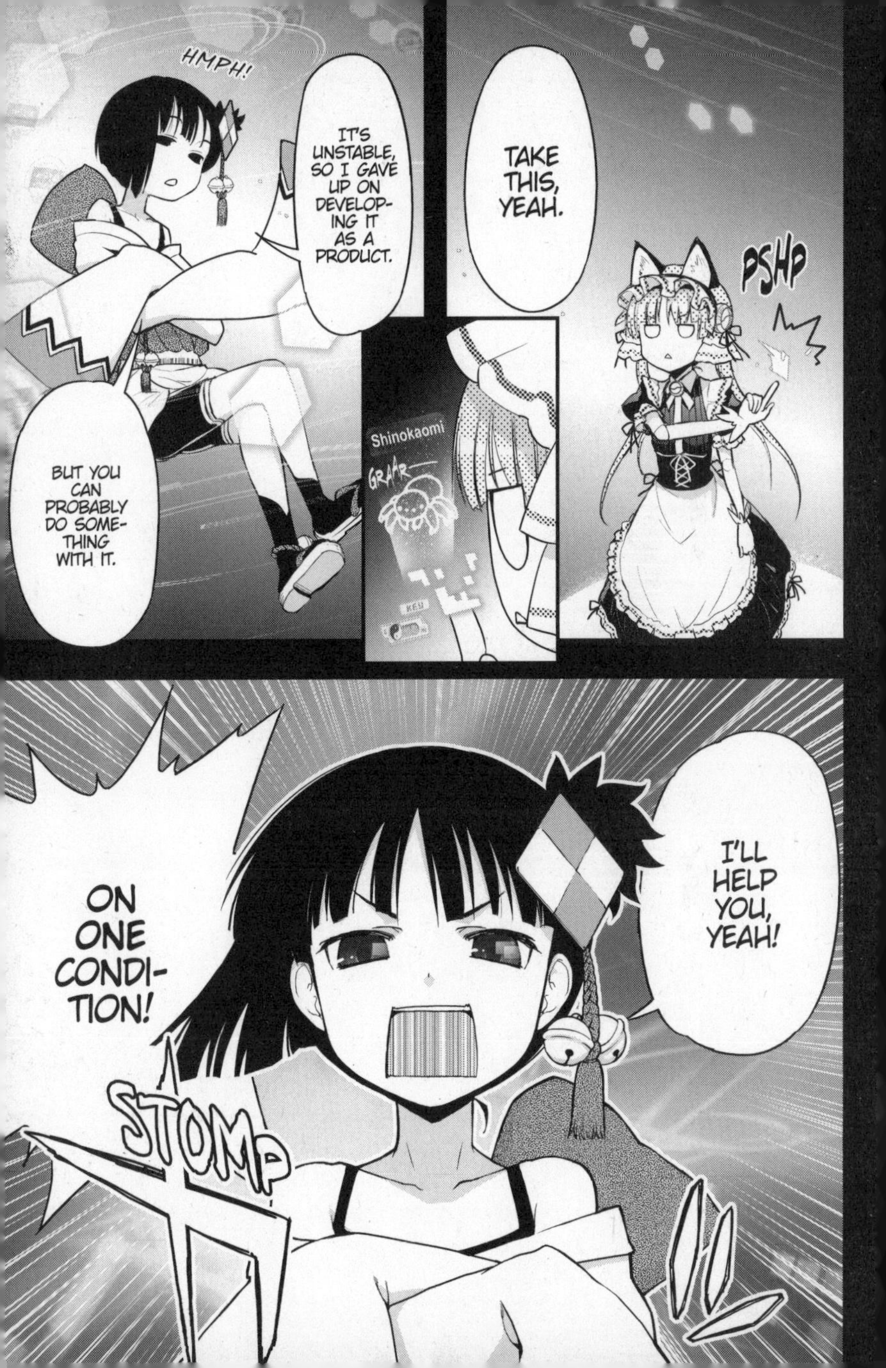
TAKE THIS, YEAH.
PSHP
Shinokaomi
GRAAR
KEY
HMPH!
IT'S UNSTABLE, SO I GAVE UP ON DEVELOPING IT AS A PRODUCT.
BUT YOU CAN PROBABLY DO SOMETHING WITH IT.
I'LL HELP YOU, YEAH!
ON ONE CONDITION!
STOMP

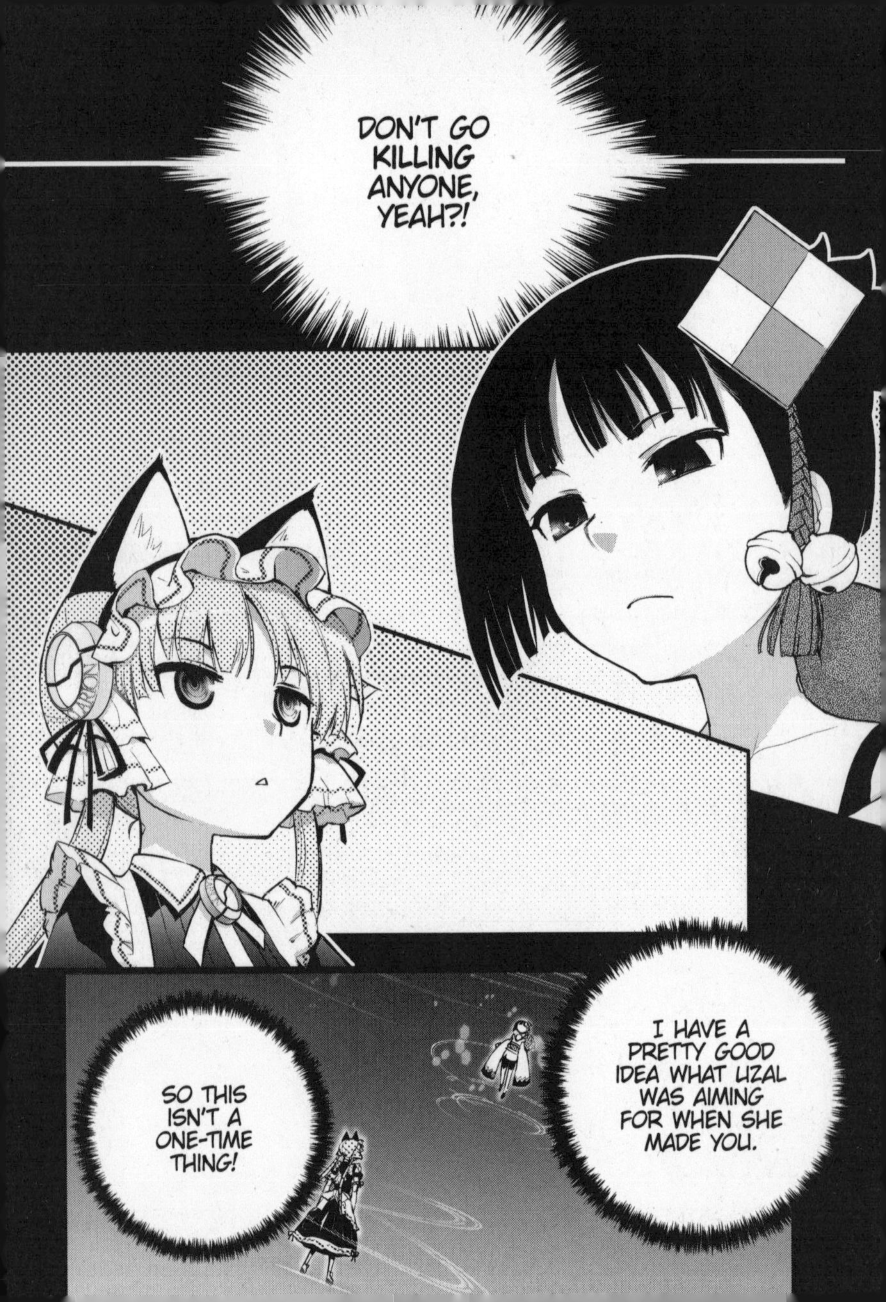
DON'T GO KILLING ANYONE, YEAH?!
I HAVE A PRETTY GOOD IDEA WHAT LIZAL WAS AIMING FOR WHEN SHE MADE YOU.
SO THIS ISN'T A ONE-TIME THING!

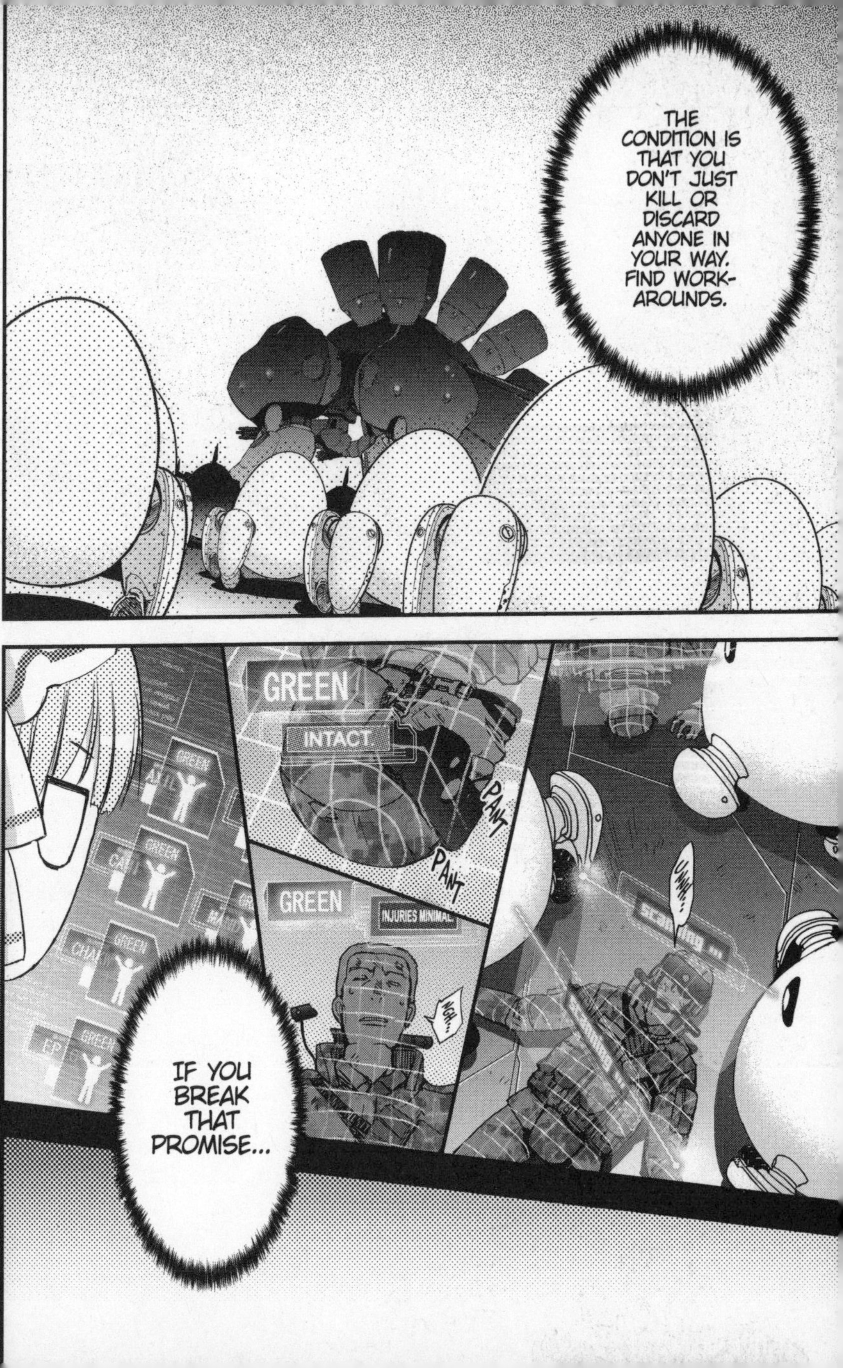
THE CONDITION IS THAT YOU DON'T JUST KILL OR DISCARD ANYONE IN YOUR WAY. FIND WORK-AROUNDS.
UNH...
GREEN
INTACT.
PANT
PANT
GREEN
INJURIES MINIMAL
NGH...
GREEN
GREEN
GREEN
GREEN
IF YOU BREAK THAT PROMISE...

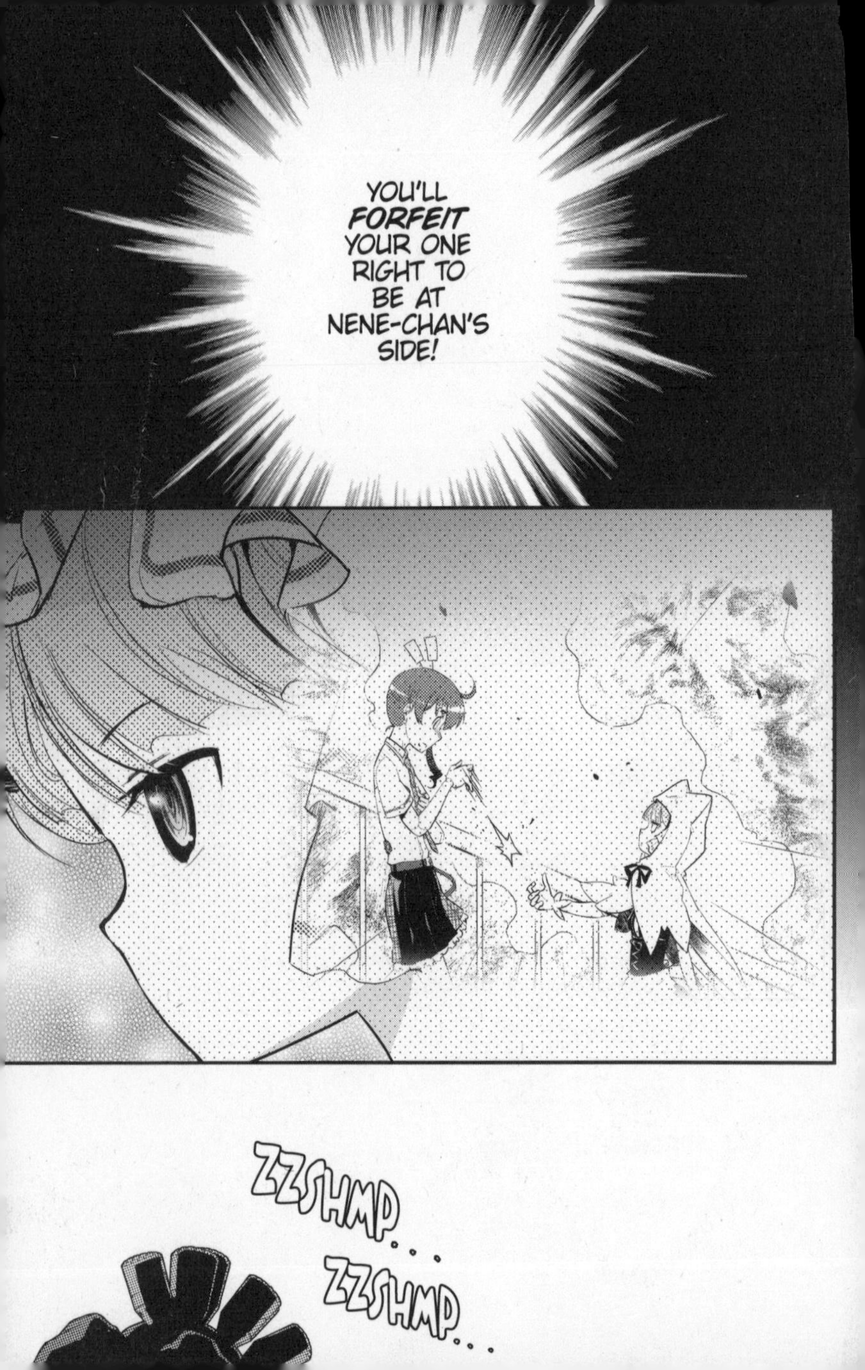
YOU'LL *FORFEIT* YOUR ONE RIGHT TO BE AT NENE-CHAN'S SIDE!
ZZSHMP...
ZZSHMP...

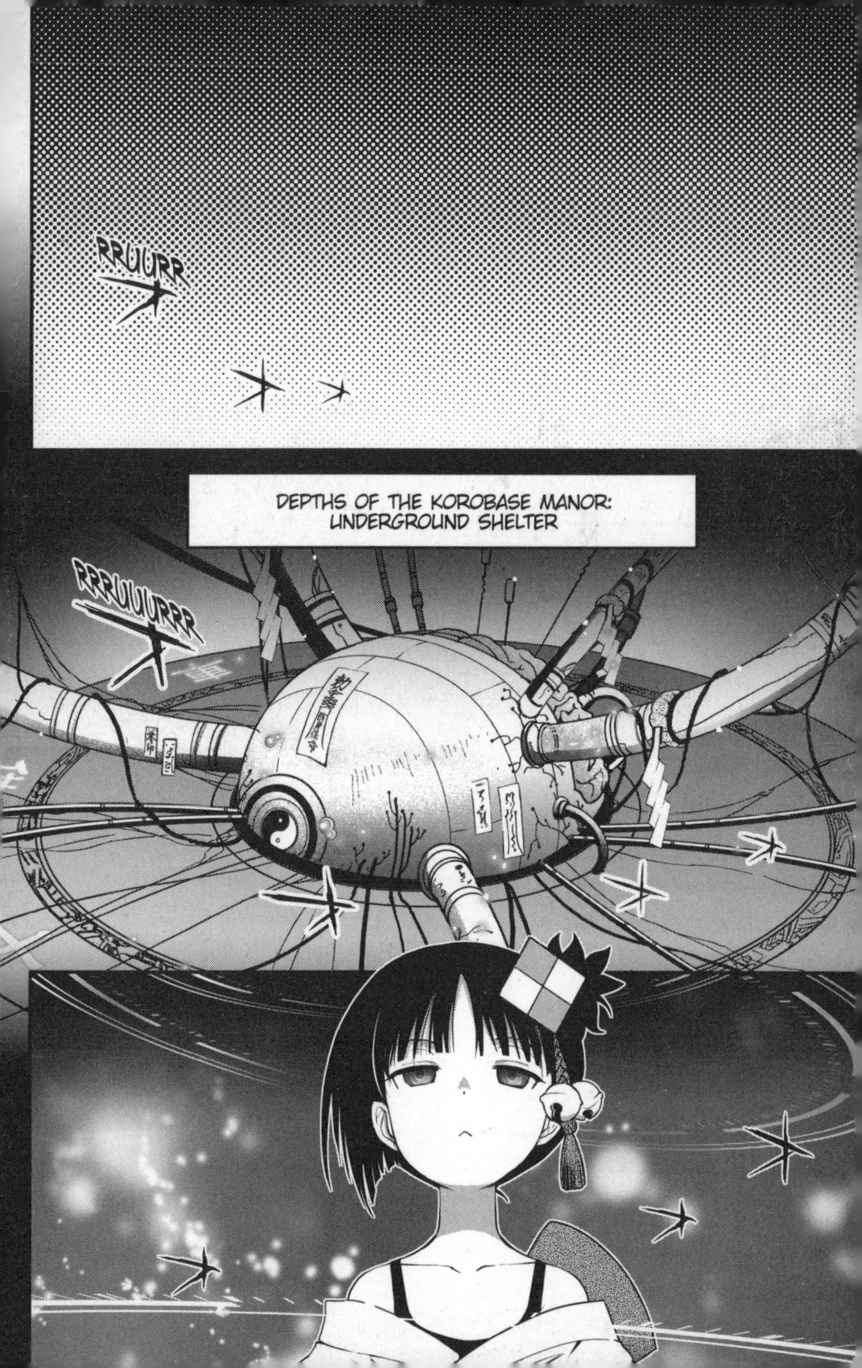
RRUURR
DEPTHS OF THE KOROBASE MANOR: UNDERGROUND SHELTER
RRRUUURRR

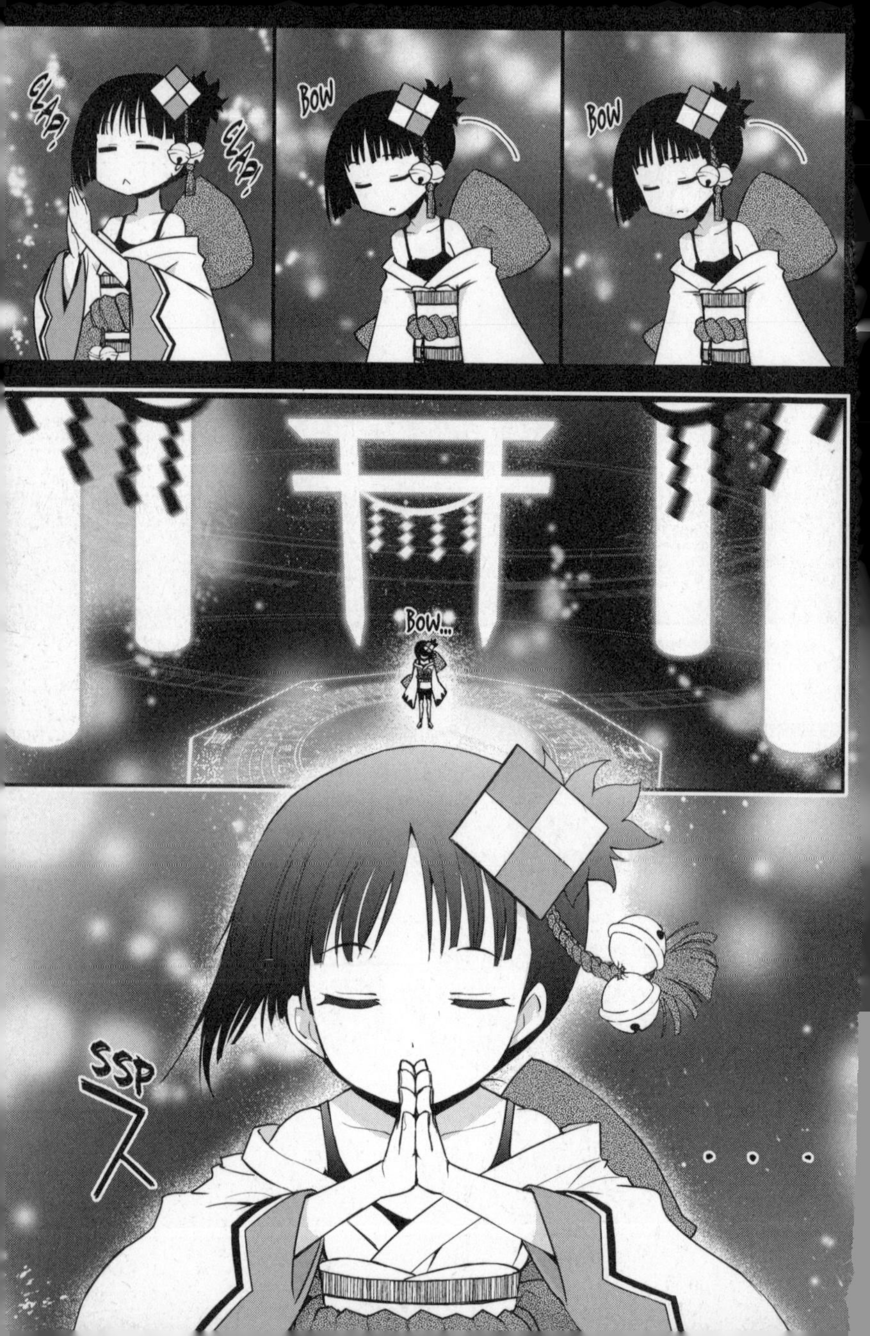
BOW
BOW
CLAP!
CLAP!
BOW...
SSP
...

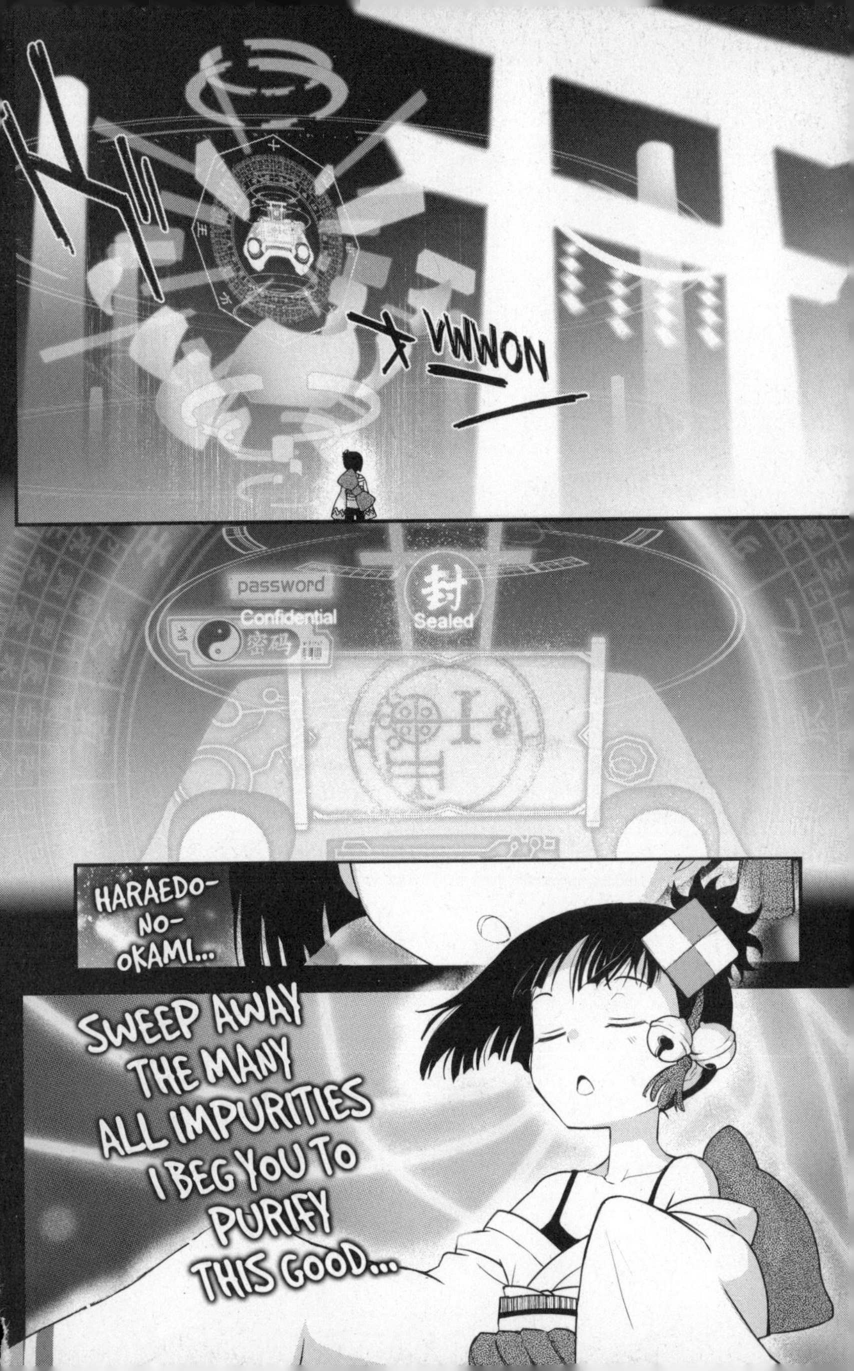
VWWON
password
Confidential
封
Sealed
密码
HARAEDO-NO-OKAMI...
SWEEP AWAY THE MANY ALL IMPURITIES I BEG YOU TO PURIFY THIS GOOD...

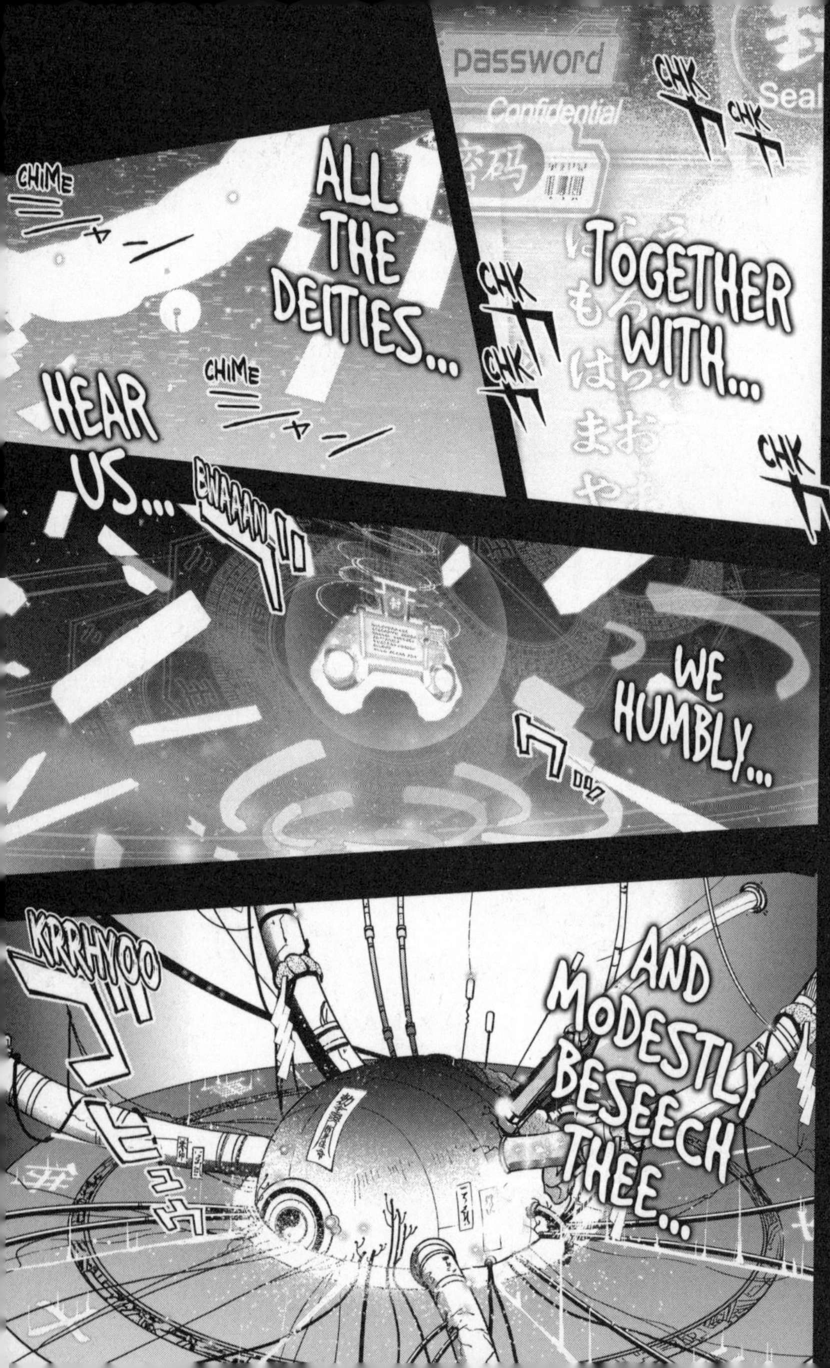
Seal
CHK
CHK
password
Confidential
TOGETHER WITH...
CHK
CHK
CHK
ALL THE DEITIES...
CHIME
CHIME
HEAR US...
BWAAAN
WE HUMBLY...
AND MODESTLY BESEECH THEE...
KRRHYOO

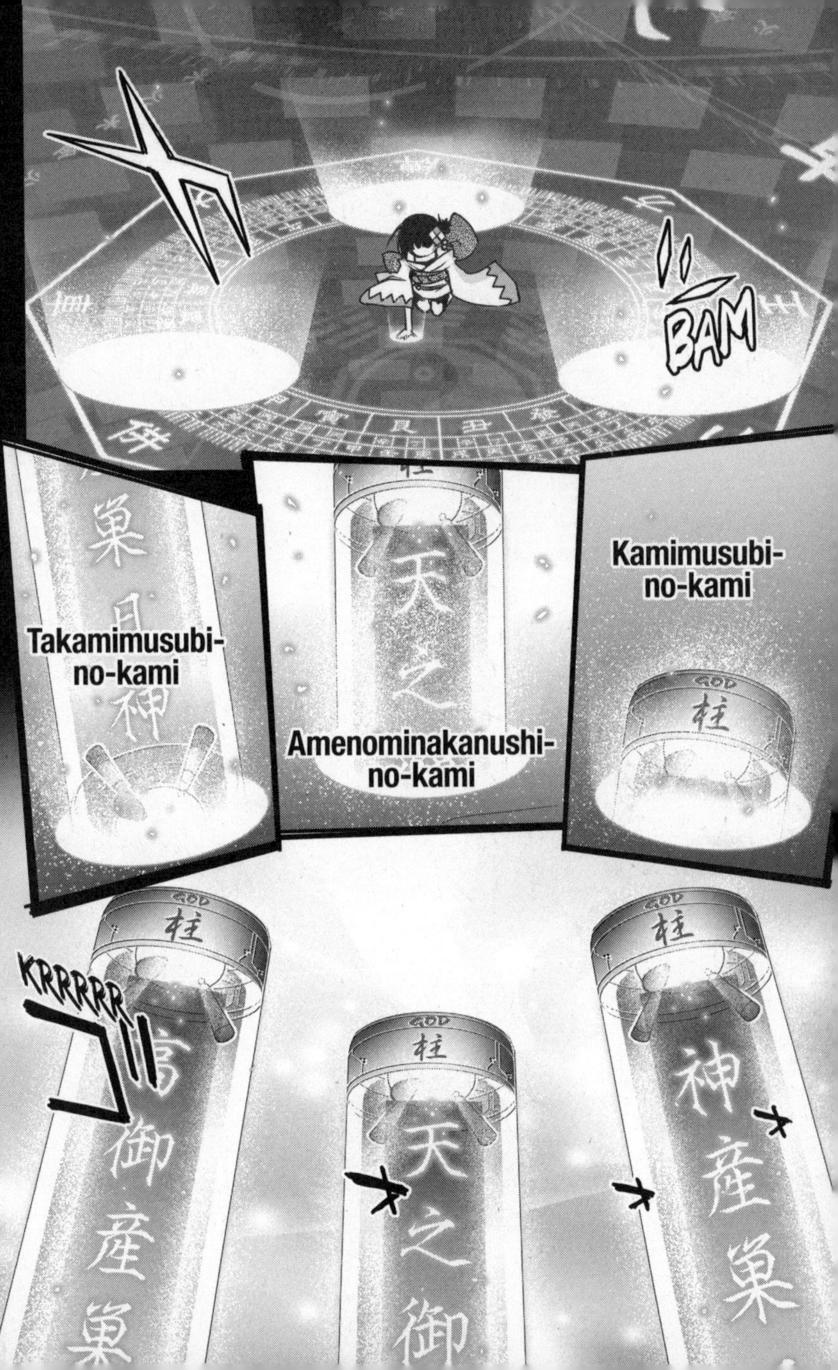
BAM
Kamimusubi-no-kami
Amenominakanushi-no-kami
Takamimusubi-no-kami
KRRRRRR

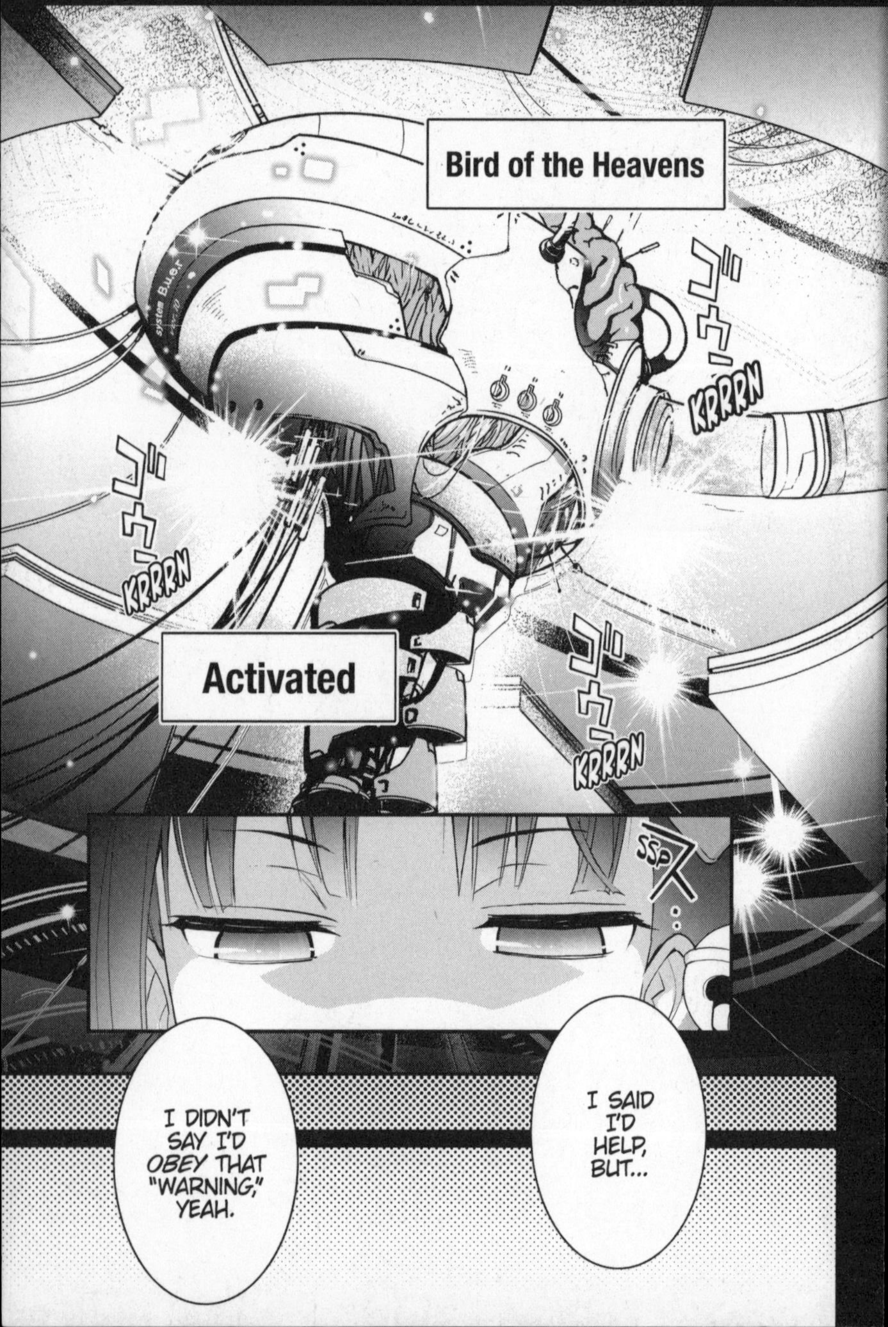
Bird of the Heavens
ゴウン
KRRRN
ゴウン
KRRRN
Activated
ゴウン
KRRRN
SSP
I SAID I'D HELP, BUT...
I DIDN'T SAY I'D *OBEY* THAT "WARNING," YEAH.

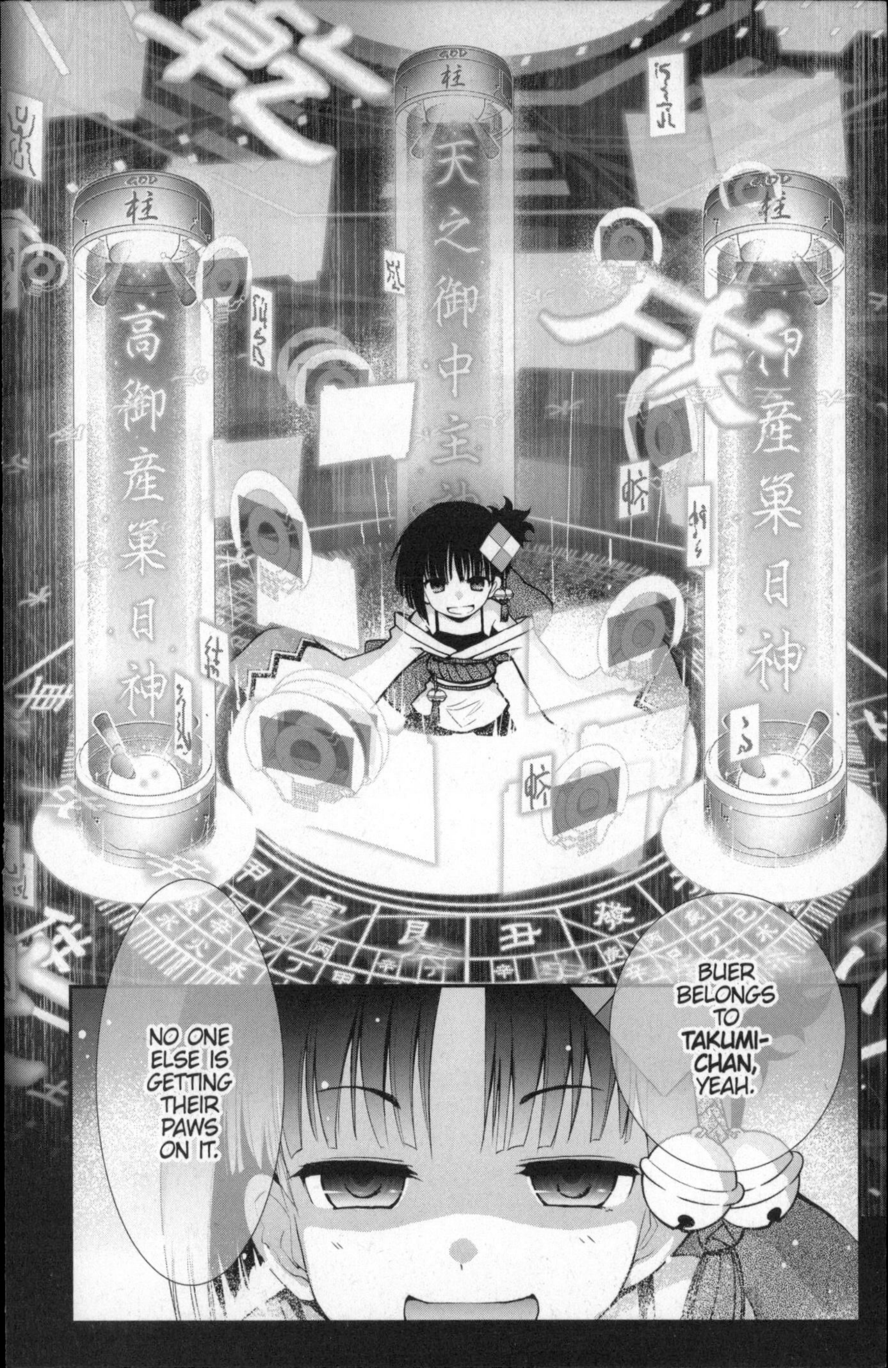
高御産巣日神
BUER BELONGS TO TAKUMI-CHAN, YEAH.
NO ONE ELSE IS GETTING THEIR PAWS ON IT.

GHOST URN

GHOST URN

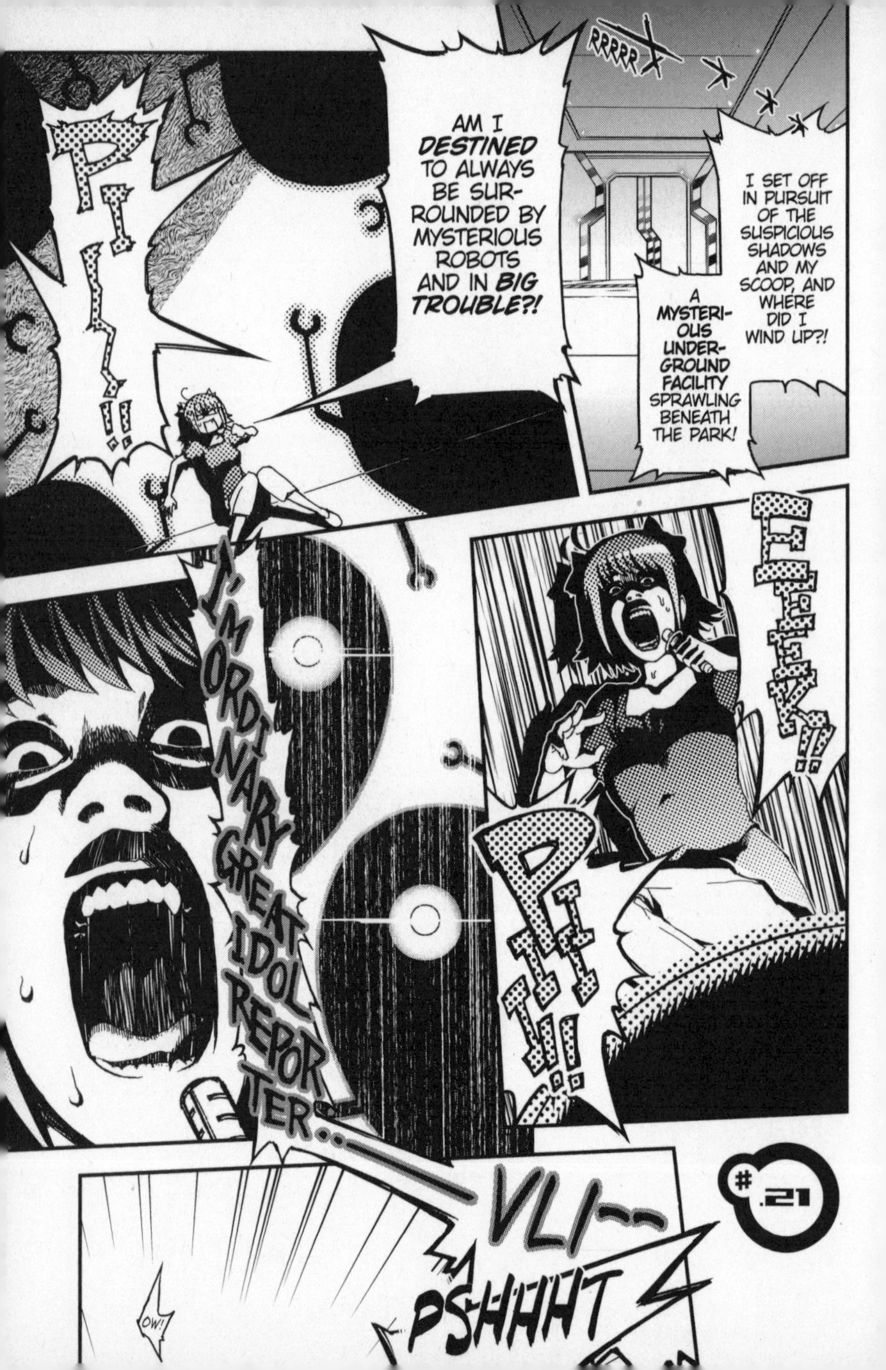
RRRRR
I SET OFF IN PURSUIT OF THE SUSPICIOUS SHADOWS AND MY SCOOP, AND WHERE DID I WIND UP?!
A MYSTERIOUS UNDERGROUND FACILITY SPRAWLING BENEATH THE PARK!
AM I *DESTINED* TO ALWAYS BE SURROUNDED BY MYSTERIOUS ROBOTS AND IN *BIG TROUBLE?!*
PI!!
EEEEK!!
PI!!
I'M ORDINARY GREAT IDOL REPORTER...
#.21
VLI--
PSHHHT
OW!

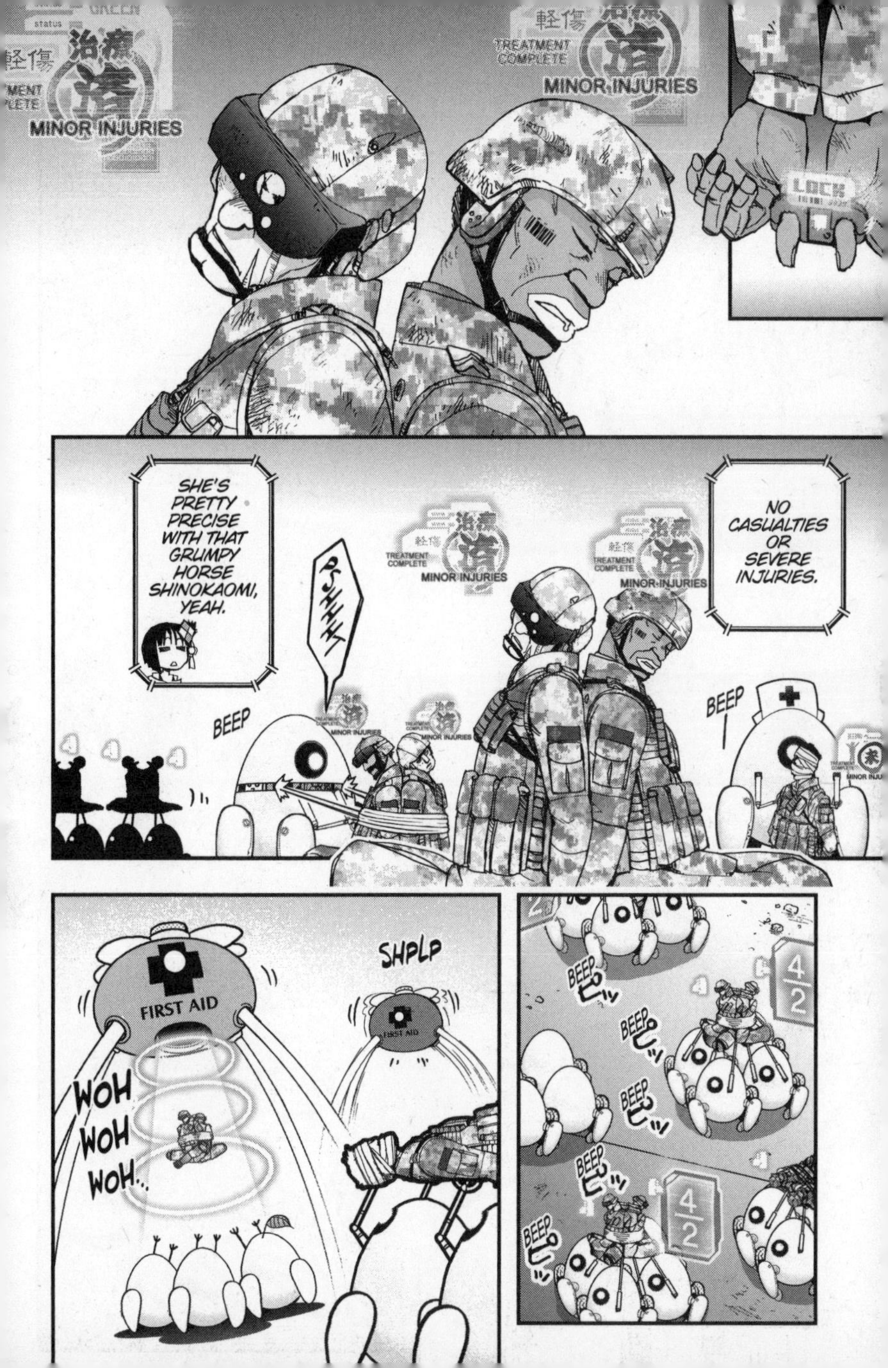
LOCK
軽傷
治療
済
TREATMENT COMPLETE
MINOR INJURIES
status
軽傷
治療
済
TREATMENT COMPLETE
MINOR INJURIES
NO CASUALTIES OR SEVERE INJURIES.
BEEP
MINOR INJURIES
TREATMENT COMPLETE
MINOR INJURIES
TREATMENT COMPLETE
MINOR INJURIES
SHE'S PRETTY PRECISE WITH THAT GRUMPY HORSE SHINOKAOMI, YEAH.
PSHHH
BEEP
4/2
BEEP ピッ
BEEP ピッ
BEEP ピッ
BEEP ピッ
BEEP ピッ
4/2
SHPLP
FIRST AID
FIRST AID
WOH WOH WOH...

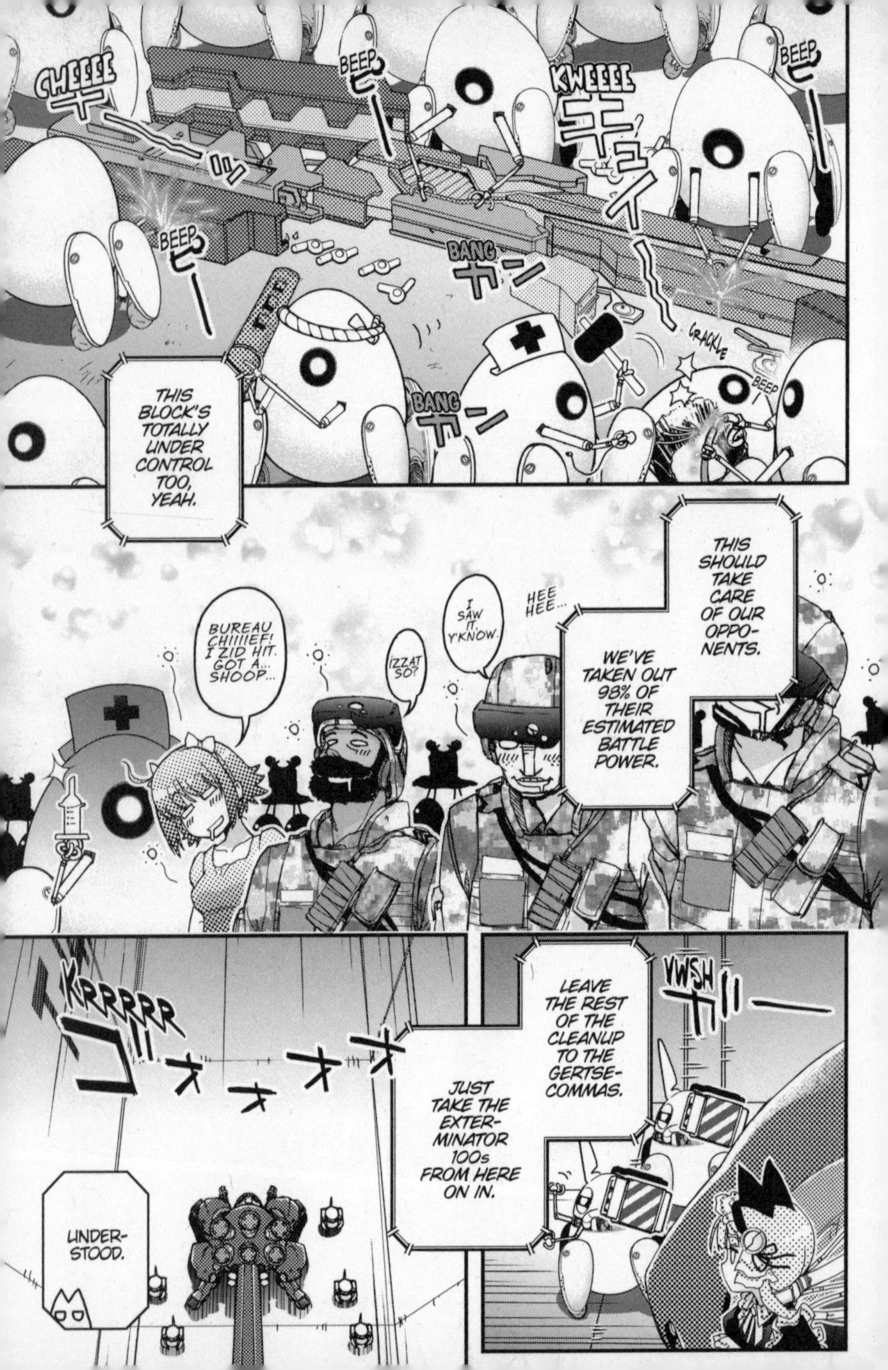
BEEP
KWEEEE
BEEP
CHEEEE
BANG
BEEP
CRACKLE
BEEP
BANG
THIS BLOCK'S TOTALLY UNDER CONTROL TOO, YEAH.
THIS SHOULD TAKE CARE OF OUR OPPO-NENTS.
WE'VE TAKEN OUT 98% OF THEIR ESTIMATED BATTLE POWER.
HEE HEE...
I SAW IT, Y'KNOW.
IZZAT SO?
BUREAU CHIIIIIEF! I ZID HIT. GOT A... SHOOP...
VWSH
LEAVE THE REST OF THE CLEANUP TO THE GERTSE-COMMAS.
JUST TAKE THE EXTER-MINATOR 100s FROM HERE ON IN.
KRRRRR
UNDER-STOOD.

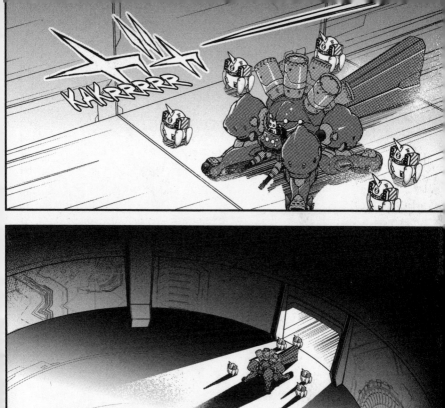

I'VE BEEN WAITING FOR YOU, CLARION!

BWA HA HA HA!

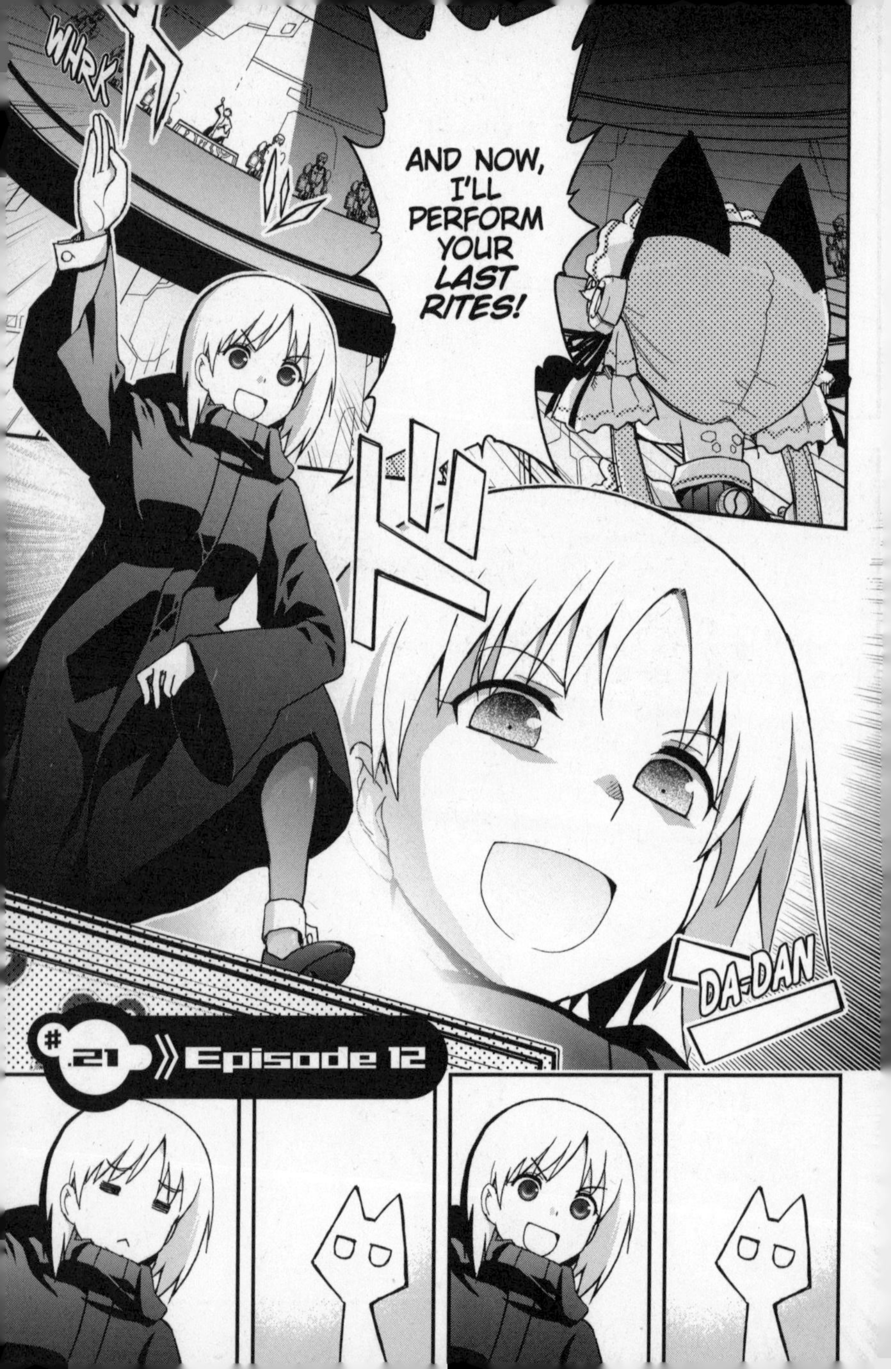
AND NOW, I'LL PERFORM YOUR LAST RITES!
WHRK
DA-DAN
#.21 》Episode 12

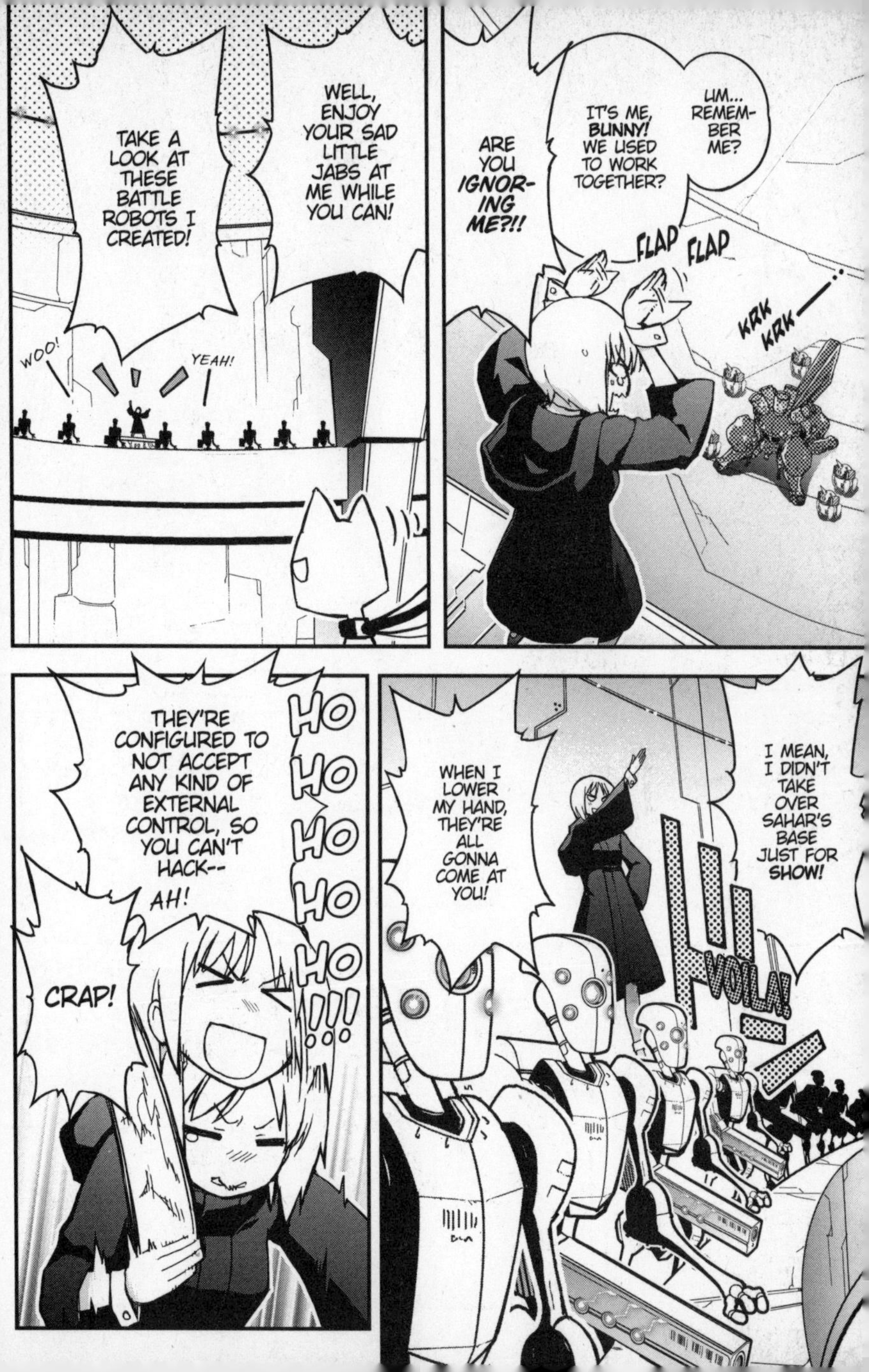
UM... REMEMBER ME?
IT'S ME, BUNNY! WE USED TO WORK TOGETHER?
ARE YOU IGNORING ME?!!
FLAP FLAP
KRK KRK
WELL, ENJOY YOUR SAD LITTLE JABS AT ME WHILE YOU CAN!
TAKE A LOOK AT THESE BATTLE ROBOTS I CREATED!
YEAH!
WOO!
I MEAN, I DIDN'T TAKE OVER SAHAR'S BASE JUST FOR SHOW!
VOILA!
WHEN I LOWER MY HAND, THEY'RE ALL GONNA COME AT YOU!
HO HO HO HO HO HO!!!
THEY'RE CONFIGURED TO NOT ACCEPT ANY KIND OF EXTERNAL CONTROL, SO YOU CAN'T HACK--
AH!
CRAP!

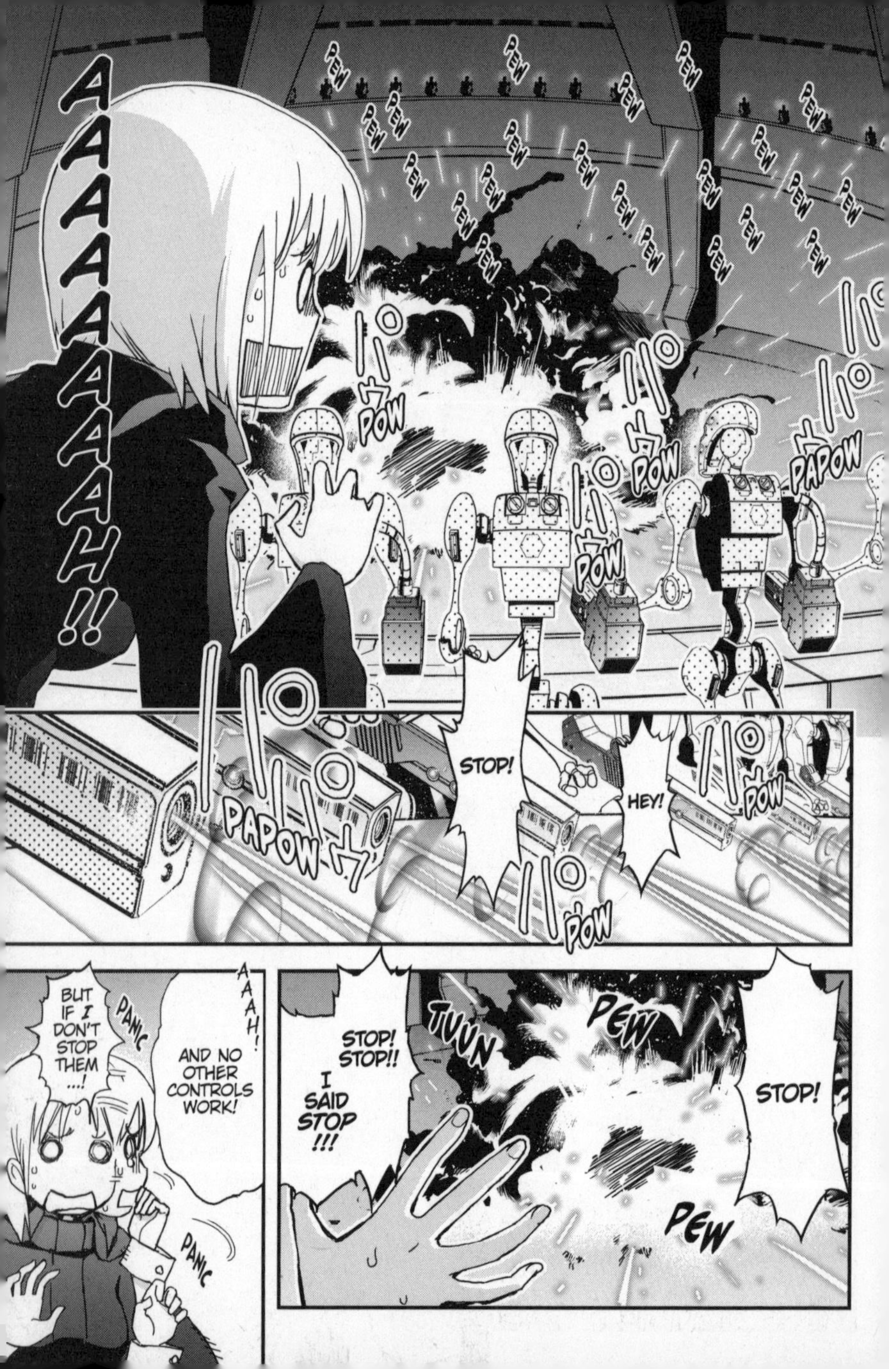
AAAAAAAAAAH!!
PEW PEW PEW PEW PEW PEW PEW PEW PEW PEW PEW PEW PEW PEW PEW PEW PEW PEW PEW PEW PEW PEW PEW
POW
POW
POW
PAPOW
STOP!
HEY!
PAPOW
POW
POW
STOP! STOP!!
I SAID STOP!!!
TUUN
PEW
STOP!
PEW
AAAH!
AND NO OTHER CONTROLS WORK!
BUT IF *I* DON'T STOP THEM ...!
PANIC
PANIC

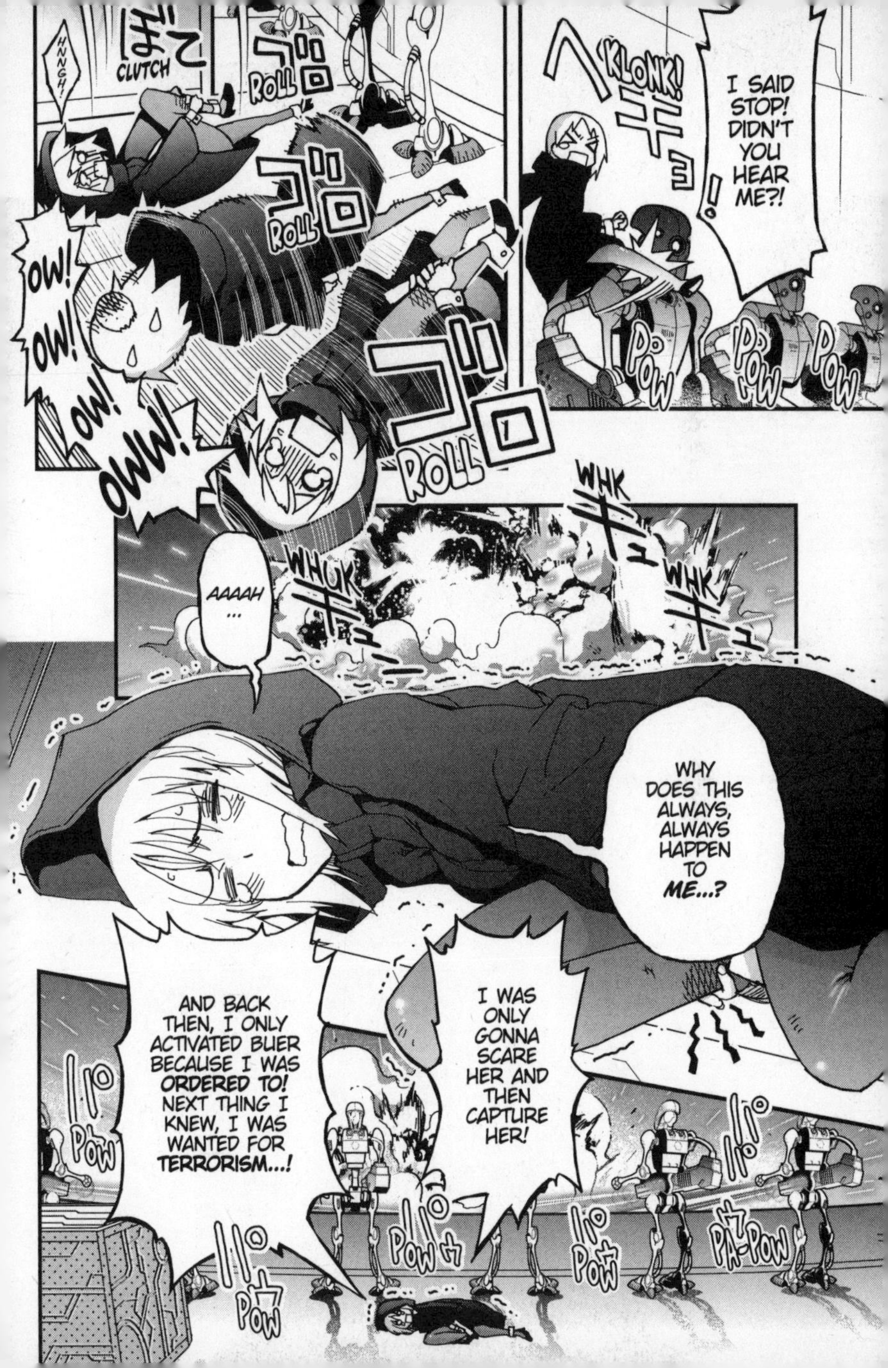
I SAID STOP! DIDN'T YOU HEAR ME?!
KLONK!
POW
POW
POW
HNNGH!
CLUTCH
ROLL
ROLL
OW! OW! OW! OWW!
ROLL
WHK
WHK
WHUK
AAAAH...
WHY DOES THIS ALWAYS, ALWAYS HAPPEN TO *ME...?*
I WAS ONLY GONNA SCARE HER AND THEN CAPTURE HER!
AND BACK THEN, I ONLY ACTIVATED BUER BECAUSE I WAS **ORDERED TO!** NEXT THING I KNEW, I WAS WANTED FOR **TERRORISM...!**
POW
PA-POW
POW
POW
POW
POW

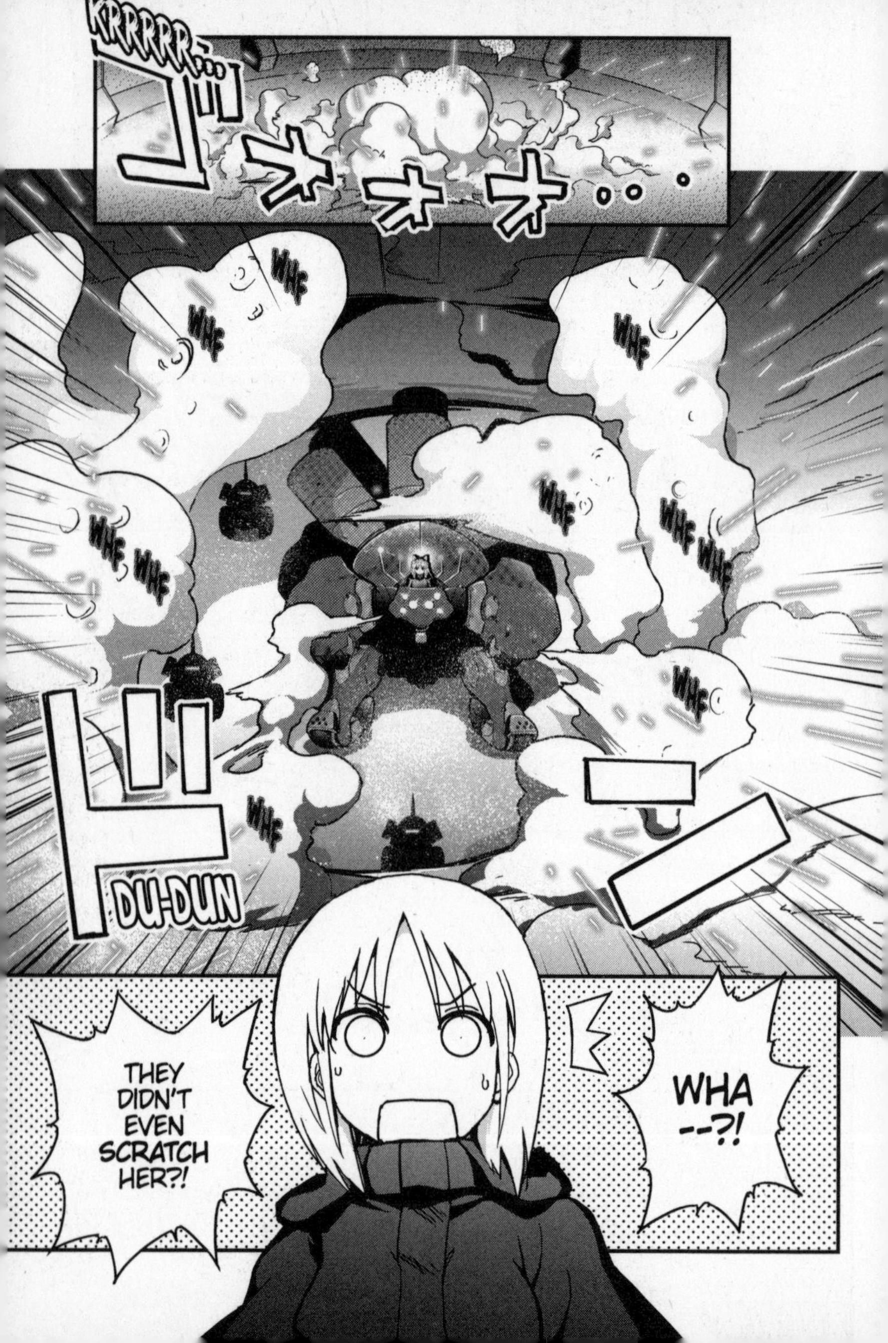
KRRRRR...
WHF
WHF
WHF
WHF
WHF
WHF
WHF
WHF
WHF
DU-DUN
WHA --?!
THEY DIDN'T EVEN SCRATCH HER?!

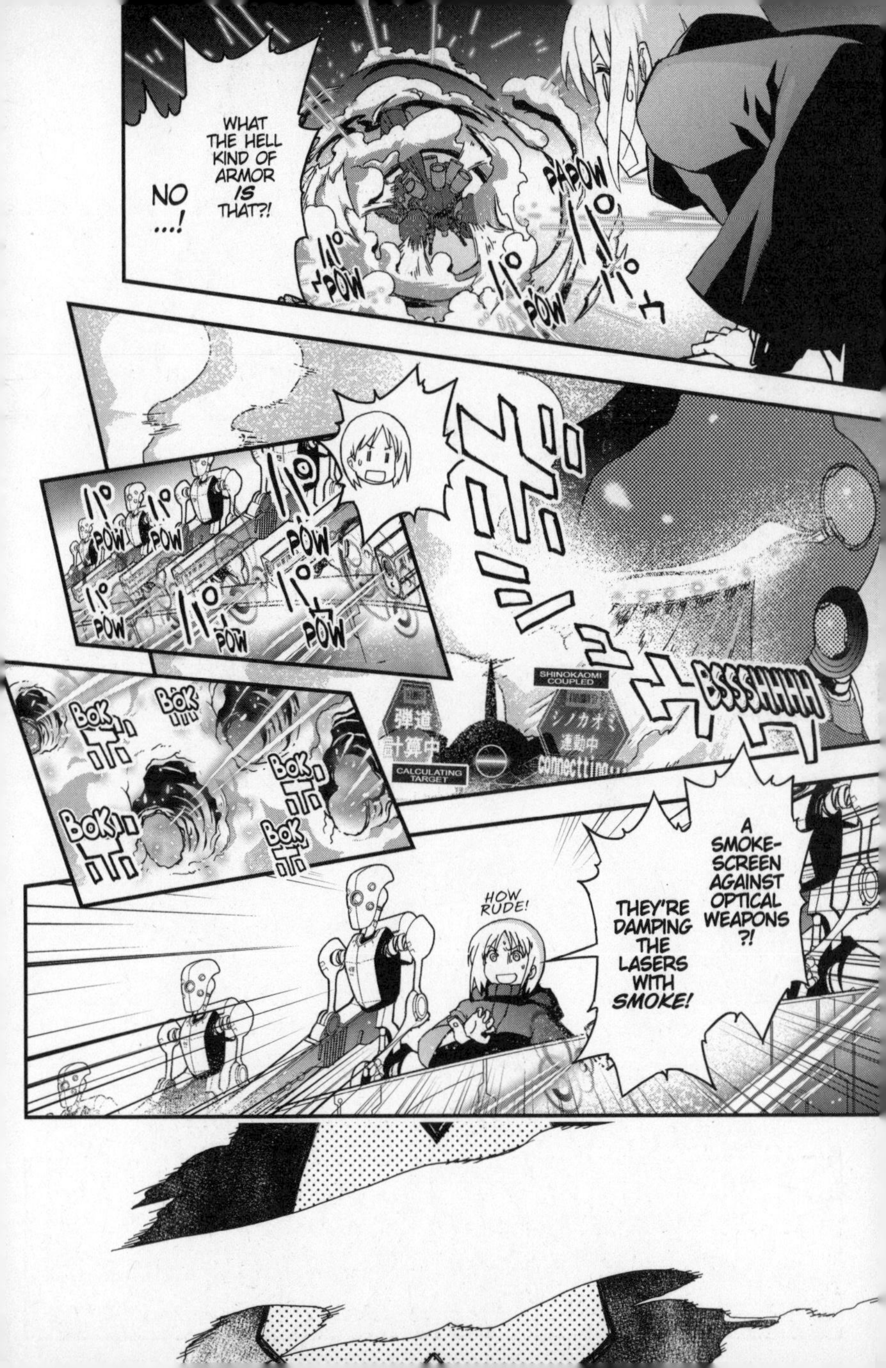
PAPOW
POW
POW
WHAT THE HELL KIND OF ARMOR *IS* THAT?!
NO ...!
BSSSHHHH
SHINOKAOMI COUPLED
シノカオミ 連動中
connecting...
弾道計算中
CALCULATING TARGET
POW
POW
POW
POW
POW
POW
BOK
BOK
BOK
BOK
BOK
A SMOKE-SCREEN AGAINST OPTICAL WEAPONS?!
THEY'RE DAMPING THE LASERS WITH *SMOKE!*
HOW RUDE!

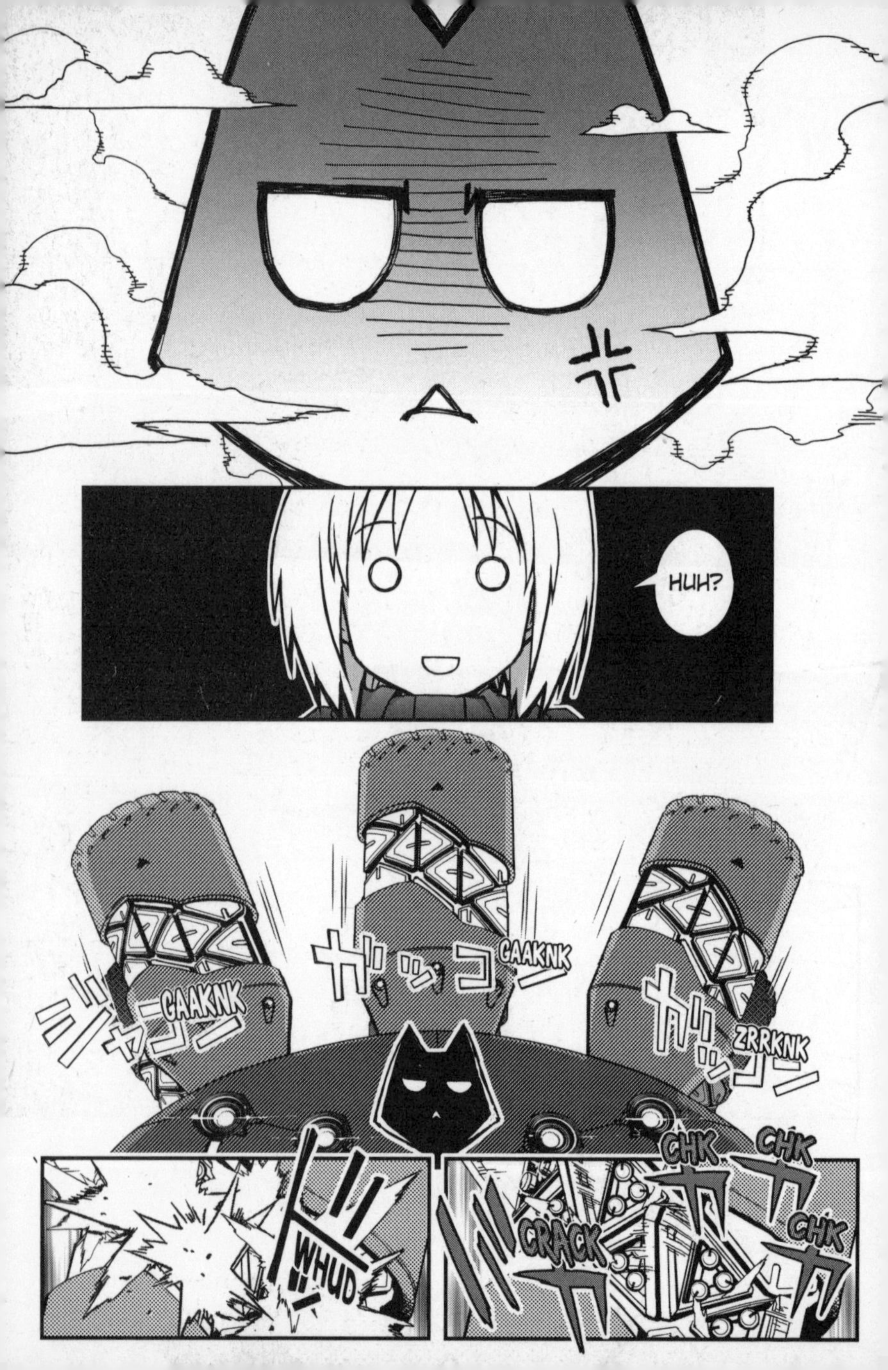

HUH?
GAAKNK
ZRRKNK
GAAKNK
CHK
CHK
CHK
CRACK
WHUD

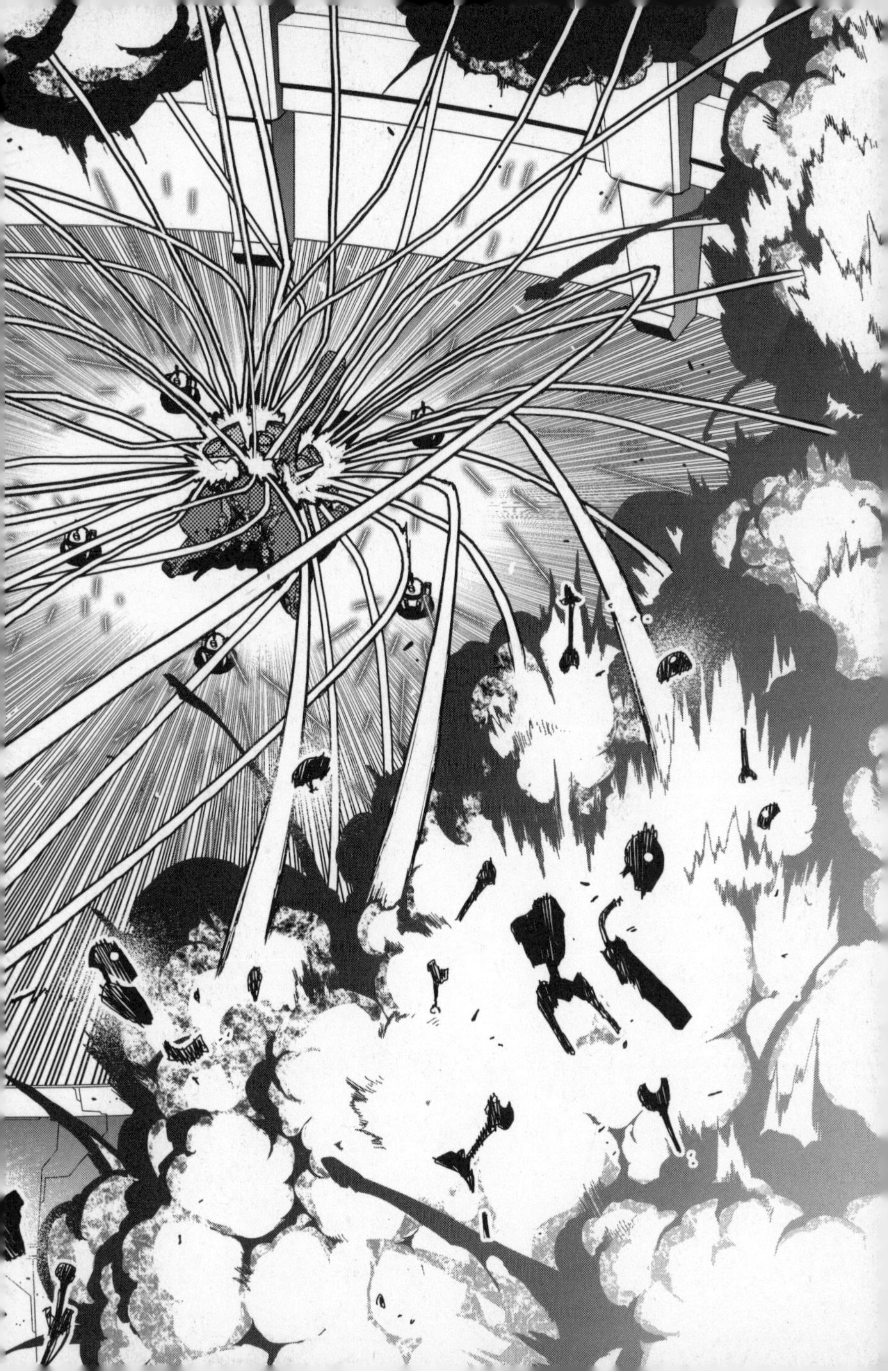

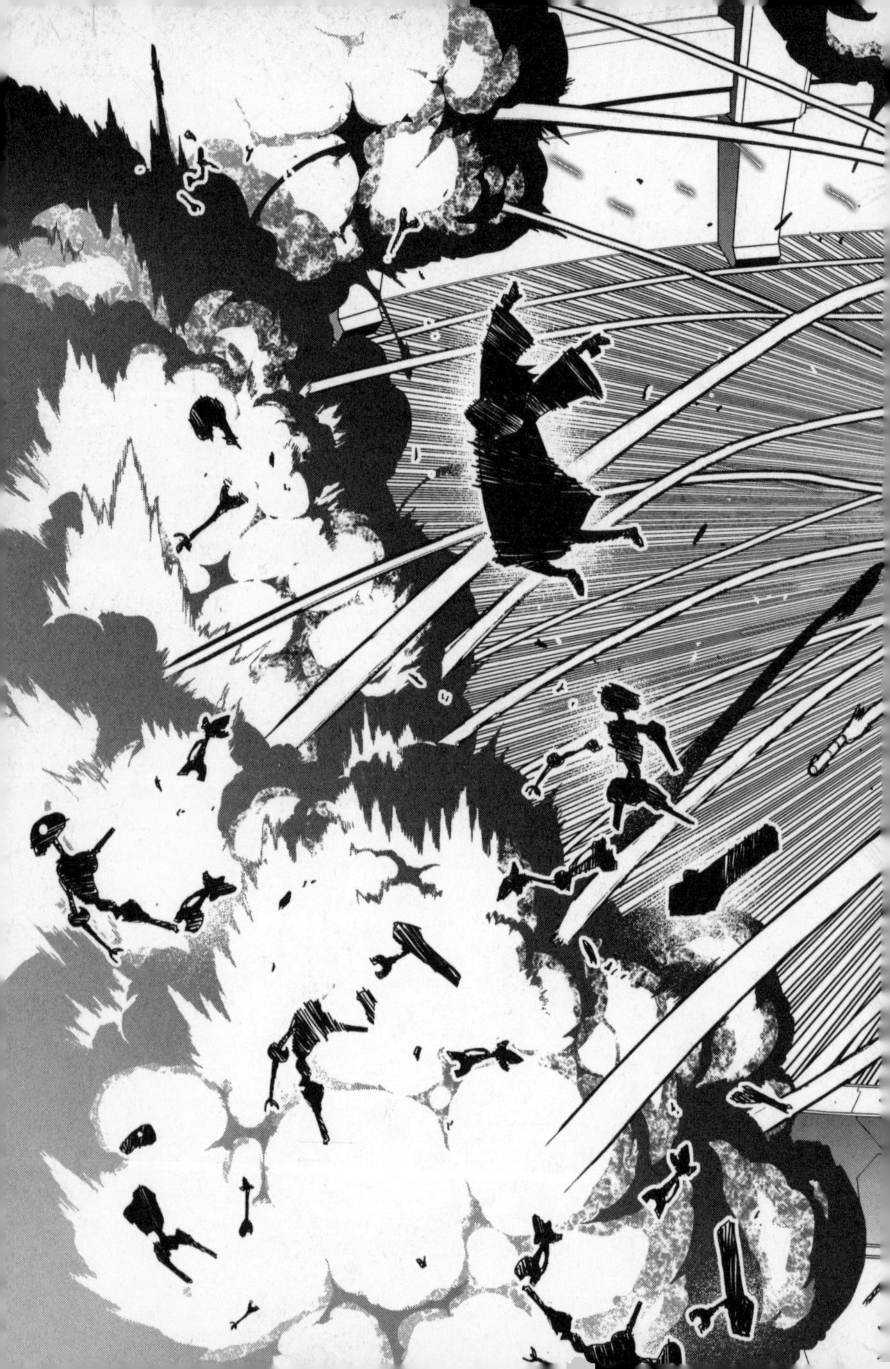

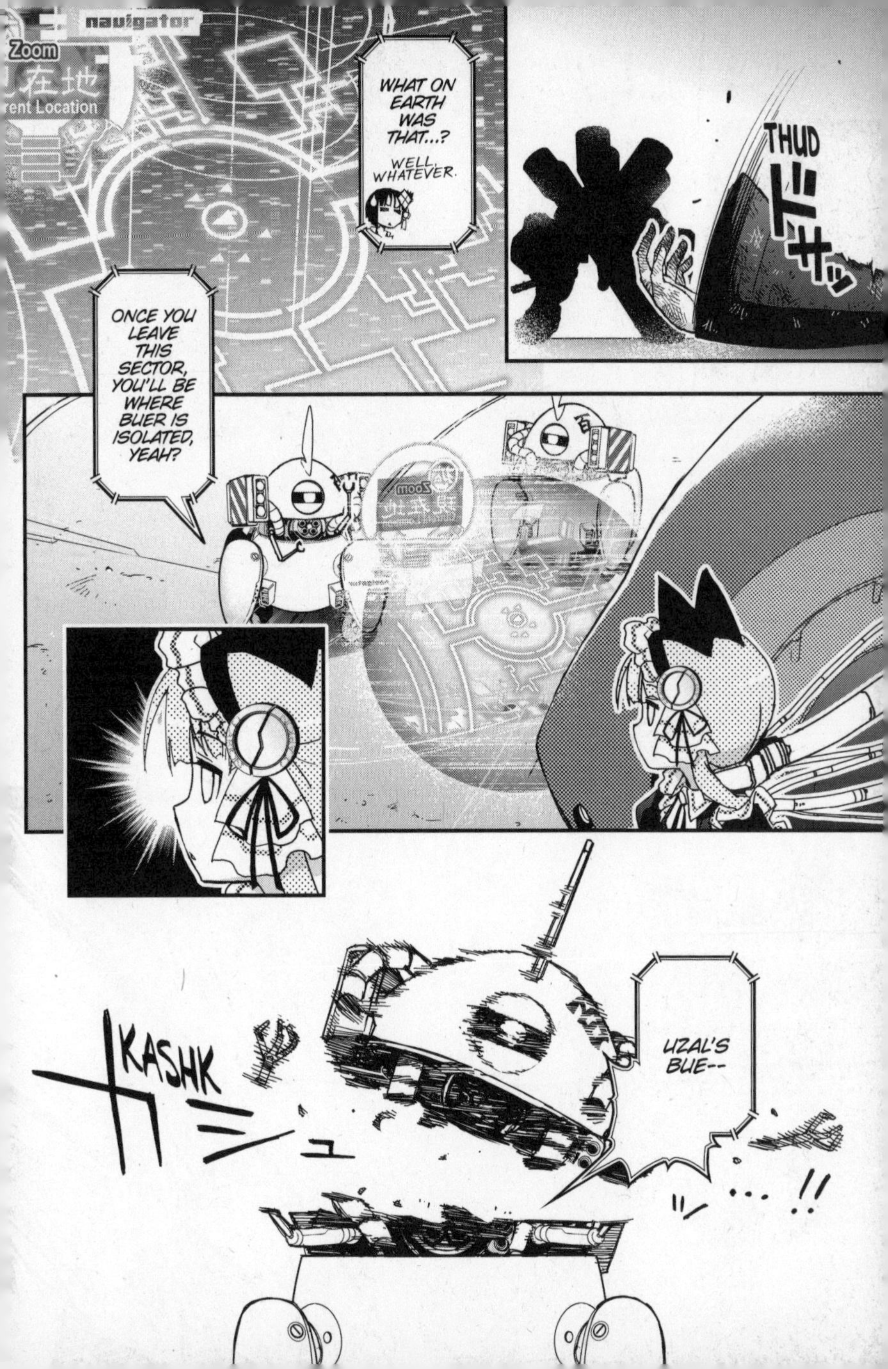
THUD
ドサッ
navigator
Zoom
WHAT ON EARTH WAS THAT...?
WELL, WHATEVER.
ONCE YOU LEAVE THIS SECTOR, YOU'LL BE WHERE BUER IS ISOLATED, YEAH?
Zoom
UZAL'S BUE--
KASHK
カシュ
...!!

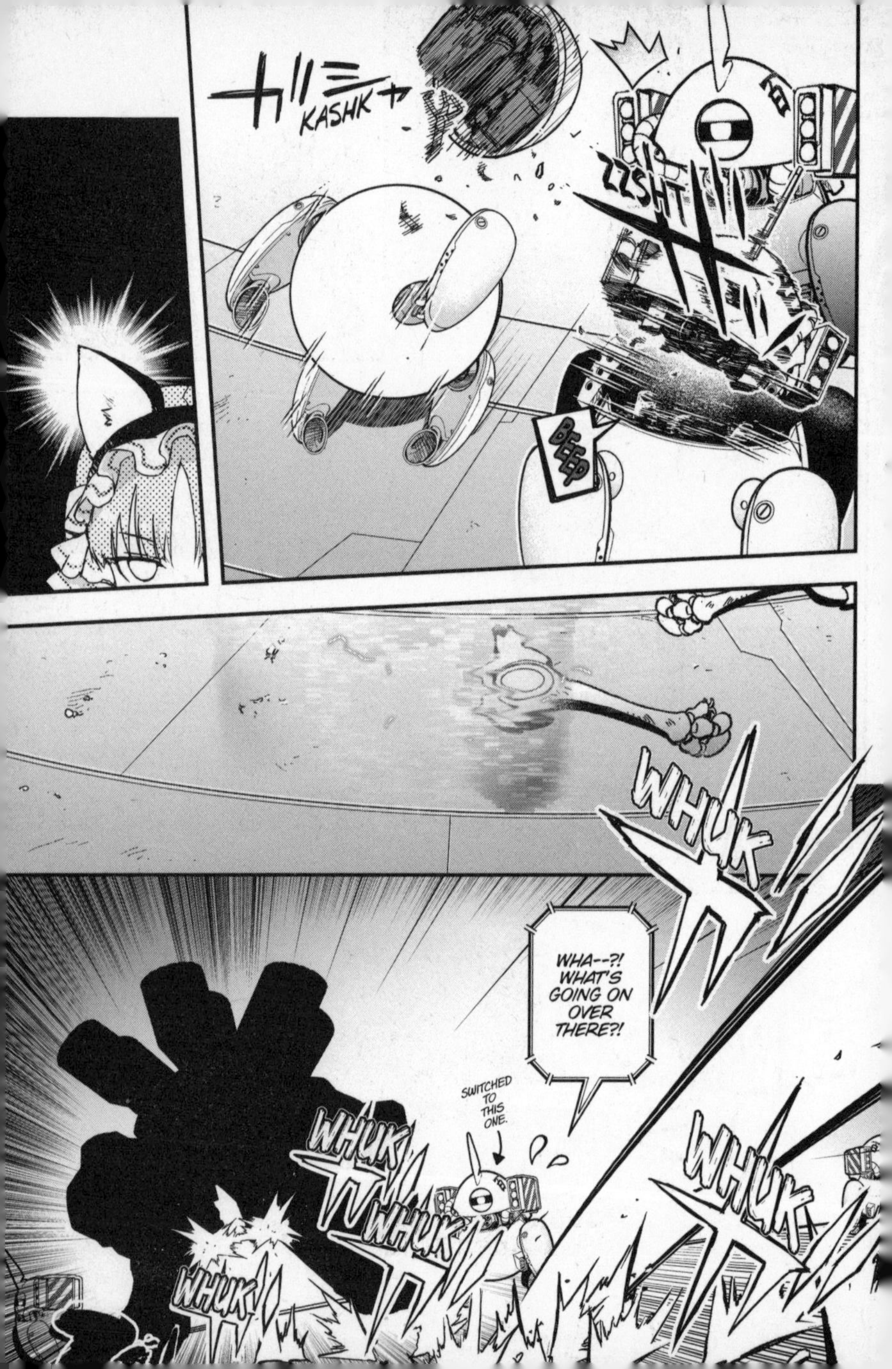

ZZSHT
KASHK
BEEP
WHUK
WHUK
WHA--?! WHAT'S GOING ON OVER THERE?!
SWITCHED TO THIS ONE.
WHUK
WHUK
WHUK

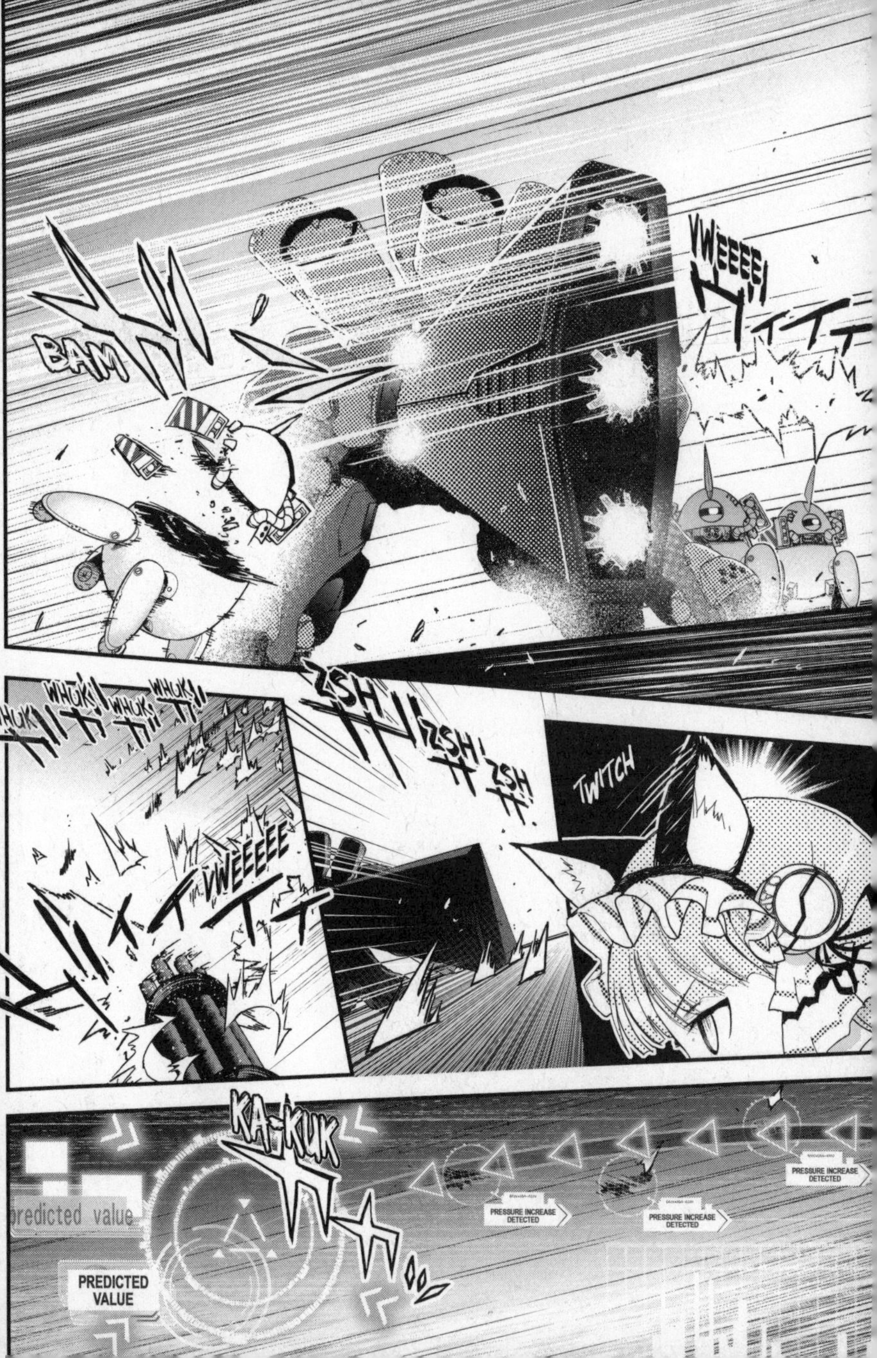
VWEEEE
BAM
TWITCH
ZSH
ZSH
ZSH
WHUK
WHUK
WHUK
WHUK
VWEEEE
PRESSURE INCREASE DETECTED
PRESSURE INCREASE DETECTED
PRESSURE INCREASE DETECTED
KA-KUK
predicted value
PREDICTED VALUE

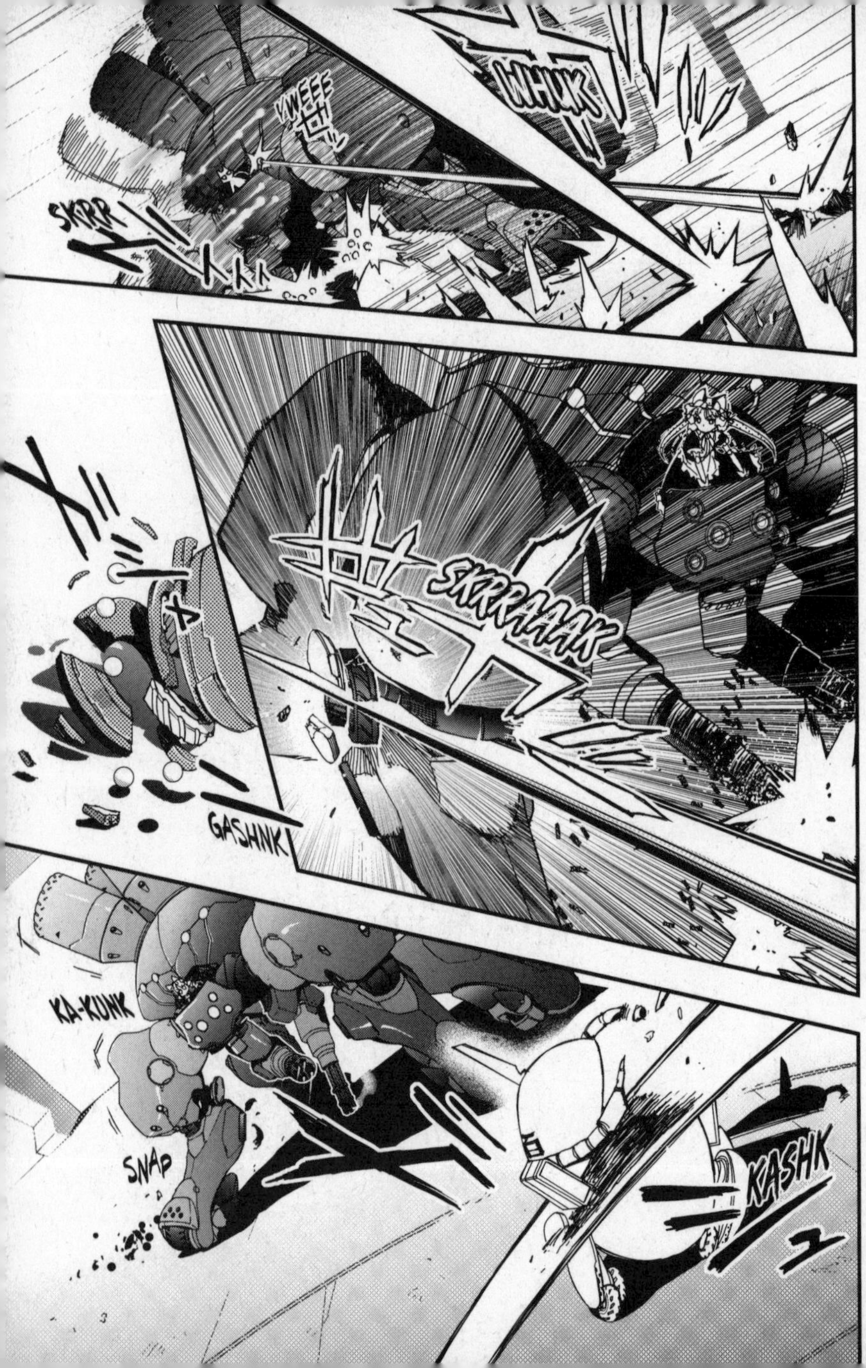
WHUK
KWEEE
SKRR
SKRRAAAK
GASHNK
KASHK
KA-KUNK
SNAP

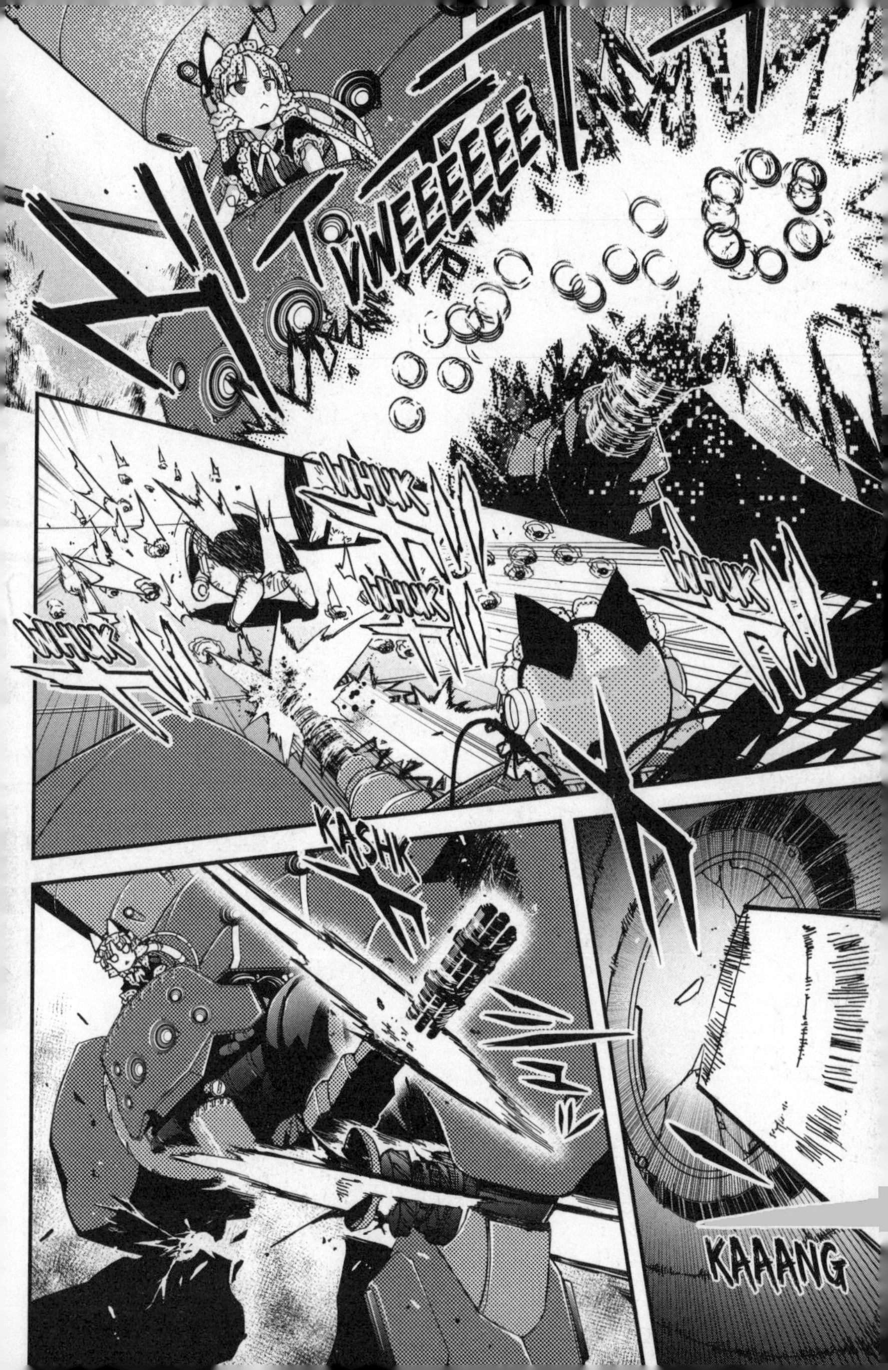
VWEEEEEEE
WHUK
WHUK
WHUK
WHUK
KAAANG
KASHK

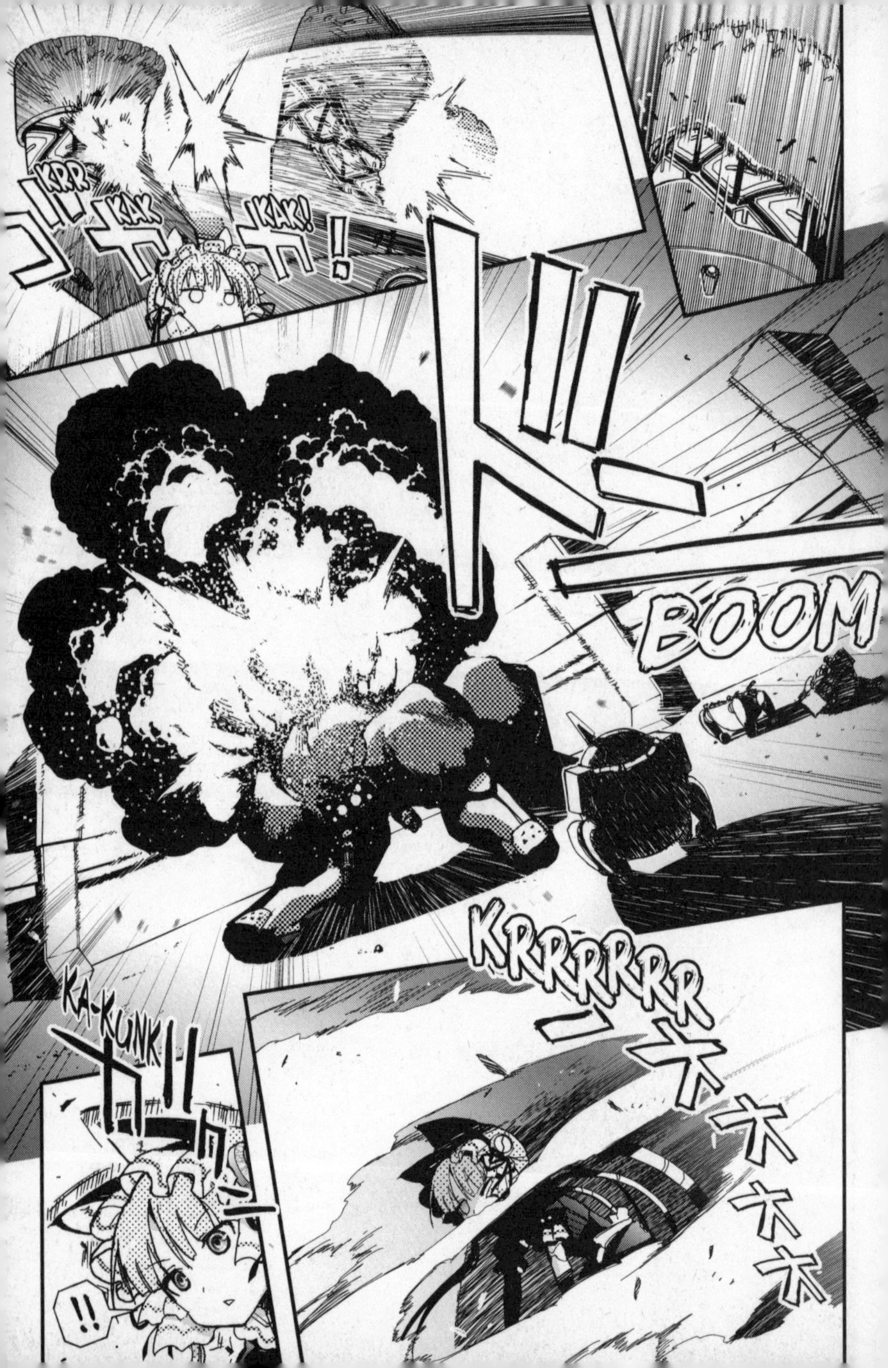
KAK!
KAK
KRR
BOOM
KRRRRRR
KA-KUNK
!!

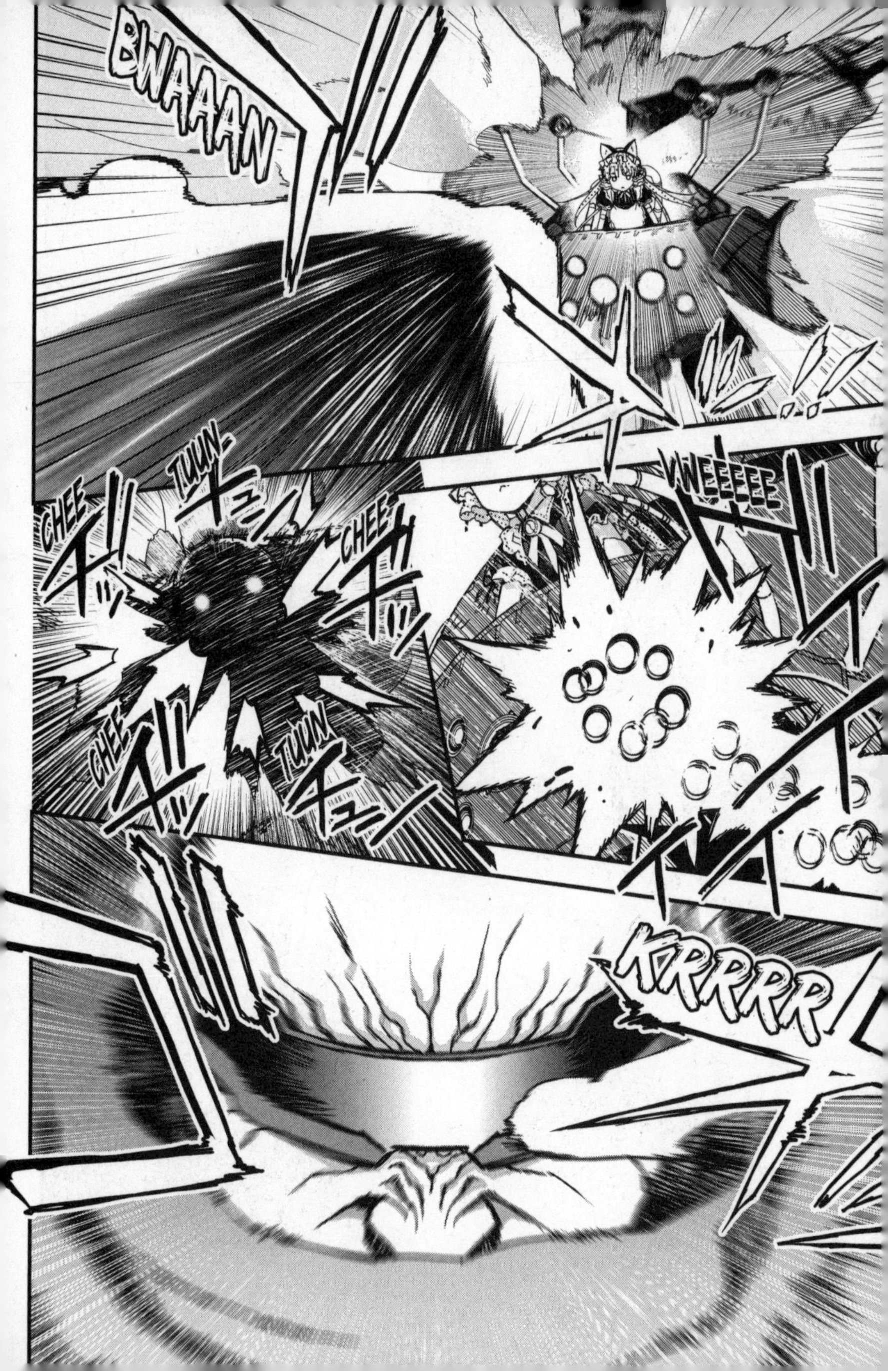
BWAAAN
VWEEEEE
CHEE
TUUN
CHEE
TUUN
CHEE
KRRRR

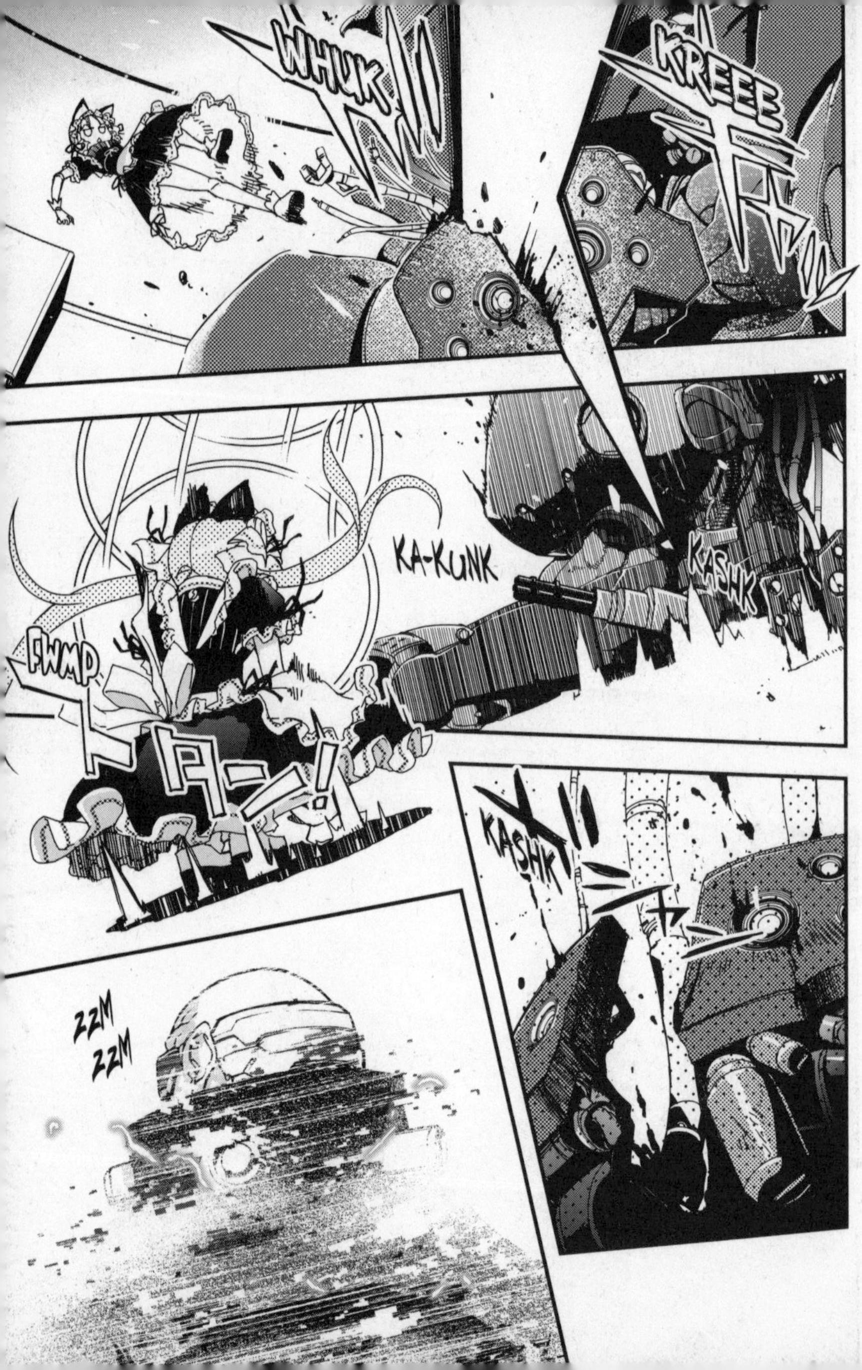
KREEE
WHUK
KASHK
KA-KUNK
FWMP
KASHK
ZZM
ZZM

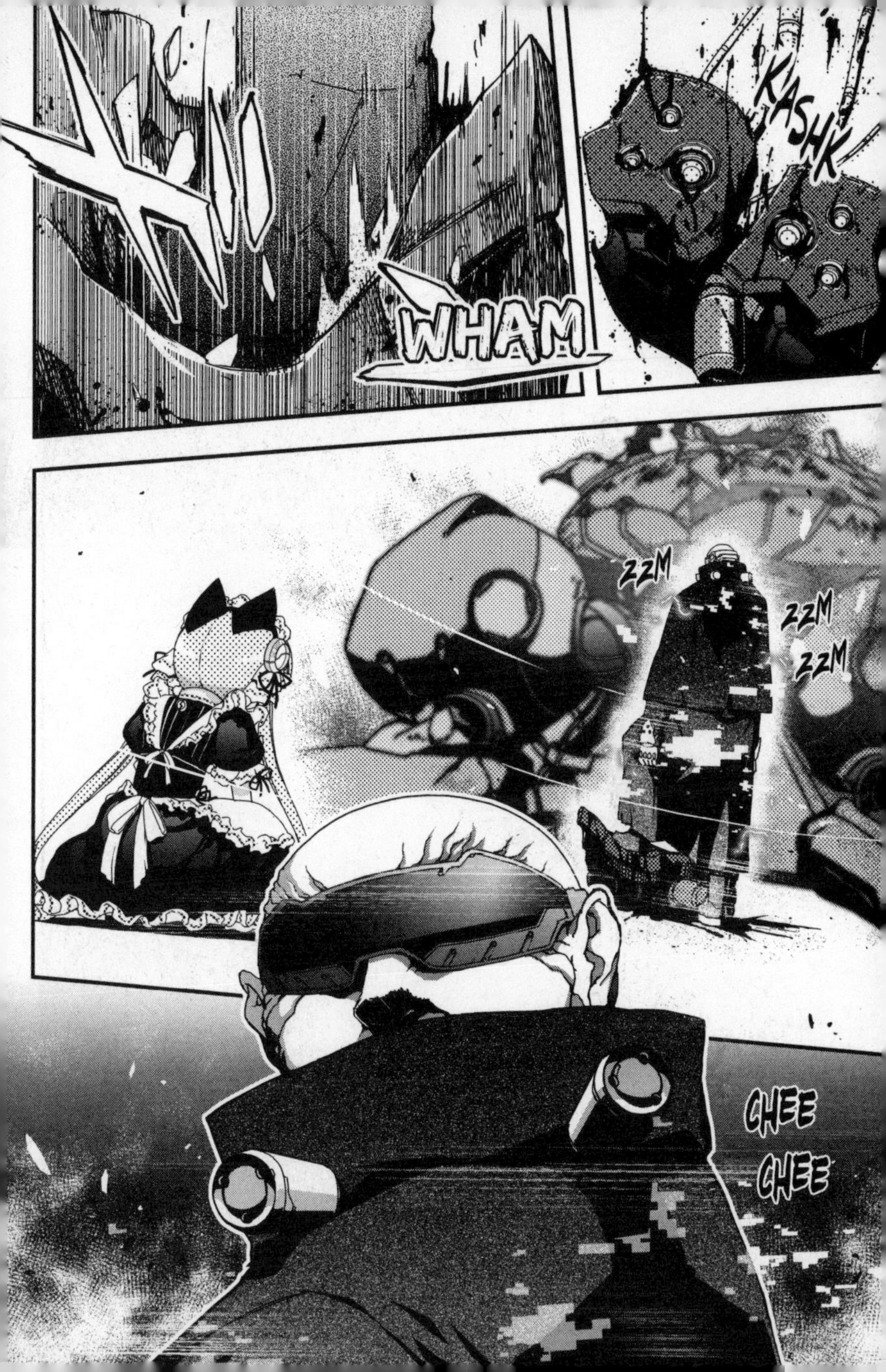
KASHK
WHAM
ZZM
ZZM
ZZM
CHEE
CHEE

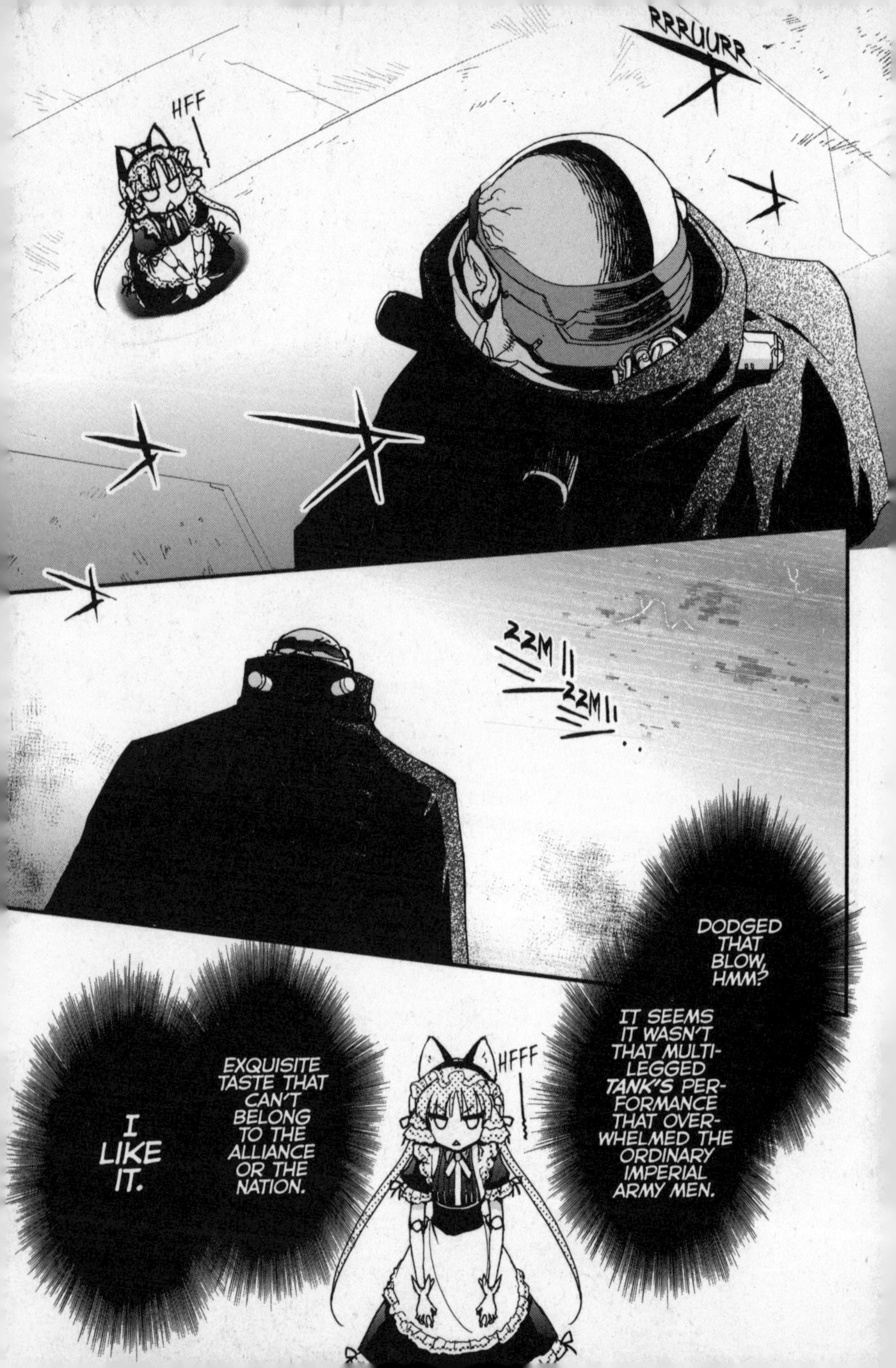

RRRUURR
HFF
ZZM
ZZM
DODGED THAT BLOW, HMM?
IT SEEMS IT WASN'T THAT MULTI-LEGGED TANK'S PERFORMANCE THAT OVERWHELMED THE ORDINARY IMPERIAL ARMY MEN.
HFFF
EXQUISITE TASTE THAT CAN'T BELONG TO THE ALLIANCE OR THE NATION.
I LIKE IT.

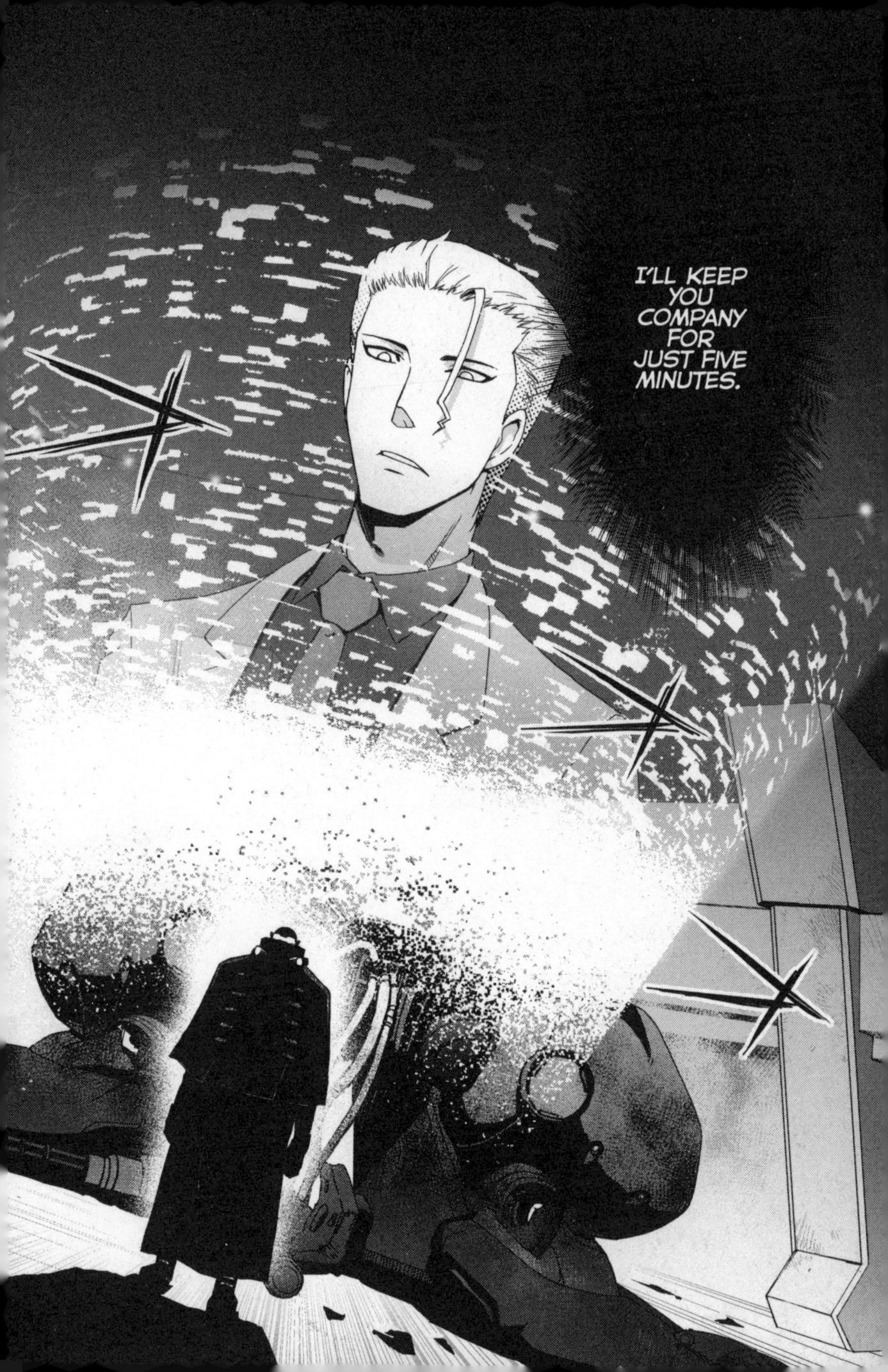
I'LL KEEP YOU COMPANY FOR JUST FIVE MINUTES.

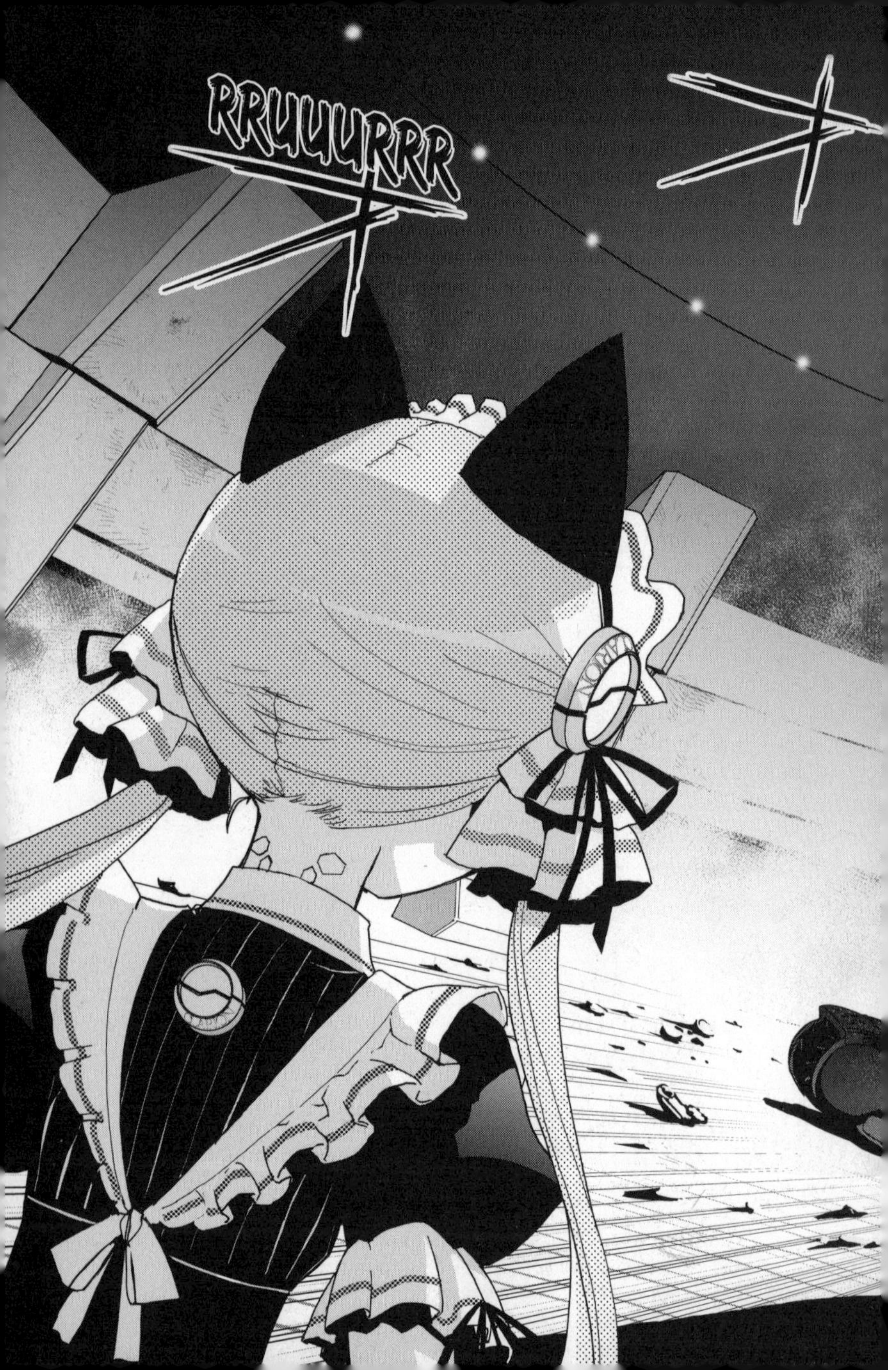
RRUUURRR

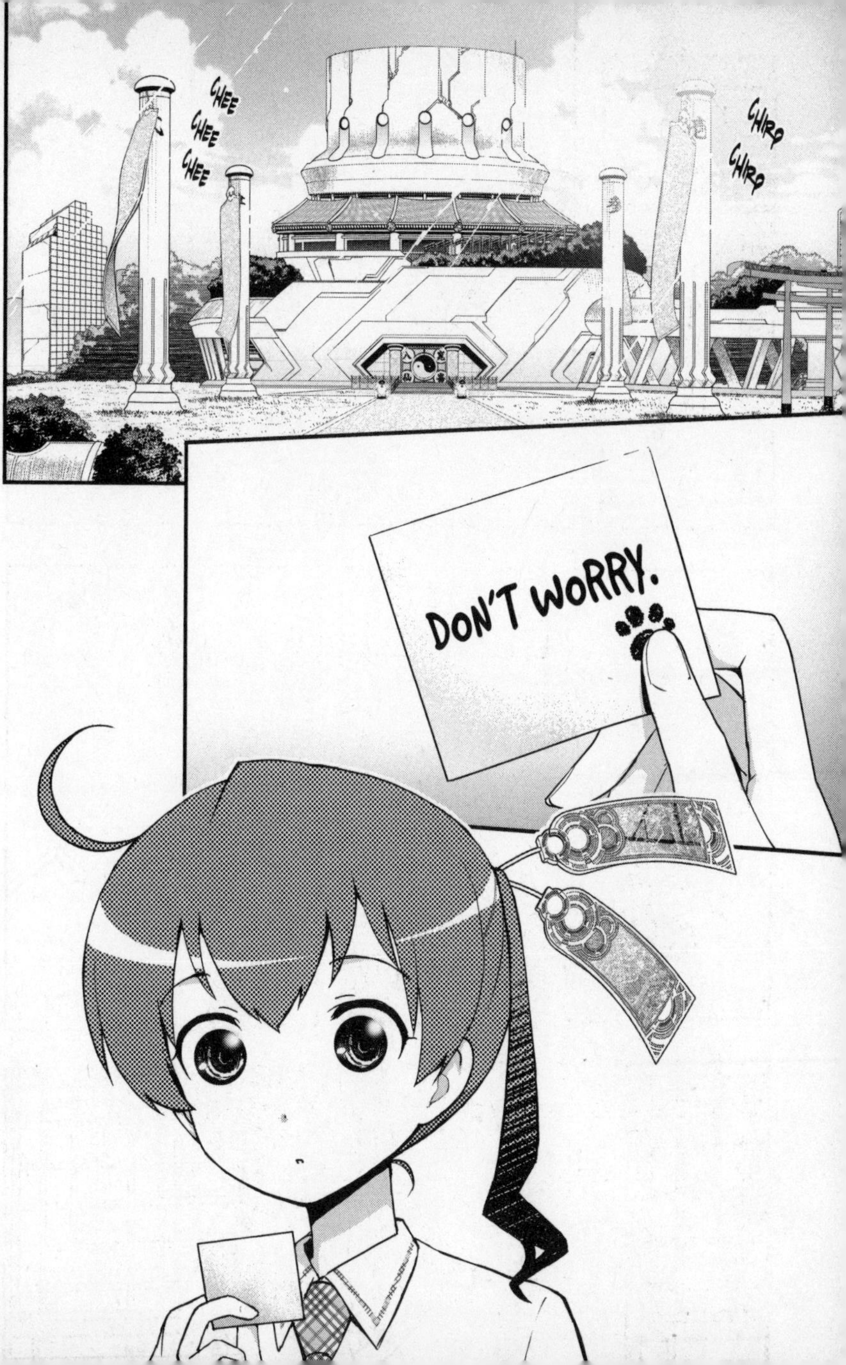
CHIRP
CHIRP
CHEE
CHEE
CHEE
DON'T WORRY.

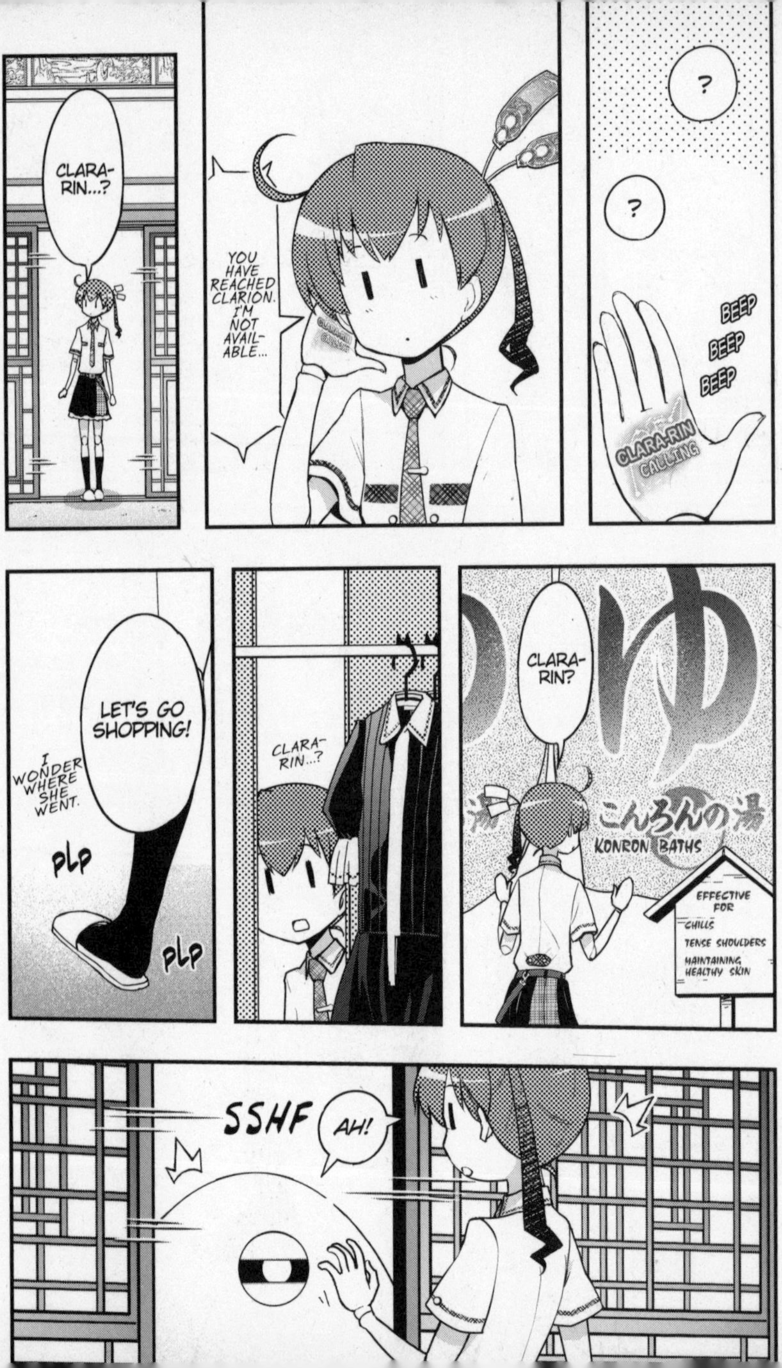
?
?
BEEP
BEEP
BEEP
CLARA-RIN CALLING
YOU HAVE REACHED CLARION. I'M NOT AVAILABLE...
CLARA-RIN...?
CLARA-RIN?
こんろんの湯
KONRON BATHS
EFFECTIVE FOR
CHILLS
TENSE SHOULDERS
MAINTAINING HEALTHY SKIN
CLARA-RIN...?
LET'S GO SHOPPING!
I WONDER WHERE SHE WENT.
PLP
PLP
SSHF
AH!

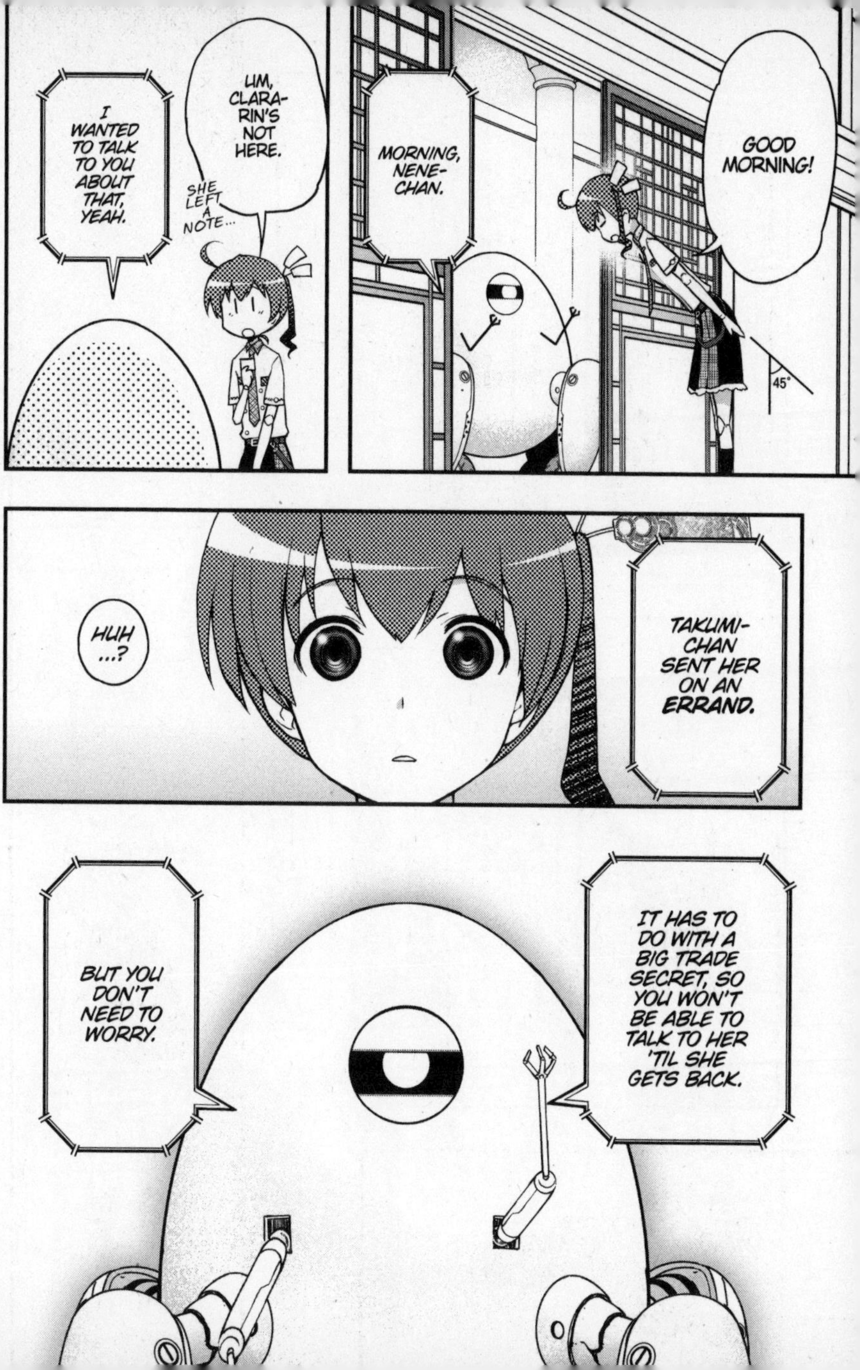
GOOD MORNING!
MORNING, NENE-CHAN.
45°
UM, CLARARIN'S NOT HERE.
SHE LEFT A NOTE...
I WANTED TO TALK TO YOU ABOUT THAT, YEAH.
TAKUMI-CHAN SENT HER ON AN ERRAND.
HUH...?
IT HAS TO DO WITH A BIG TRADE SECRET, SO YOU WON'T BE ABLE TO TALK TO HER 'TIL SHE GETS BACK.
BUT YOU DON'T NEED TO WORRY.

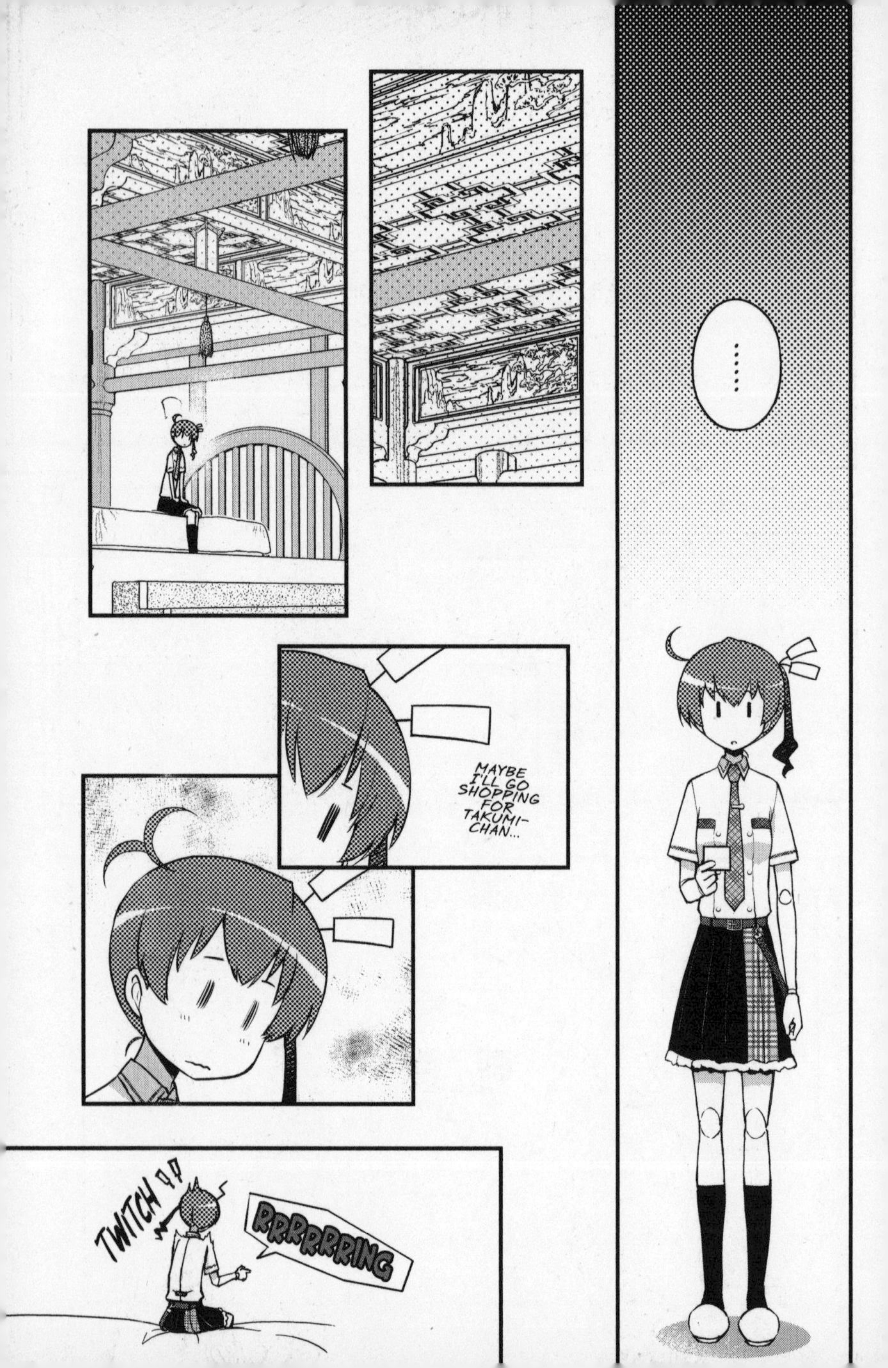
……
MAYBE I'LL GO SHOPPING FOR TAKUMI-CHAN...
TWITCH
RRRRRRING

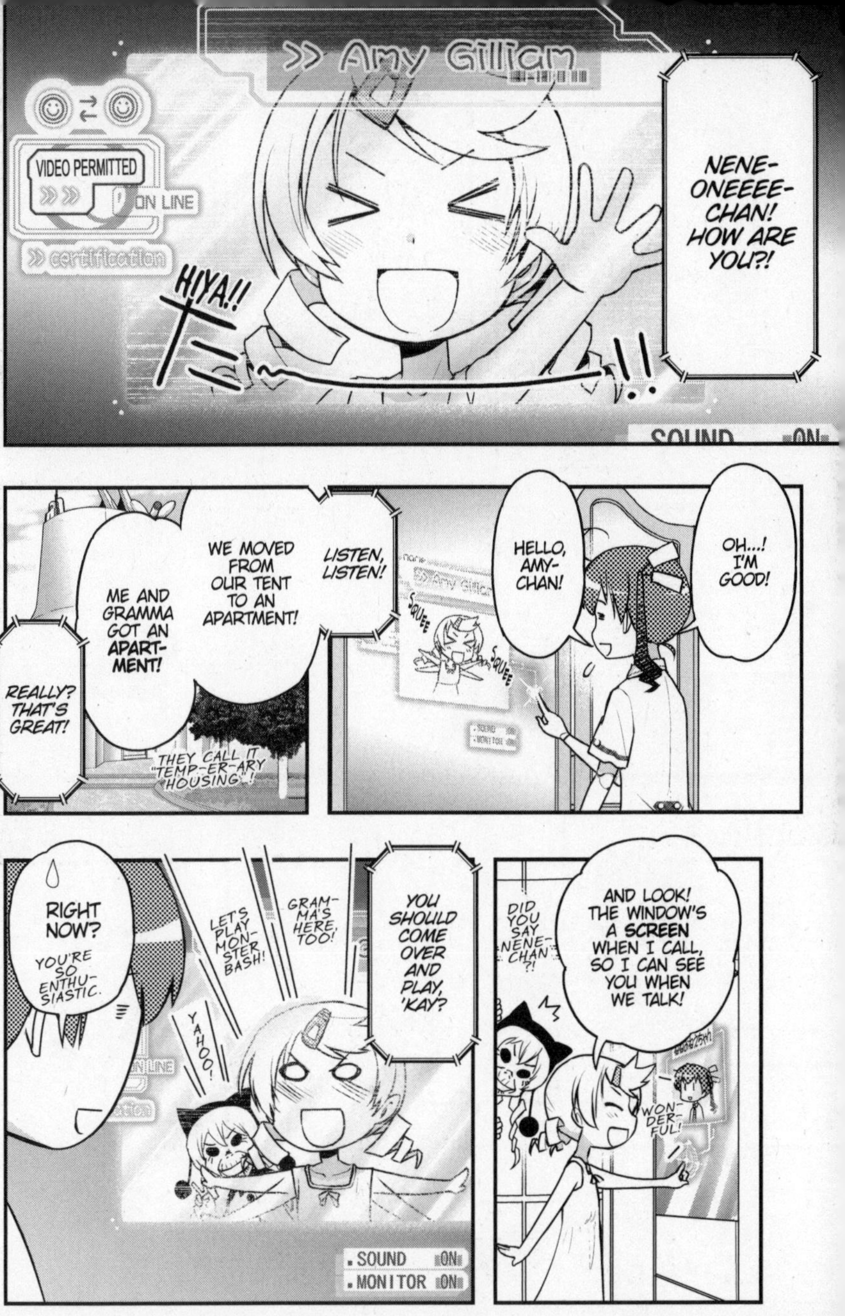
>> Amy Gilliam
VIDEO PERMITTED
ON LINE
>> certification
HIYA!!
NENE-ONEEEE-CHAN! HOW ARE YOU?!
SOUND ON
OH...! I'M GOOD!
HELLO, AMY-CHAN!
SQUEE
SQUEE
LISTEN, LISTEN!
WE MOVED FROM OUR TENT TO AN APARTMENT!
ME AND GRAMMA GOT AN APARTMENT!
REALLY? THAT'S GREAT!
THEY CALL IT "TEMP-ER-ARY HOUSING"!
AND LOOK! THE WINDOW'S A SCREEN WHEN I CALL, SO I CAN SEE YOU WHEN WE TALK!
DID YOU SAY NENE-CHAN?!
WONDERFUL!
YOU SHOULD COME OVER AND PLAY, 'KAY?
GRAMMA'S HERE, TOO!
LET'S PLAY MONSTER BASH!
YAHOO!
RIGHT NOW?
YOU'RE SO ENTHUSIASTIC.
SOUND ON
MONITOR ON

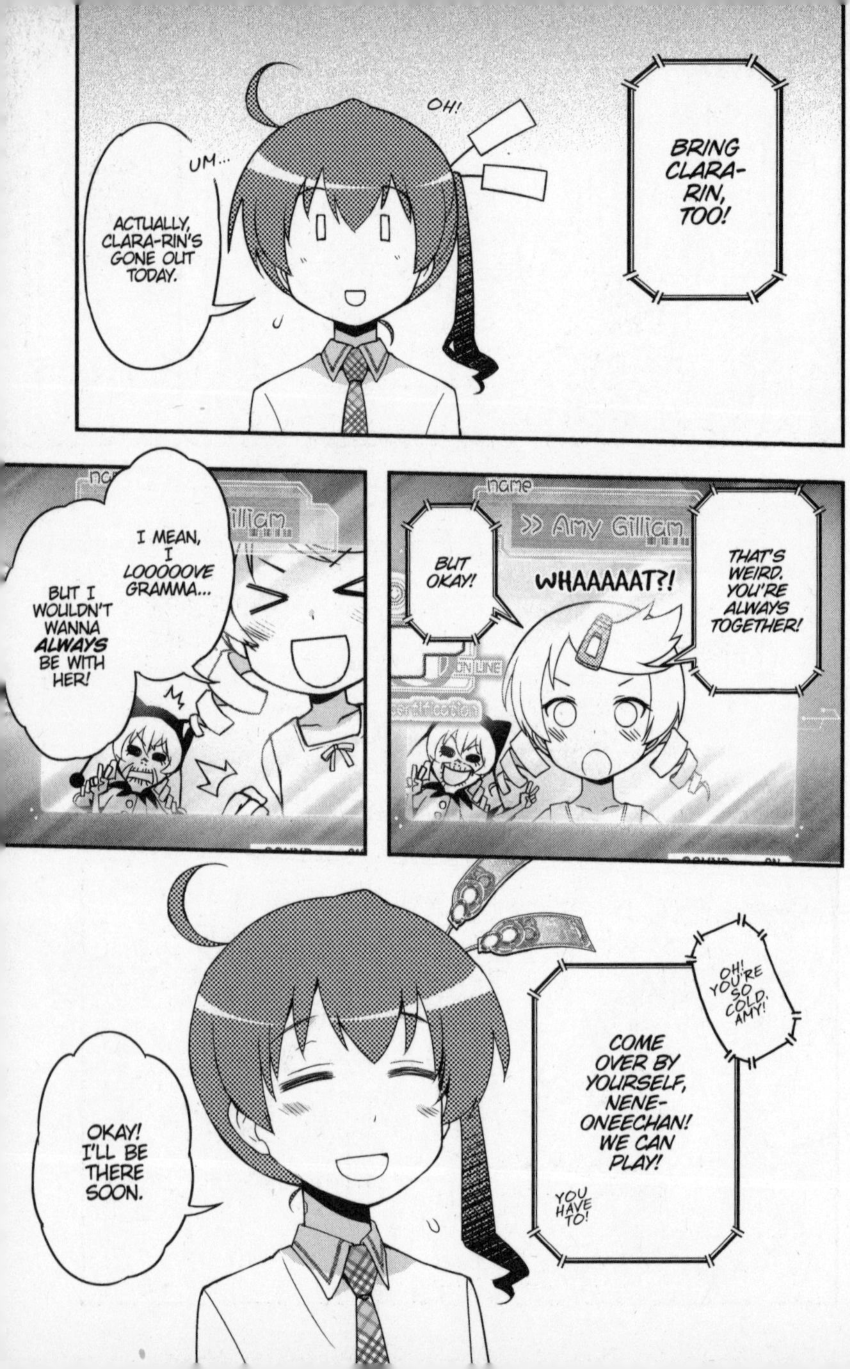
BRING CLARA-RIN, TOO!
OH!
UM...
ACTUALLY, CLARA-RIN'S GONE OUT TODAY.
name
>> Amy Gilliam
THAT'S WEIRD. YOU'RE ALWAYS TOGETHER!
WHAAAAAT?!
BUT OKAY!
ON LINE
I MEAN, I LOOOOOVE GRAMMA...
BUT I WOULDN'T WANNA **ALWAYS** BE WITH HER!
OH! YOU'RE SO COLD, AMY!
COME OVER BY YOURSELF, NENE-ONEECHAN! WE CAN PLAY!
YOU HAVE TO!
OKAY! I'LL BE THERE SOON.

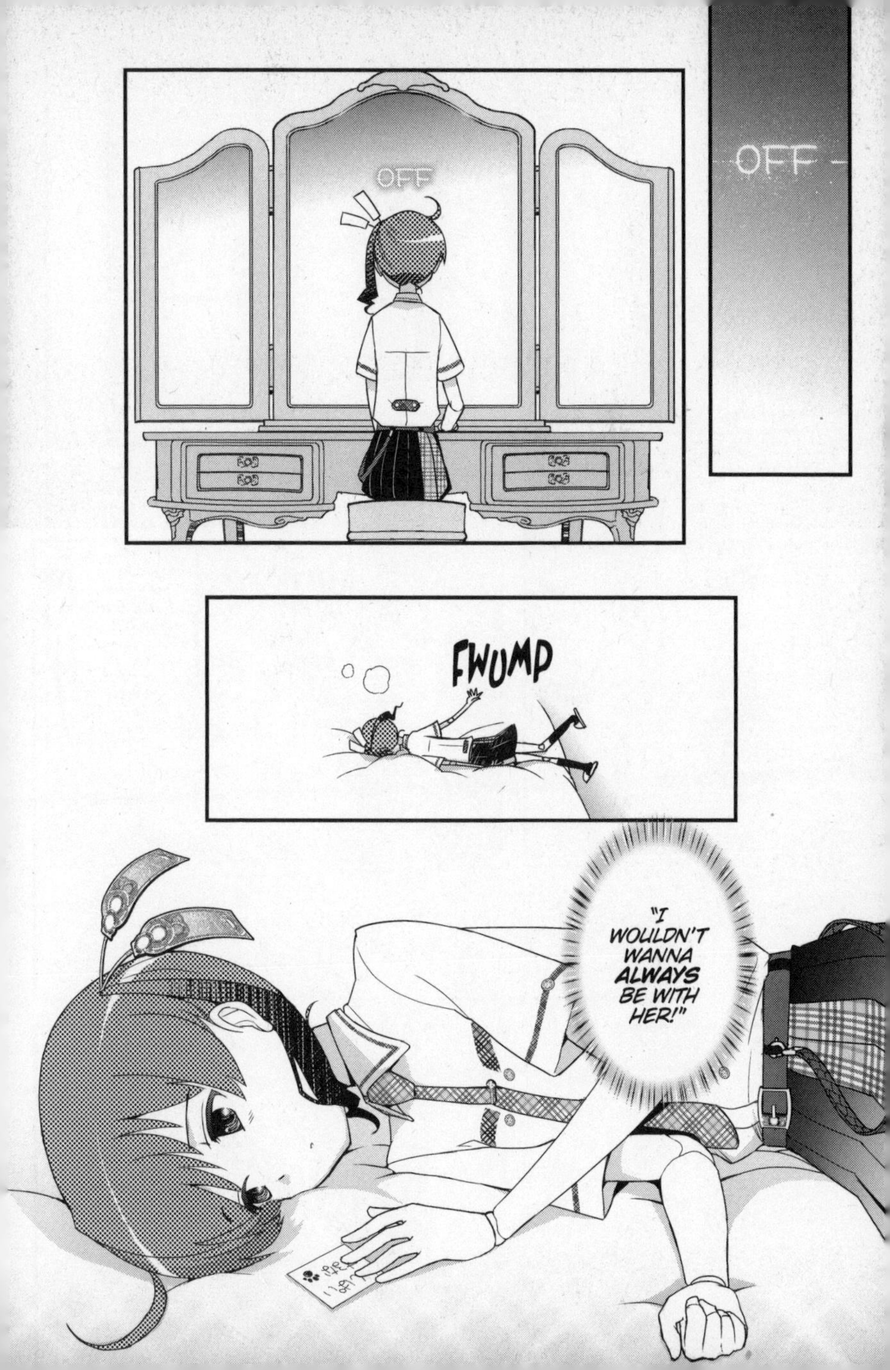
OFF –
OFF
FWUMP
"I WOULDN'T WANNA ALWAYS BE WITH HER!"

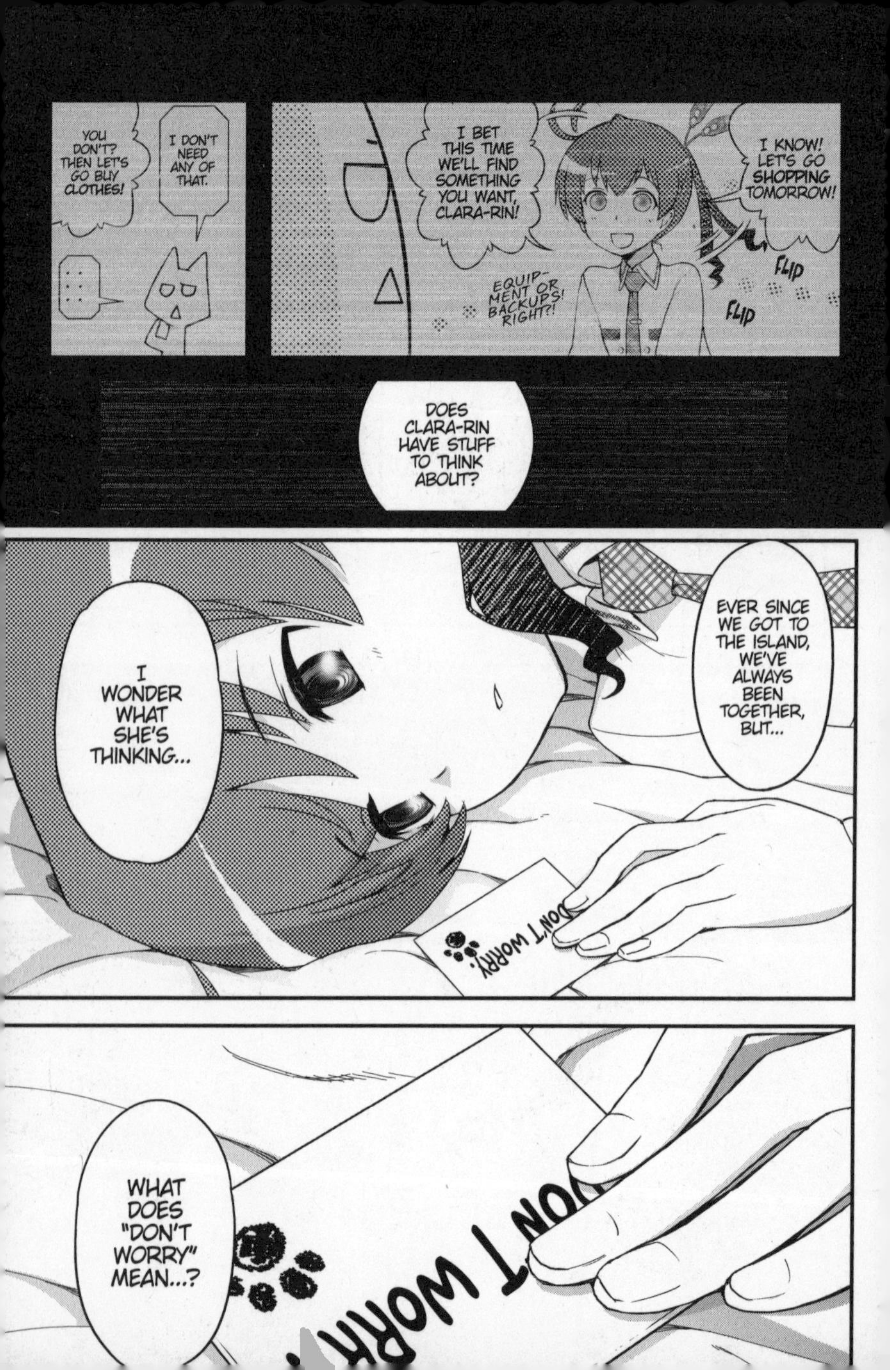
I KNOW! LET'S GO SHOPPING TOMORROW!
FLIP
FLIP
I BET THIS TIME WE'LL FIND SOMETHING YOU WANT, CLARA-RIN!
EQUIPMENT OR BACKUPS! RIGHT?!
I DON'T NEED ANY OF THAT.
YOU DON'T? THEN LET'S GO BUY CLOTHES!
...
DOES CLARA-RIN HAVE STUFF TO THINK ABOUT?
EVER SINCE WE GOT TO THE ISLAND, WE'VE ALWAYS BEEN TOGETHER, BUT...
I WONDER WHAT SHE'S THINKING...
DON'T WORRY.
WHAT DOES "DON'T WORRY" MEAN...?
DON'T WORRY

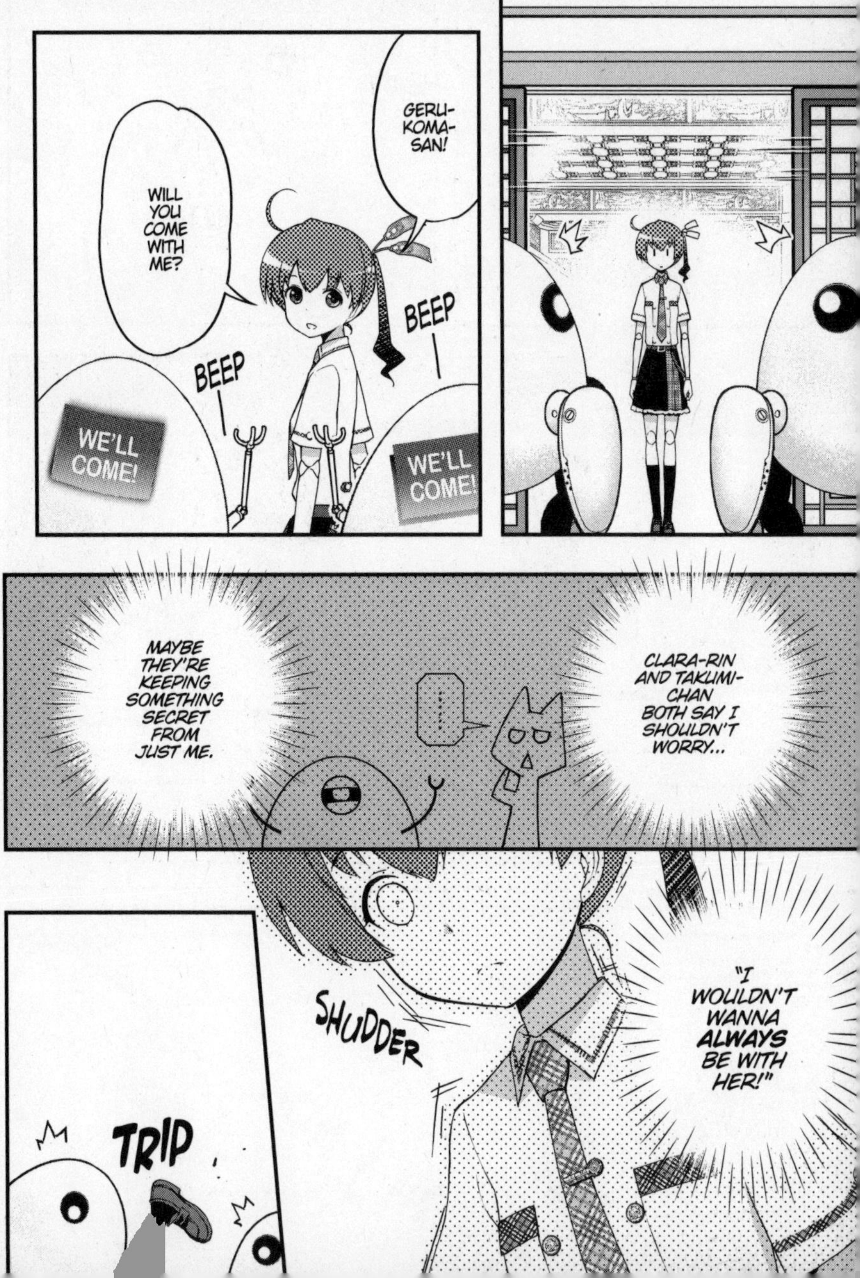
GERU-KOMA-SAN!
WILL YOU COME WITH ME?
BEEP
WE'LL COME!
BEEP
WE'LL COME!
CLARA-RIN AND TAKUMI-CHAN BOTH SAY I SHOULDN'T WORRY...
......
MAYBE THEY'RE KEEPING SOMETHING SECRET FROM JUST ME.
"I WOULDN'T WANNA **ALWAYS** BE WITH HER!"
SHUDDER
TRIP

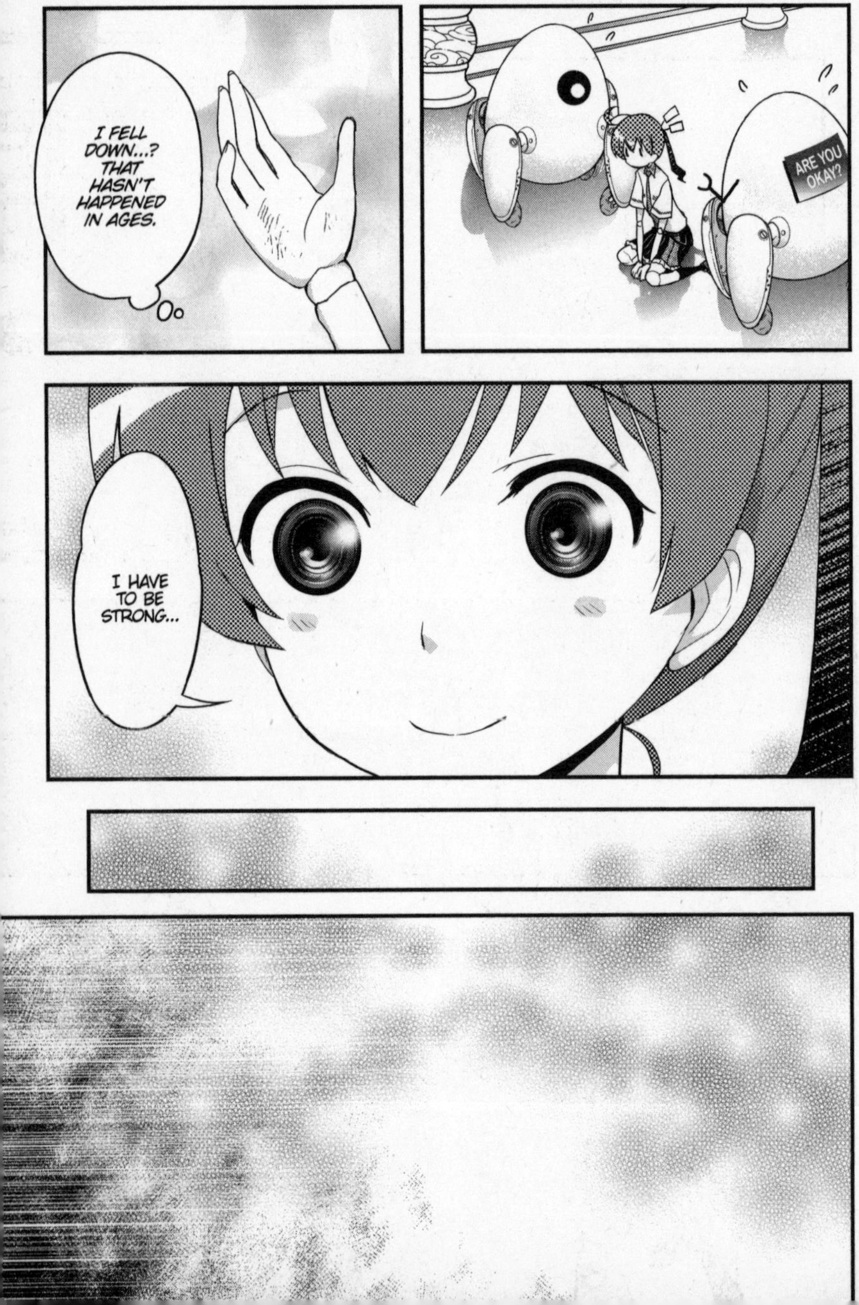
ARE YOU OKAY?
I FELL DOWN...? THAT HASN'T HAPPENED IN AGES.
I HAVE TO BE STRONG...

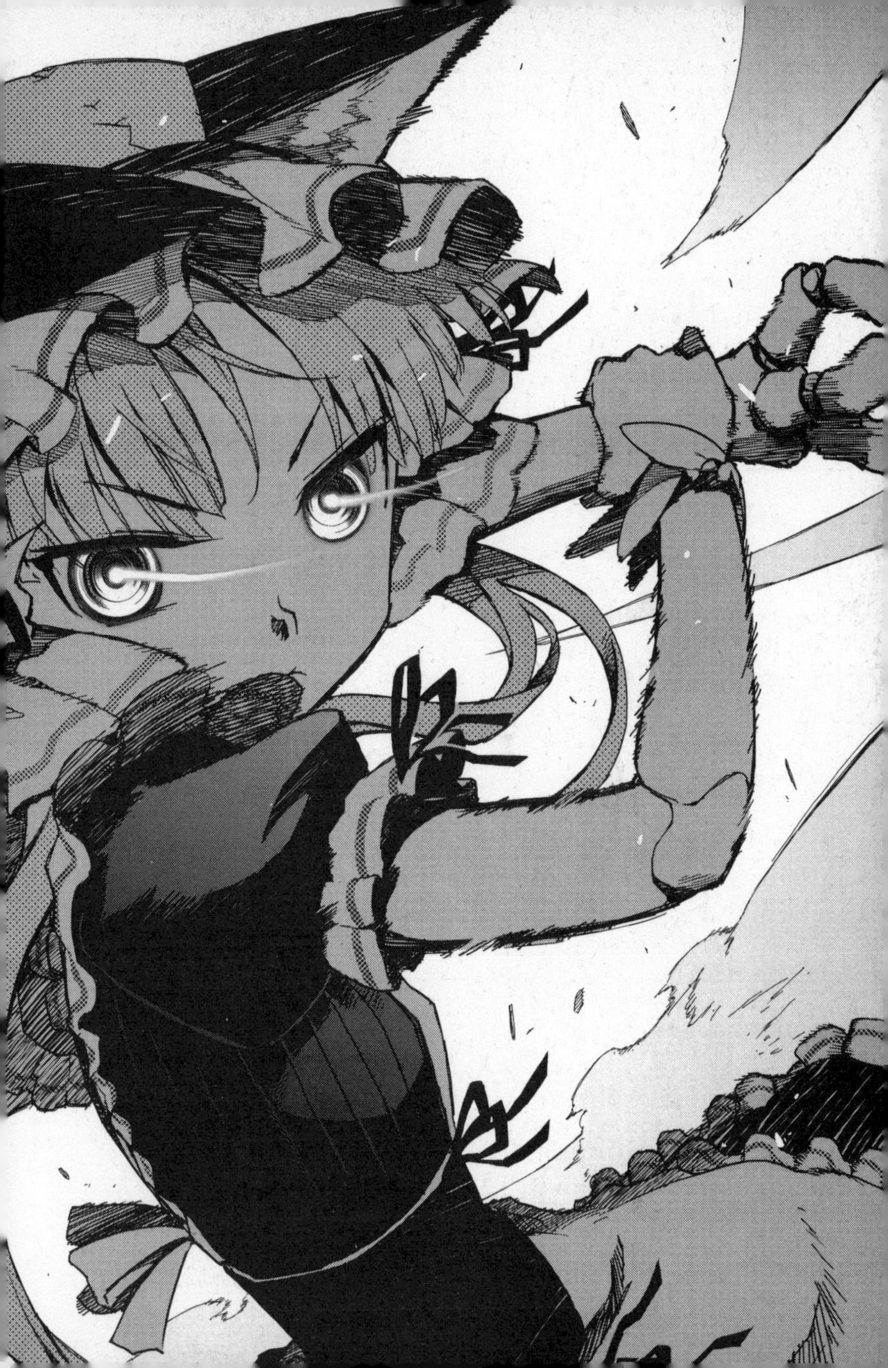

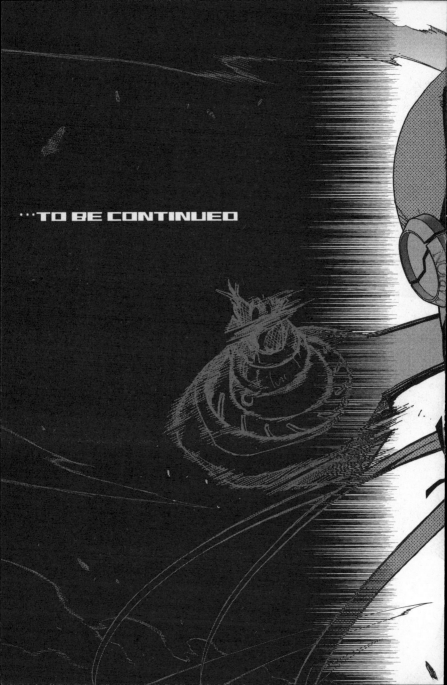

···TO BE CONTINUED

GHOST URN

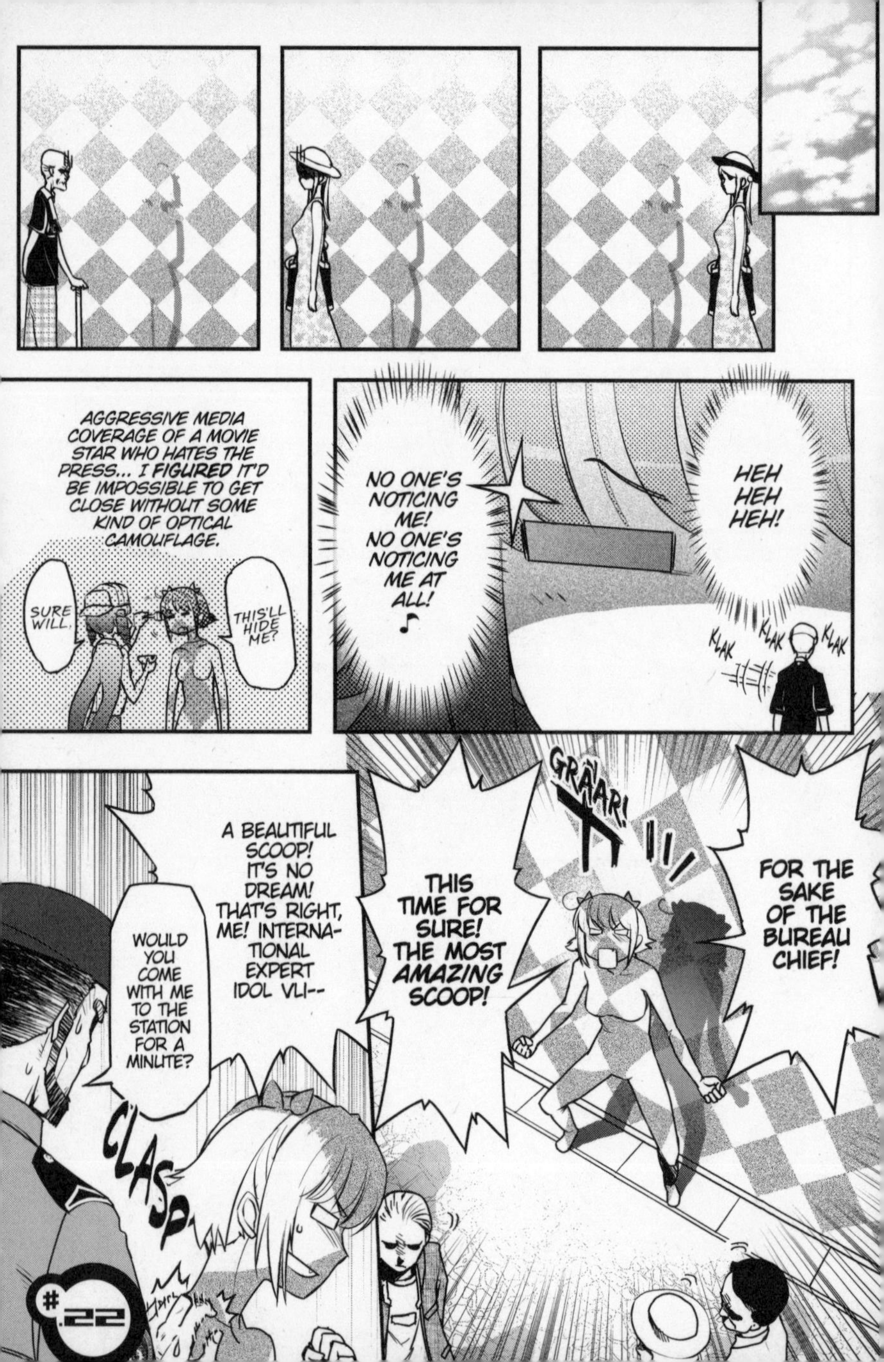
HEH HEH HEH!
NO ONE'S NOTICING ME! NO ONE'S NOTICING ME AT ALL! ♪
KLAK
KLAK
KLAK
AGGRESSIVE MEDIA COVERAGE OF A MOVIE STAR WHO HATES THE PRESS... I **FIGURED** IT'D BE IMPOSSIBLE TO GET CLOSE WITHOUT SOME KIND OF OPTICAL CAMOUFLAGE.
THIS'LL HIDE ME?
SURE WILL.
FOR THE SAKE OF THE BUREAU CHIEF!
GRAAR!
THIS TIME FOR SURE! THE MOST *AMAZING* SCOOP!
A BEAUTIFUL SCOOP! IT'S NO DREAM! THAT'S RIGHT, ME! INTERNATIONAL EXPERT IDOL VLI--
WOULD YOU COME WITH ME TO THE STATION FOR A MINUTE?
CLASP

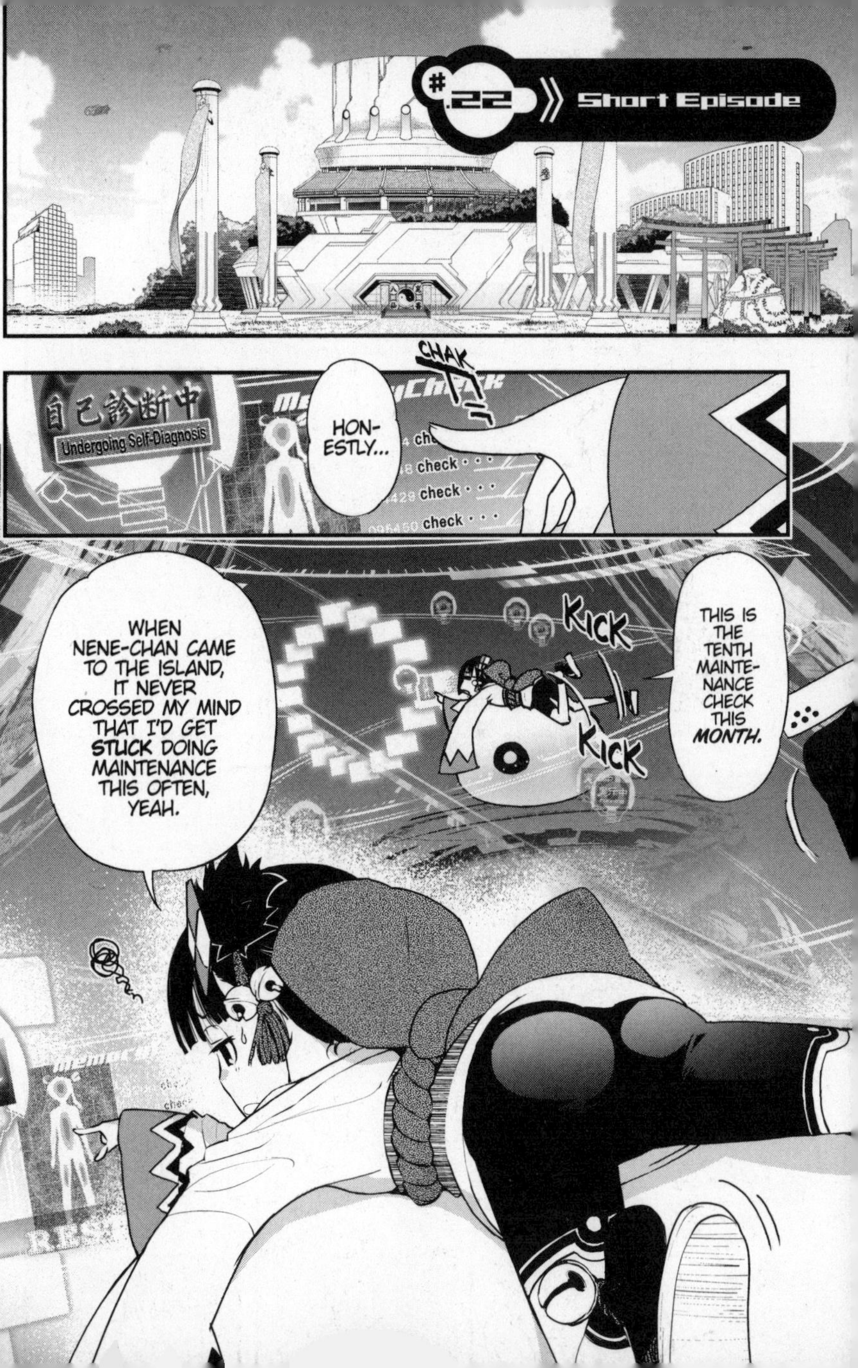
#.22 Short Episode
CHAK
HON-ESTLY...
自己診断中
Undergoing Self-Diagnosis
check
48 check
429 check
095460 check
THIS IS THE TENTH MAINTE-NANCE CHECK THIS MONTH.
KICK
KICK
WHEN NENE-CHAN CAME TO THE ISLAND, IT NEVER CROSSED MY MIND THAT I'D GET STUCK DOING MAINTENANCE THIS OFTEN, YEAH.

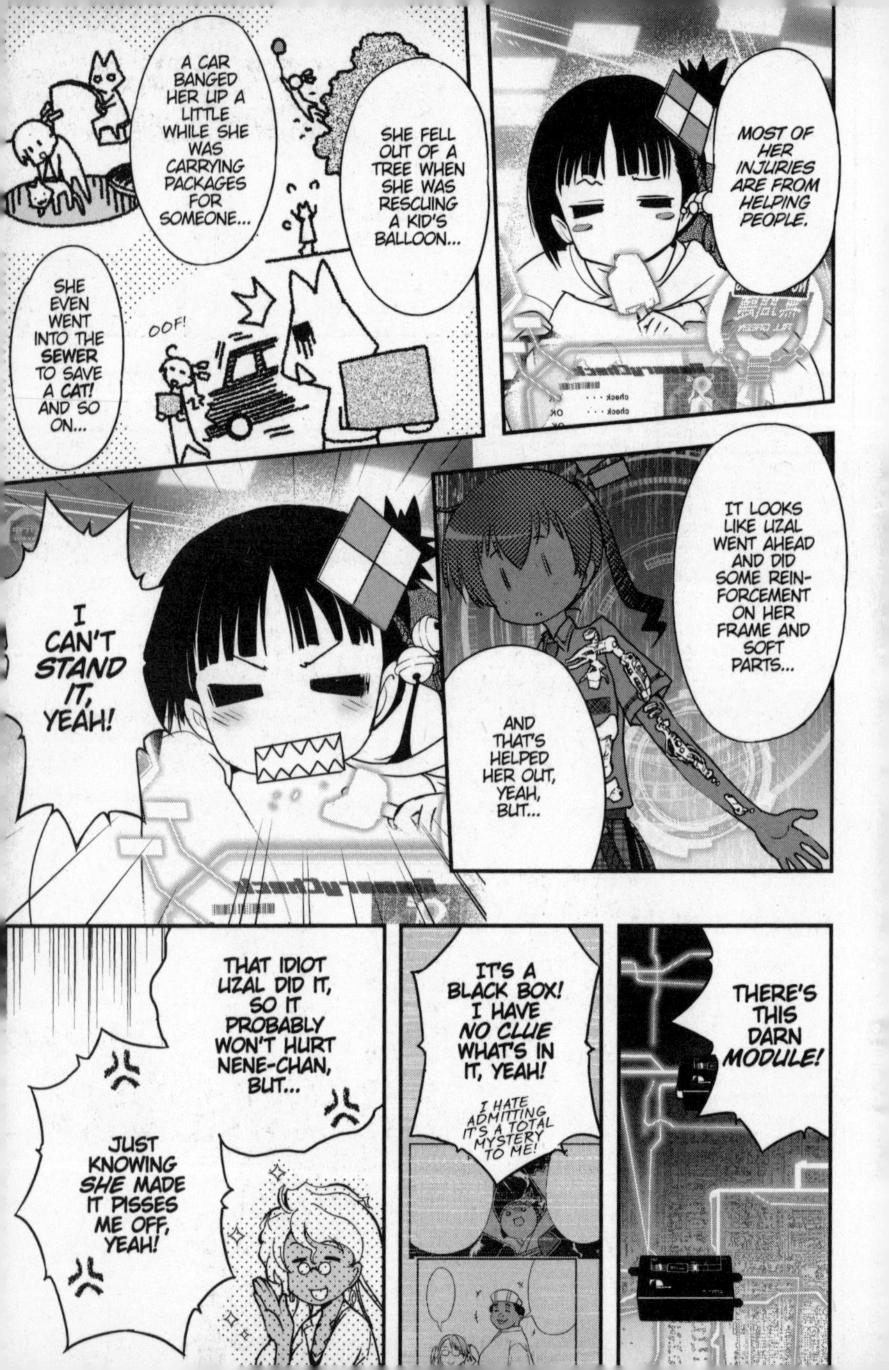

MOST OF HER INJURIES ARE FROM HELPING PEOPLE.
SHE FELL OUT OF A TREE WHEN SHE WAS RESCUING A KID'S BALLOON...
A CAR BANGED HER UP A LITTLE WHILE SHE WAS CARRYING PACKAGES FOR SOMEONE...
SHE EVEN WENT INTO THE SEWER TO SAVE A CAT! AND SO ON...
OOF!
IT LOOKS LIKE UZAL WENT AHEAD AND DID SOME REIN-FORCEMENT ON HER FRAME AND SOFT PARTS...
AND THAT'S HELPED HER OUT, YEAH, BUT...
I CAN'T STAND IT, YEAH!
THERE'S THIS DARN MODULE!
IT'S A BLACK BOX! I HAVE NO CLUE WHAT'S IN IT, YEAH!
I HATE ADMITTING IT'S A TOTAL MYSTERY TO ME!
THAT IDIOT UZAL DID IT, SO IT PROBABLY WON'T HURT NENE-CHAN, BUT...
JUST KNOWING SHE MADE IT PISSES ME OFF, YEAH!

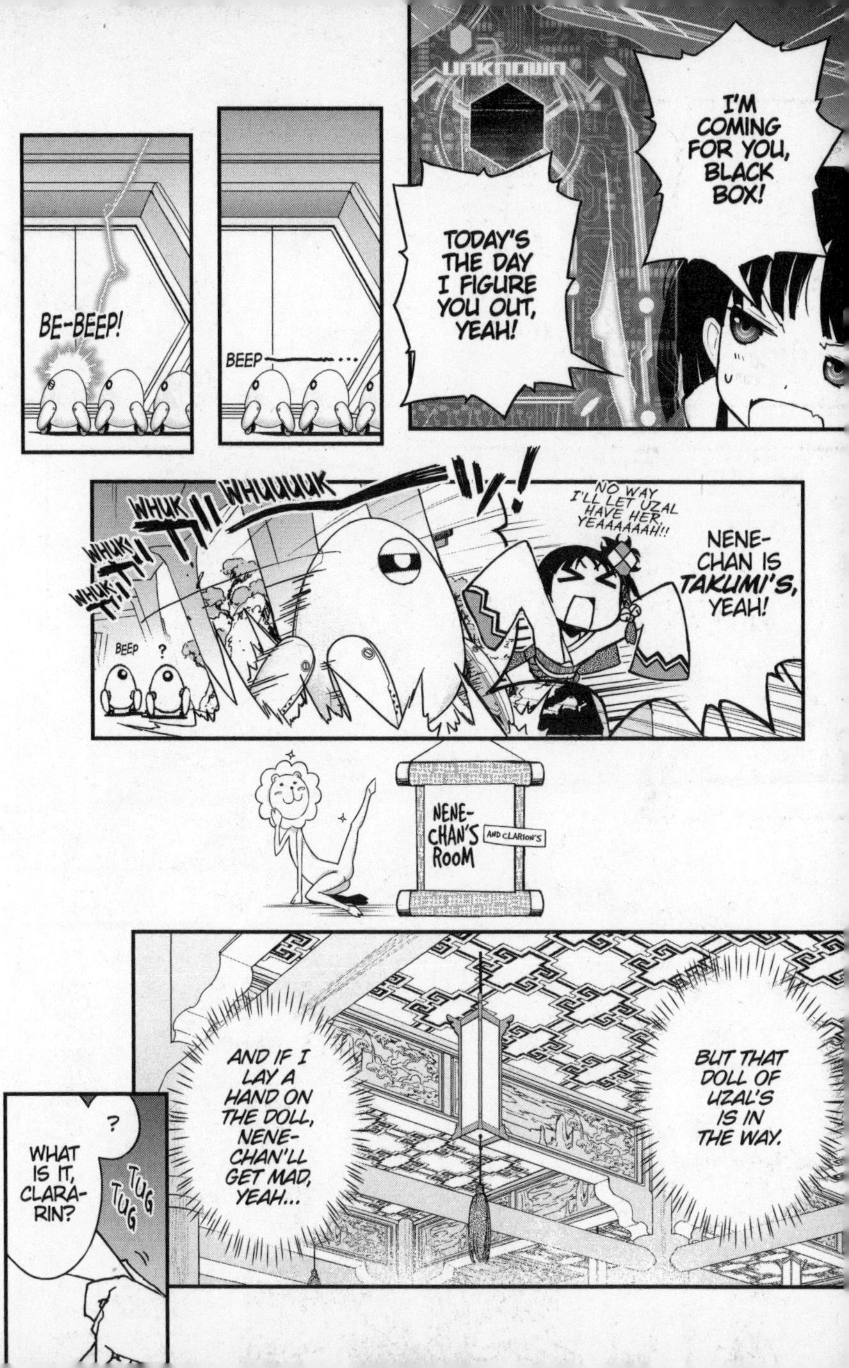
UNKNOWN
I'M COMING FOR YOU, BLACK BOX!
TODAY'S THE DAY I FIGURE YOU OUT, YEAH!
BEEP———...
BE-BEEP!
NENE-CHAN IS TAKUMI'S, YEAH!
NO WAY I'LL LET UZAL HAVE HER, YEAAAAAAAH!!
WHUUUUK
WHUK
WHUK
WHUK
BEEP
?
NENE-CHAN'S ROOM
AND CLARION'S
BUT THAT DOLL OF UZAL'S IS IN THE WAY.
AND IF I LAY A HAND ON THE DOLL, NENE-CHAN'LL GET MAD, YEAH...
?
WHAT IS IT, CLARA-RIN?
TUG TUG

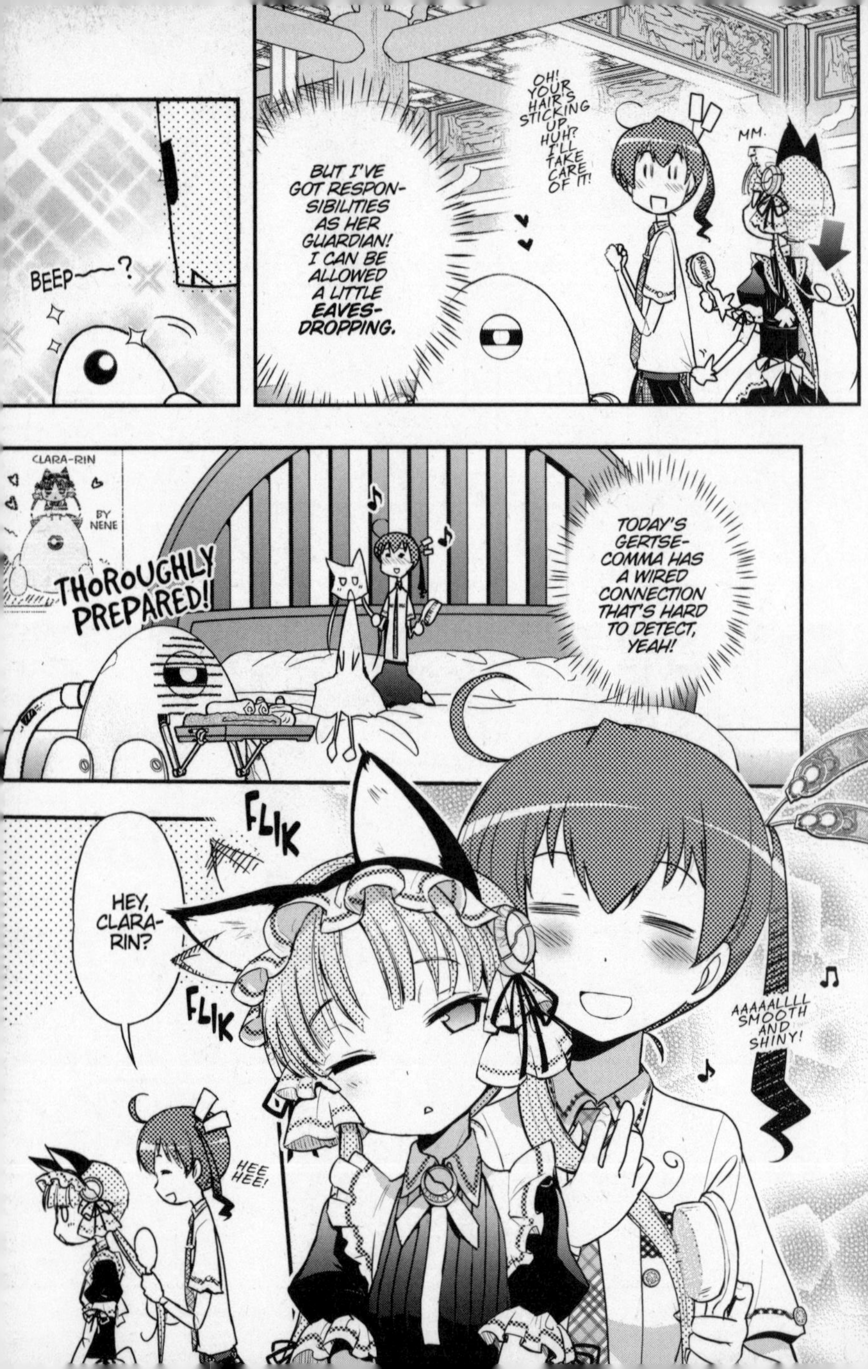
OH! YOUR HAIR'S STICKING UP HUH? I'LL TAKE CARE OF IT!
MM.
BRUSH
BUT I'VE GOT RESPONSIBILITIES AS HER GUARDIAN! I CAN BE ALLOWED A LITTLE EAVESDROPPING.
BEEP~~?
TODAY'S GERTSE-COMMA HAS A WIRED CONNECTION THAT'S HARD TO DETECT, YEAH!
THOROUGHLY PREPARED!
CLARA-RIN
BY NENE
AAAAALLLL SMOOTH AND SHINY!
FLIK
FLIK
HEY, CLARA-RIN?
HEE HEE!

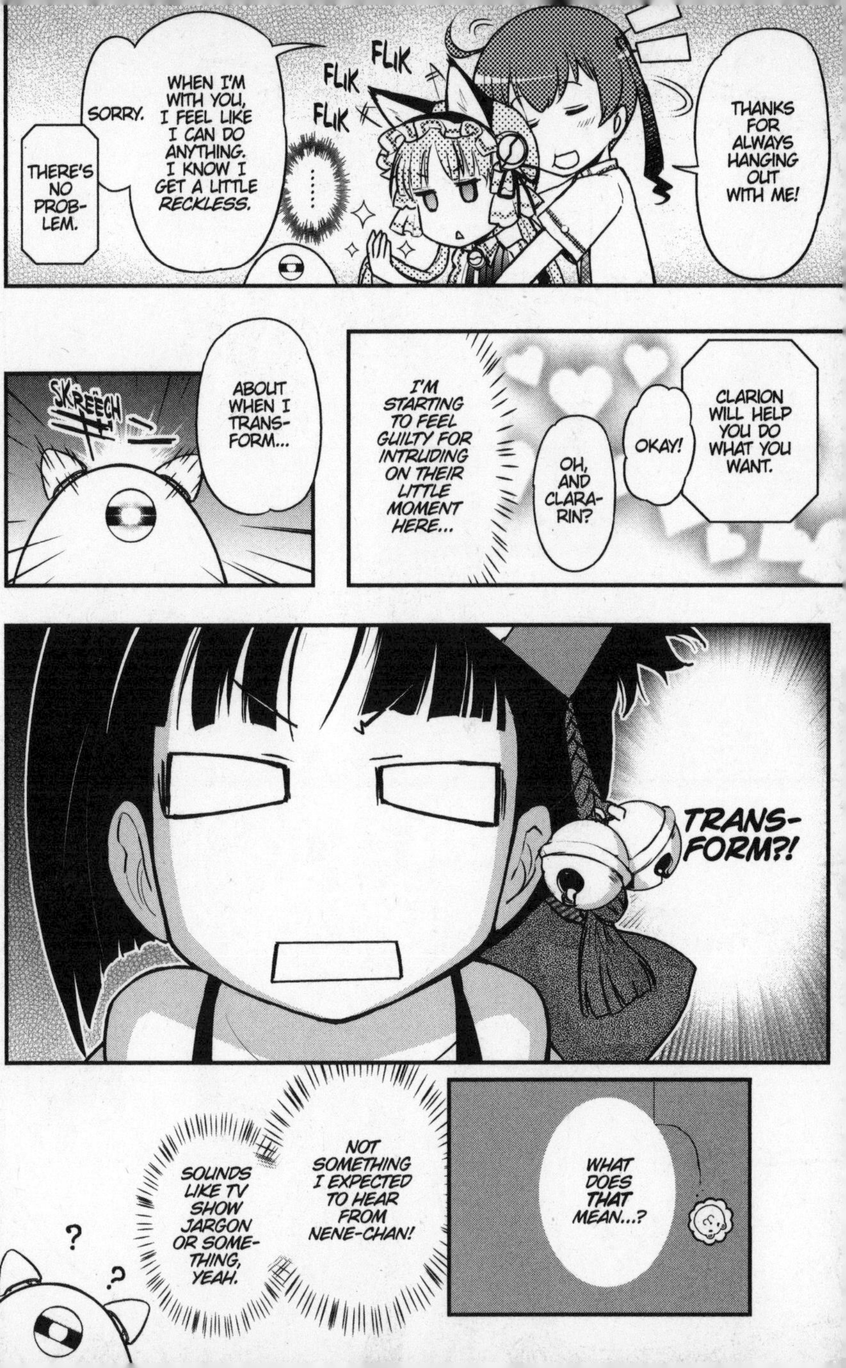
THANKS FOR ALWAYS HANGING OUT WITH ME!
FLIK
FLIK
FLIK
......
WHEN I'M WITH YOU, I FEEL LIKE I CAN DO ANYTHING. I KNOW I GET A LITTLE RECKLESS.
SORRY.
THERE'S NO PROB-LEM.
CLARION WILL HELP YOU DO WHAT YOU WANT.
OKAY!
OH, AND CLARA-RIN?
I'M STARTING TO FEEL GUILTY FOR INTRUDING ON THEIR LITTLE MOMENT HERE...
ABOUT WHEN I TRANS-FORM...
SKREECH
TRANS-FORM?!
WHAT DOES THAT MEAN...?
NOT SOMETHING I EXPECTED TO HEAR FROM NENE-CHAN!
SOUNDS LIKE TV SHOW JARGON OR SOME-THING, YEAH.
?
?

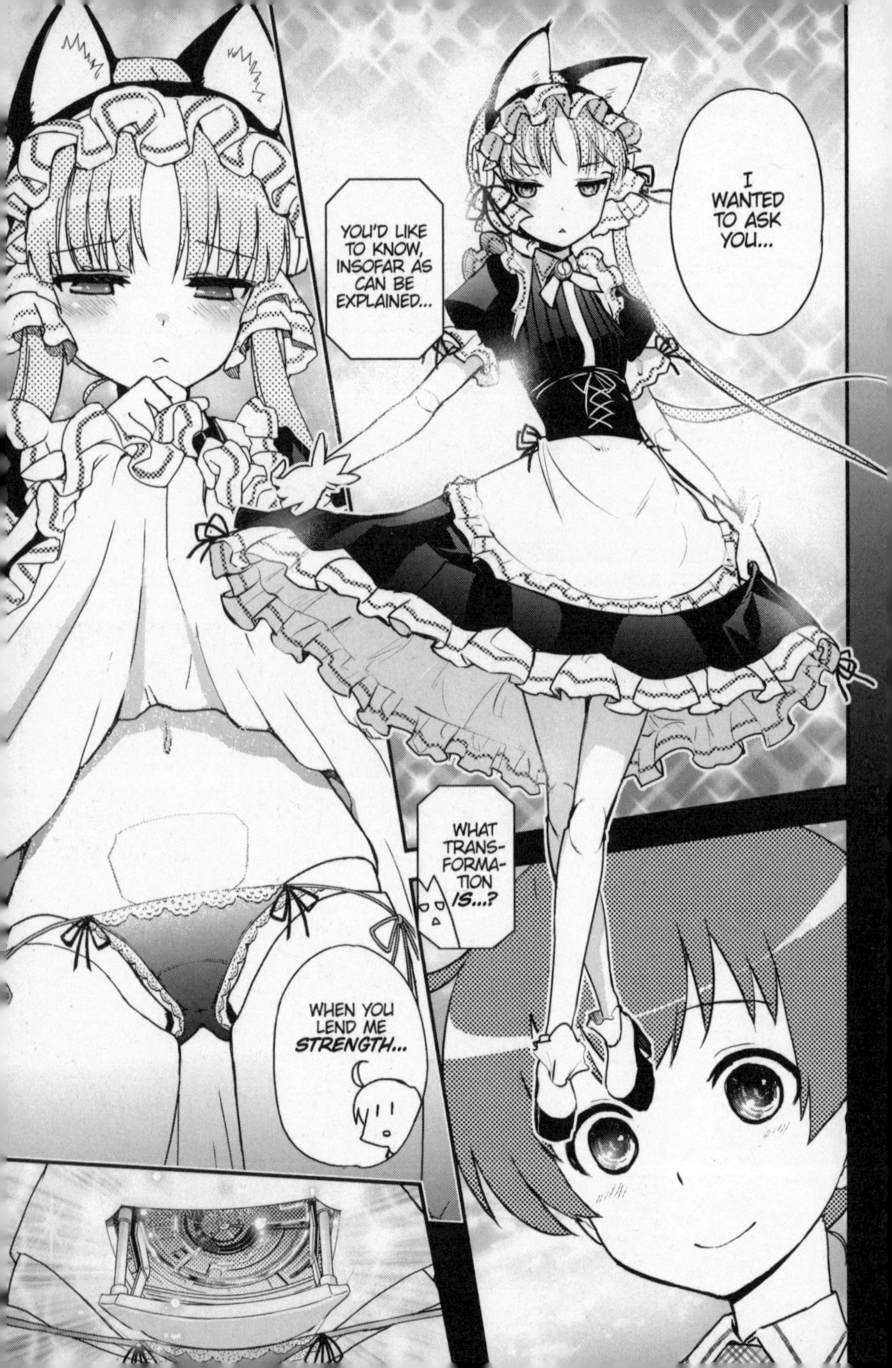
I WANTED TO ASK YOU...
YOU'D LIKE TO KNOW, INSOFAR AS CAN BE EXPLAINED...
WHAT TRANSFORMATION IS...?
WHEN YOU LEND ME STRENGTH...

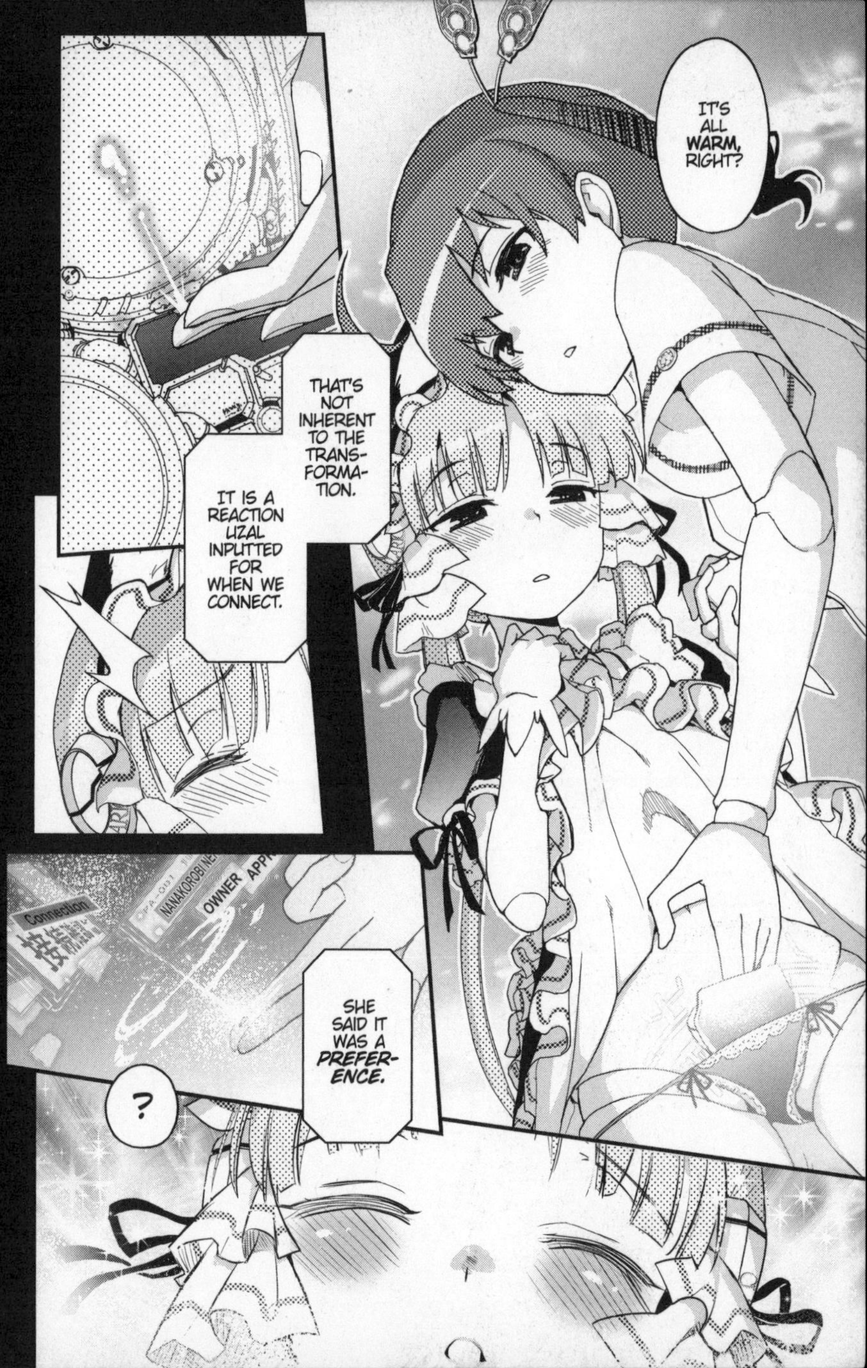
IT'S ALL WARM, RIGHT?
THAT'S NOT INHERENT TO THE TRANS-FORMA-TION.
IT IS A REACTION UZAL INPUTTED FOR WHEN WE CONNECT.
Connection
SHE SAID IT WAS A *PREFER-ENCE.*
?

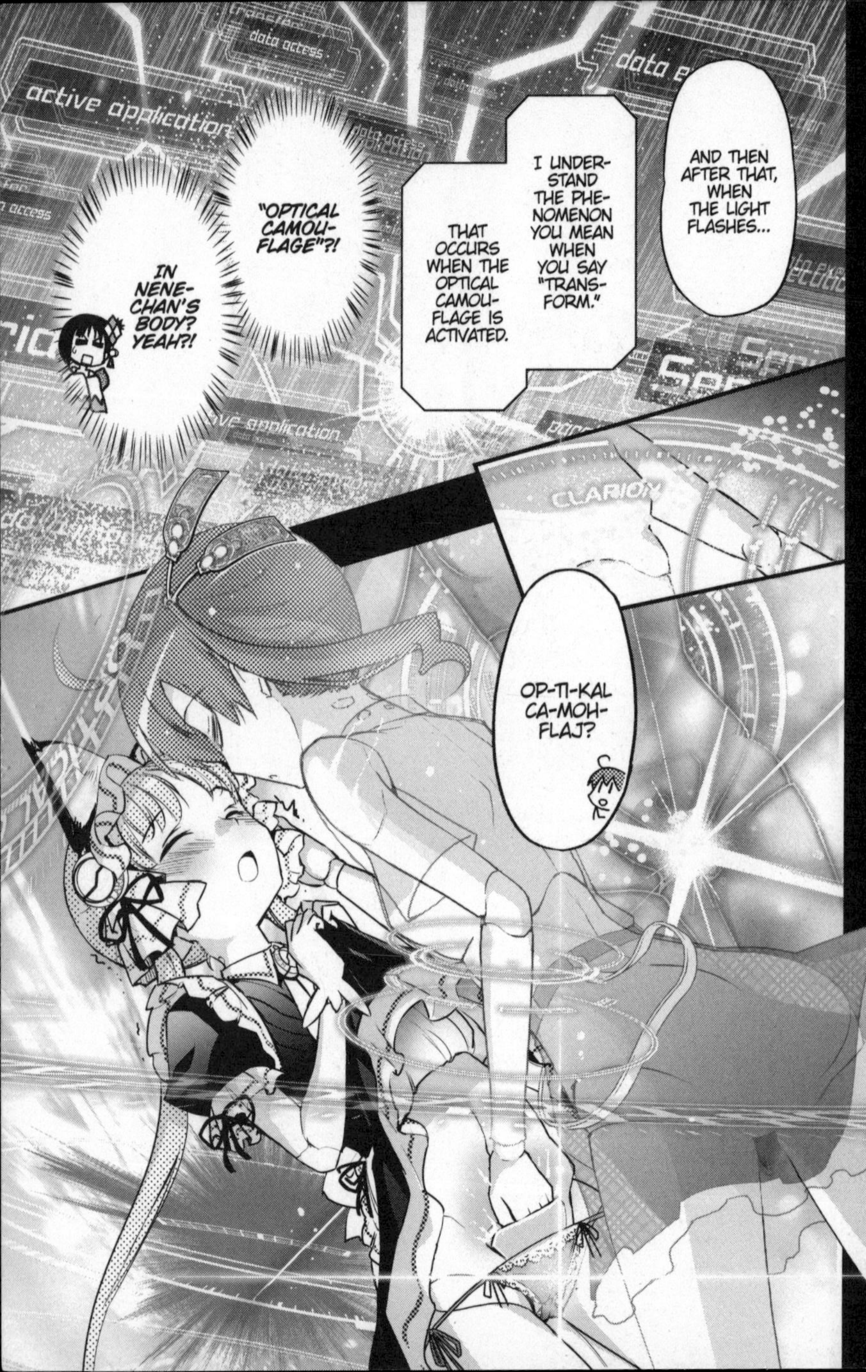
AND THEN AFTER THAT, WHEN THE LIGHT FLASHES...
I UNDERSTAND THE PHENOMENON YOU MEAN WHEN YOU SAY "TRANSFORM."
THAT OCCURS WHEN THE OPTICAL CAMOUFLAGE IS ACTIVATED.
"OPTICAL CAMOUFLAGE"?!
IN NENE-CHAN'S BODY? YEAH?!
data access
active application
CLARION
OP-TI-KAL CA-MOH-FLAJ?

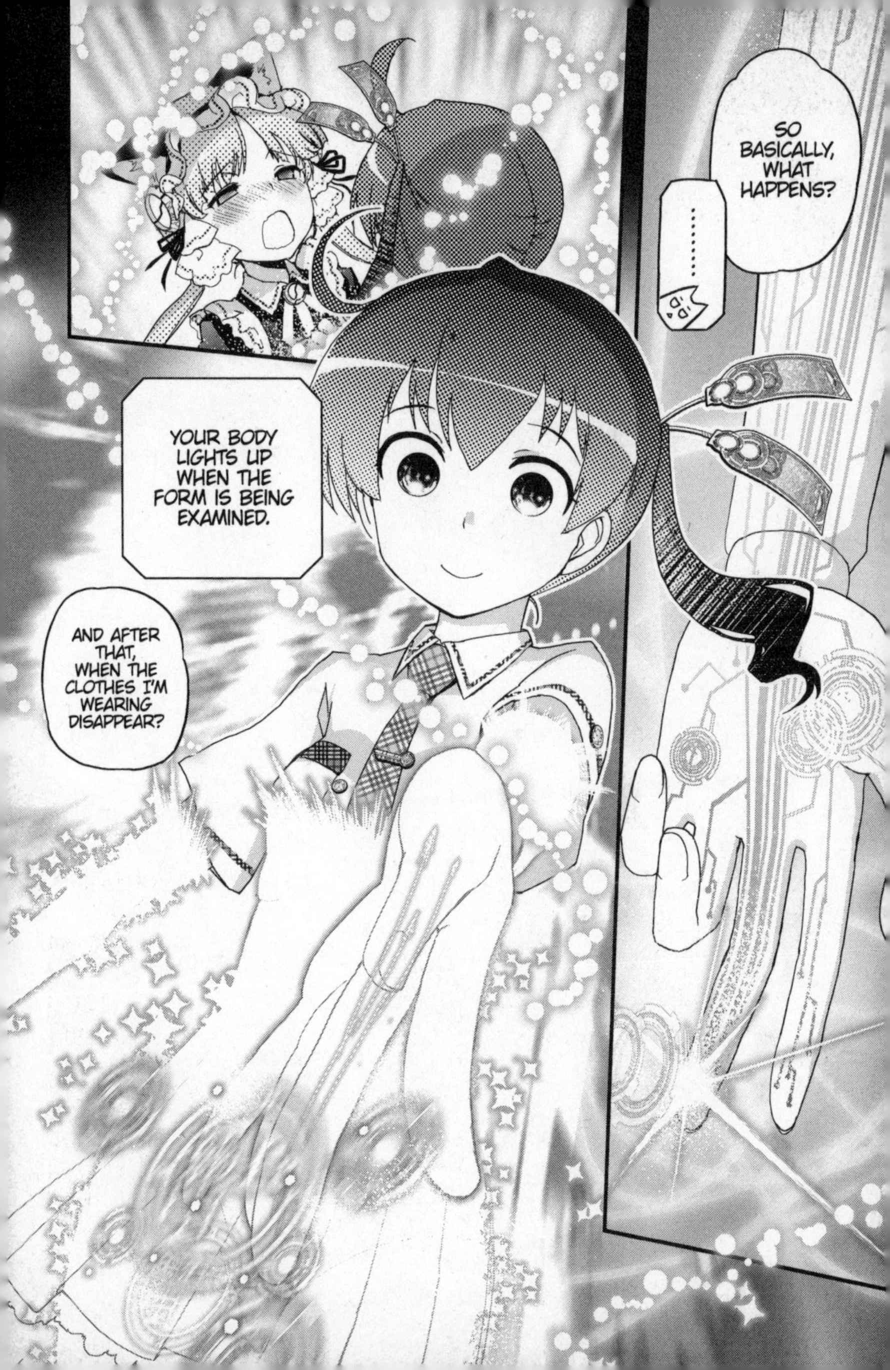
SO BASICALLY, WHAT HAPPENS?
......
YOUR BODY LIGHTS UP WHEN THE FORM IS BEING EXAMINED.
AND AFTER THAT, WHEN THE CLOTHES I'M WEARING DISAPPEAR?

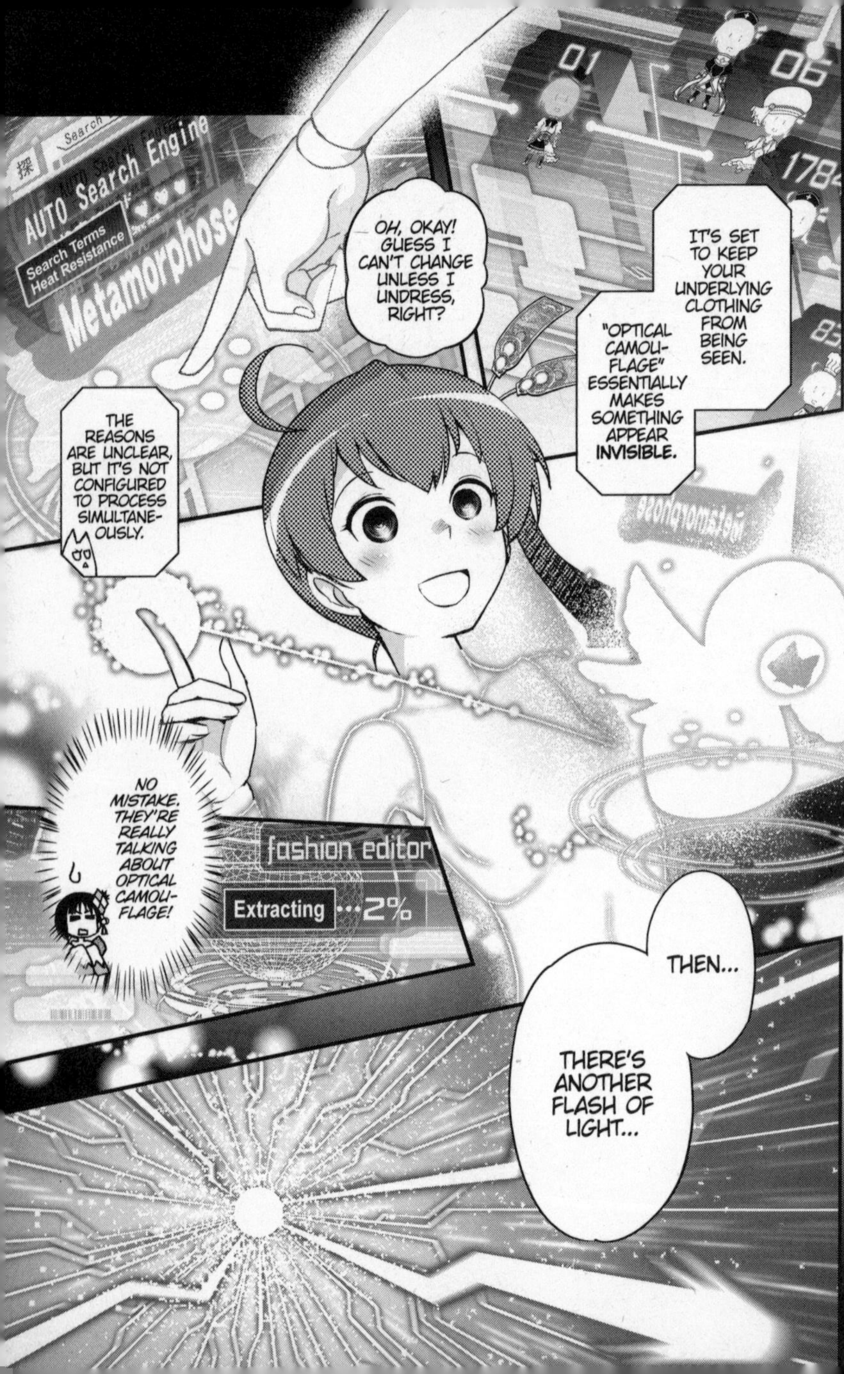

AUTO Search Engine
Search Terms
Heat Resistance
Metamorphose
01
06
IT'S SET TO KEEP YOUR UNDERLYING CLOTHING FROM BEING SEEN.
"OPTICAL CAMOUFLAGE" ESSENTIALLY MAKES SOMETHING APPEAR **INVISIBLE.**
OH, OKAY! GUESS I CAN'T CHANGE UNLESS I UNDRESS, RIGHT?
THE REASONS ARE UNCLEAR, BUT IT'S NOT CONFIGURED TO PROCESS SIMULTANEOUSLY.
NO MISTAKE. THEY'RE REALLY TALKING ABOUT OPTICAL CAMOUFLAGE!
fashion editor
Extracting ···2%
THEN...
THERE'S ANOTHER FLASH OF LIGHT...

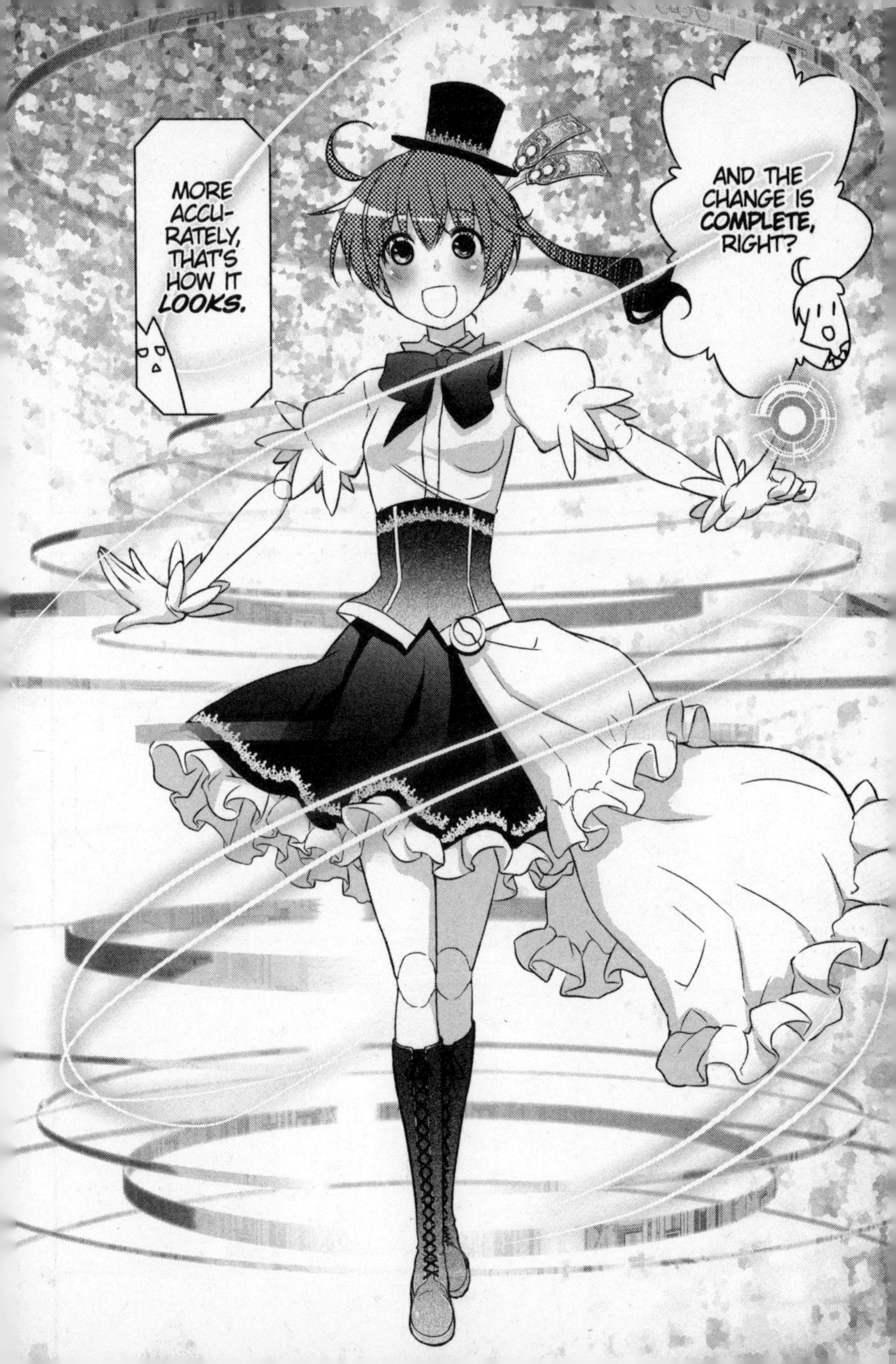
AND THE CHANGE IS COMPLETE, RIGHT?
MORE ACCU-RATELY, THAT'S HOW IT LOOKS.

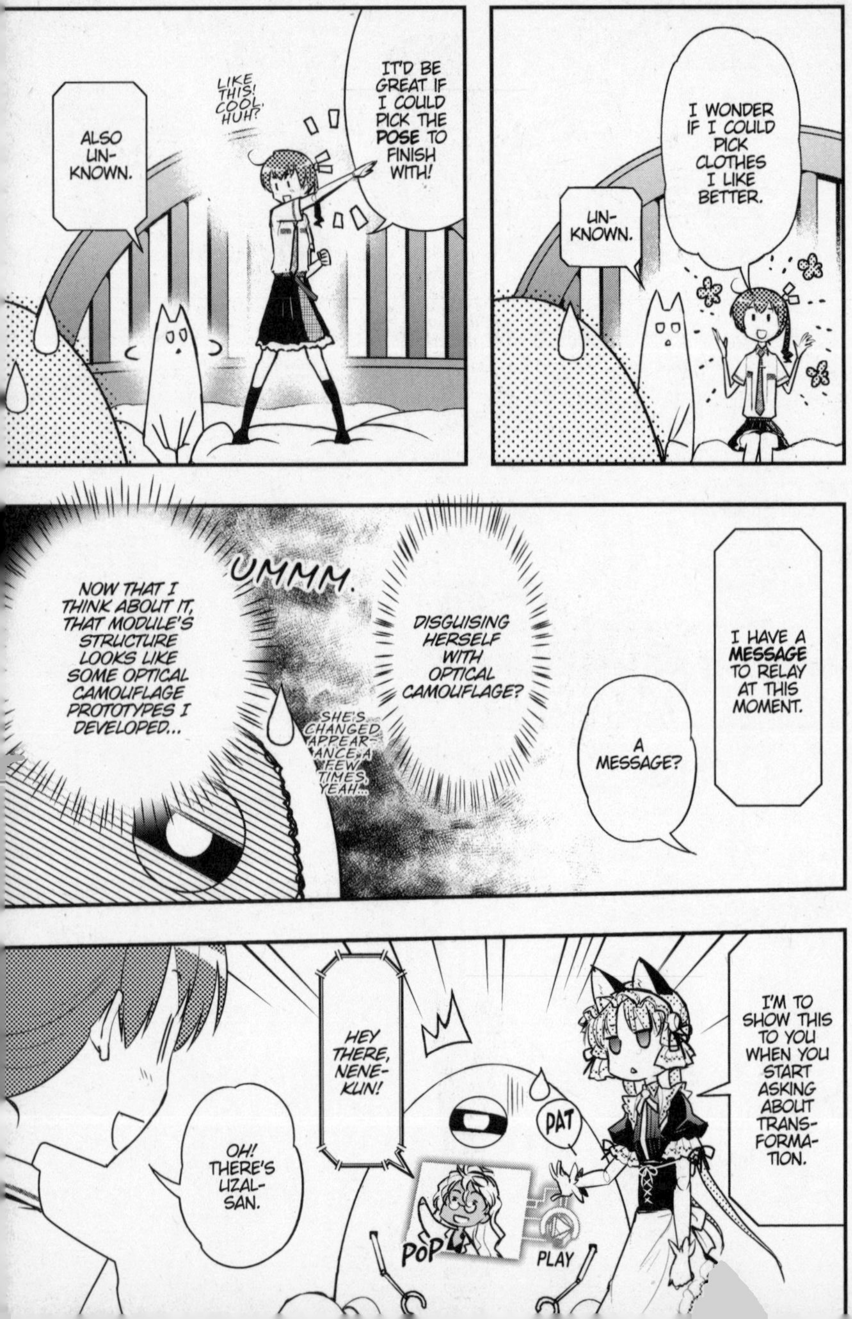
I WONDER IF I COULD PICK CLOTHES I LIKE BETTER.
UN-KNOWN.
IT'D BE GREAT IF I COULD PICK THE POSE TO FINISH WITH!
LIKE THIS! COOL, HUH?
ALSO UN-KNOWN.
I HAVE A MESSAGE TO RELAY AT THIS MOMENT.
A MESSAGE?
DISGUISING HERSELF WITH OPTICAL CAMOUFLAGE?
UMMM.
SHE'S CHANGED APPEAR-ANCE A FEW TIMES, YEAH...
NOW THAT I THINK ABOUT IT, THAT MODULE'S STRUCTURE LOOKS LIKE SOME OPTICAL CAMOUFLAGE PROTOTYPES I DEVELOPED...
I'M TO SHOW THIS TO YOU WHEN YOU START ASKING ABOUT TRANS-FORMA-TION.
PAT
PLAY
POP
HEY THERE, NENE-KUN!
OH! THERE'S LIZAL-SAN.

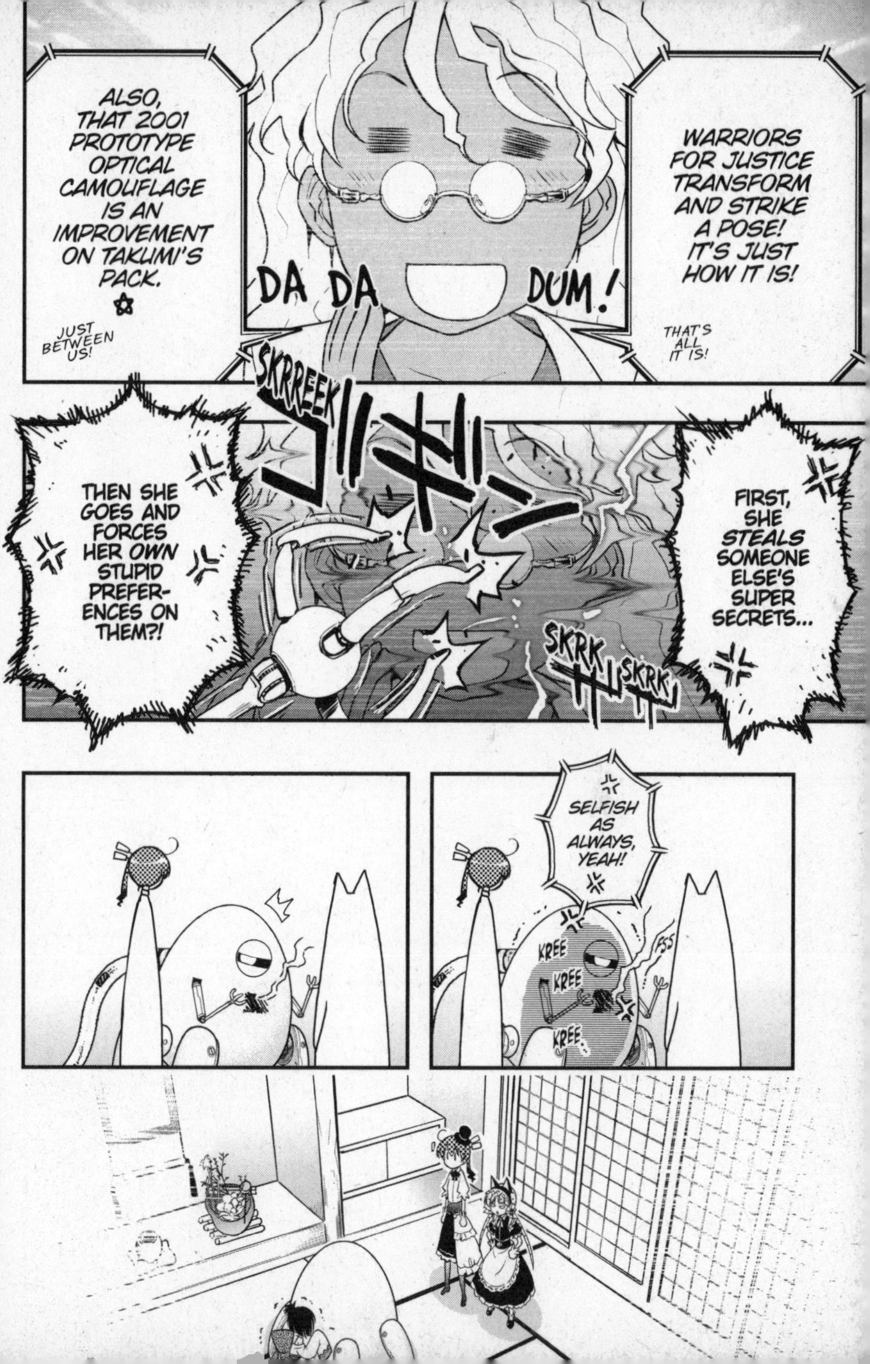
WARRIORS FOR JUSTICE TRANSFORM AND STRIKE A POSE! IT'S JUST HOW IT IS!
THAT'S ALL IT IS!
DA DA DUM!
ALSO, THAT 2001 PROTOTYPE OPTICAL CAMOUFLAGE IS AN IMPROVEMENT ON TAKUMI'S PACK. ✩
JUST BETWEEN US!
SKRREEK
FIRST, SHE STEALS SOMEONE ELSE'S SUPER SECRETS...
SKRK SKRK
THEN SHE GOES AND FORCES HER OWN STUPID PREFER-ENCES ON THEM?!
SELFISH AS ALWAYS, YEAH!
KREE KREE KREE...
FSS

GHOST URN

TRANSMITTED SOMEHOW! PANDORADIO

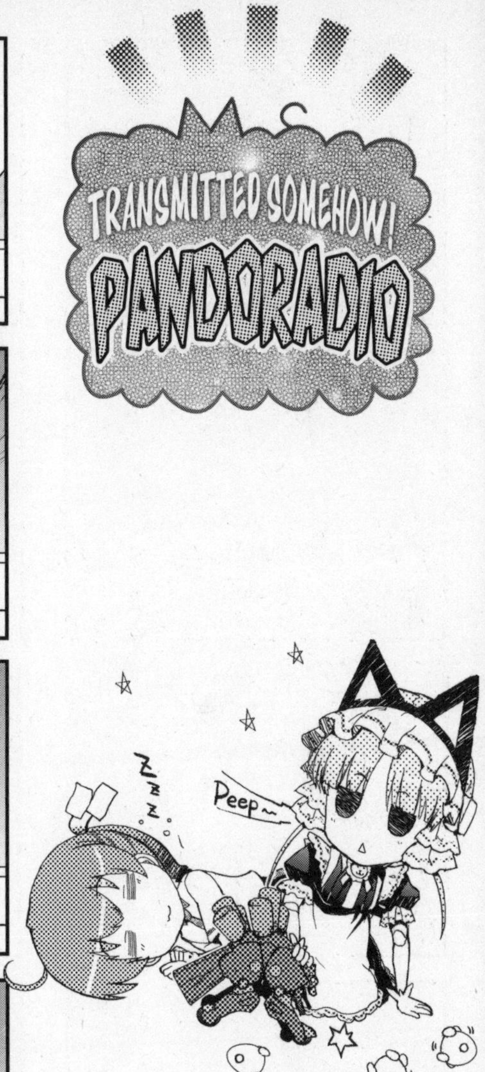

Z Z Z
Peep~

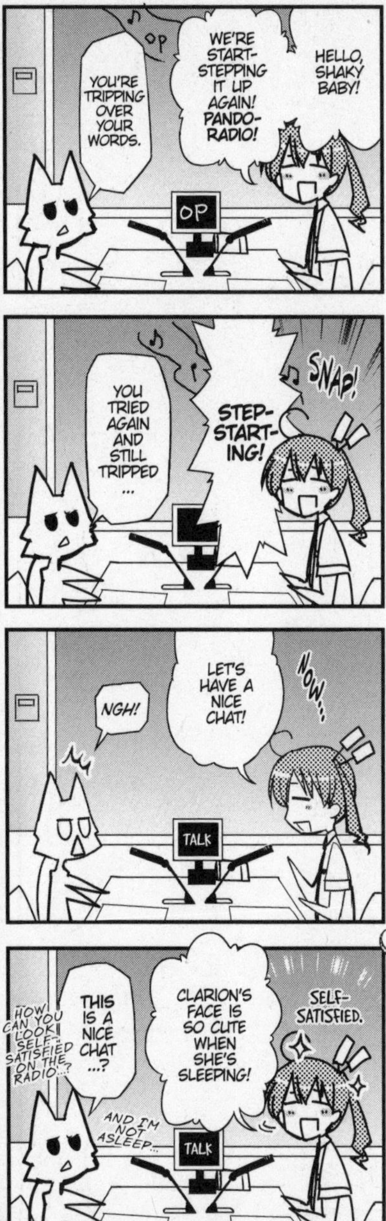

HELLO, SHAKY BABY!
WE'RE START-STEPPING IT UP AGAIN! PANDO-RADIO!
OP
YOU'RE TRIPPING OVER YOUR WORDS.
OP
SNAP!
STEP-STARTING!
YOU TRIED AGAIN AND STILL TRIPPED ...
NOW...
LET'S HAVE A NICE CHAT!
NGH!
TALK
SELF-SATISFIED.
CLARION'S FACE IS SO CUTE WHEN SHE'S SLEEPING!
THIS IS A NICE CHAT ...?
HOW CAN YOU LOOK SELF-SATISFIED ON THE RADIO...?
AND I'M NOT ASLEEP...
TALK

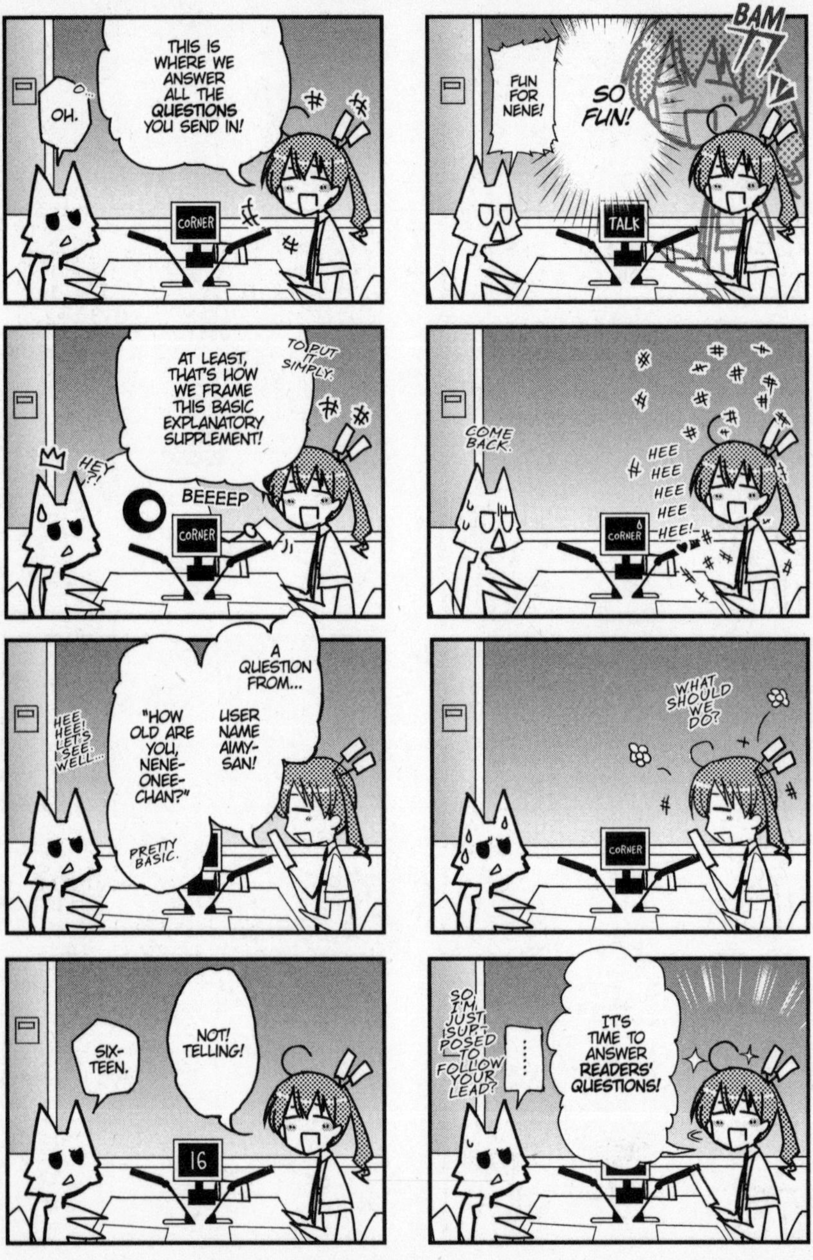
BAM
SO FUN!
FUN FOR NENE!
TALK
THIS IS WHERE WE ANSWER ALL THE QUESTIONS YOU SEND IN!
OH.
CORNER
HEE HEE HEE HEE HEE!
COME BACK.
CORNER
TO PUT IT SIMPLY.
AT LEAST, THAT'S HOW WE FRAME THIS BASIC EXPLANATORY SUPPLEMENT!
HEY ?!
BEEEEP
CORNER
WHAT SHOULD WE DO?
CORNER
A QUESTION FROM...
USER NAME AIMY-SAN!
"HOW OLD ARE YOU, NENE-ONEE-CHAN?"
PRETTY BASIC.
HEE HEE! LET'S SEE. WELL...
IT'S TIME TO ANSWER READERS' QUESTIONS!
......
SO, I'M JUST SUP-POSED TO FOLLOW YOUR LEAD?
NOT! TELLING!
SIX-TEEN.
16

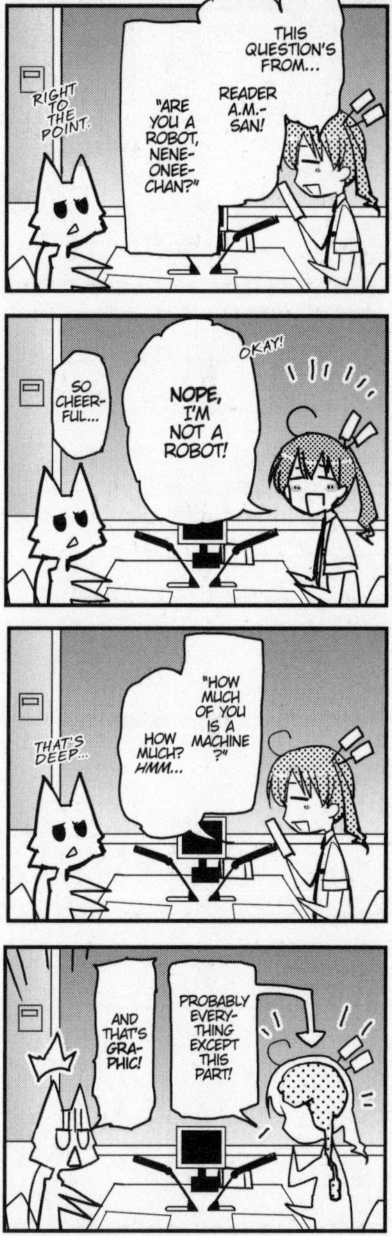
THIS QUESTION'S FROM... READER A.M.-SAN!
"ARE YOU A ROBOT, NENE-ONEECHAN?"
RIGHT TO THE POINT.
OKAY!
NOPE, I'M NOT A ROBOT!
SO CHEERFUL...
"HOW MUCH OF YOU IS A MACHINE?"
HOW MUCH? HMM...
THAT'S DEEP...
PROBABLY EVERYTHING EXCEPT THIS PART!
AND THAT'S GRAPHIC!
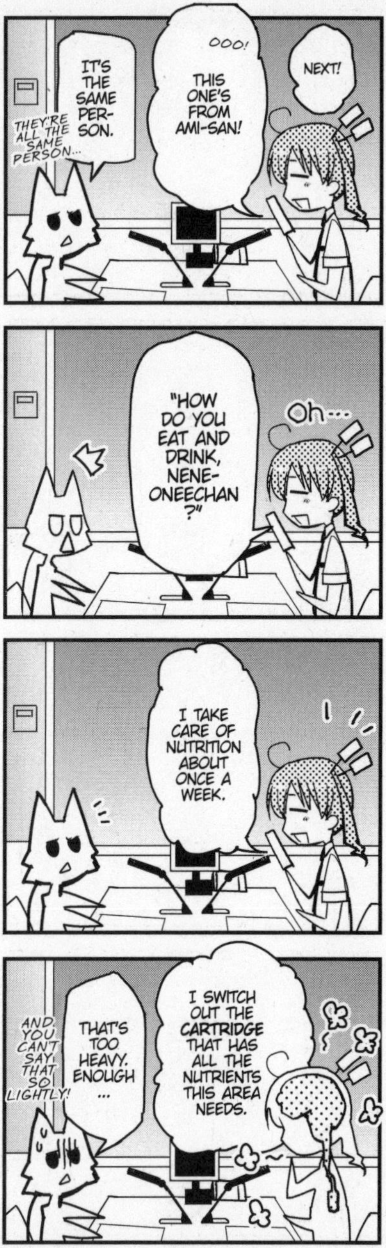
NEXT!
OOO!
THIS ONE'S FROM AMI-SAN!
IT'S THE SAME PERSON.
THEY'RE ALL THE SAME PERSON...
"HOW DO YOU EAT AND DRINK, NENE-ONEECHAN?"
Oh...
I TAKE CARE OF NUTRITION ABOUT ONCE A WEEK.
I SWITCH OUT THE CARTRIDGE THAT HAS ALL THE NUTRIENTS THIS AREA NEEDS.
THAT'S TOO HEAVY. ENOUGH...
AND YOU CAN'T SAY THAT SO LIGHTLY!

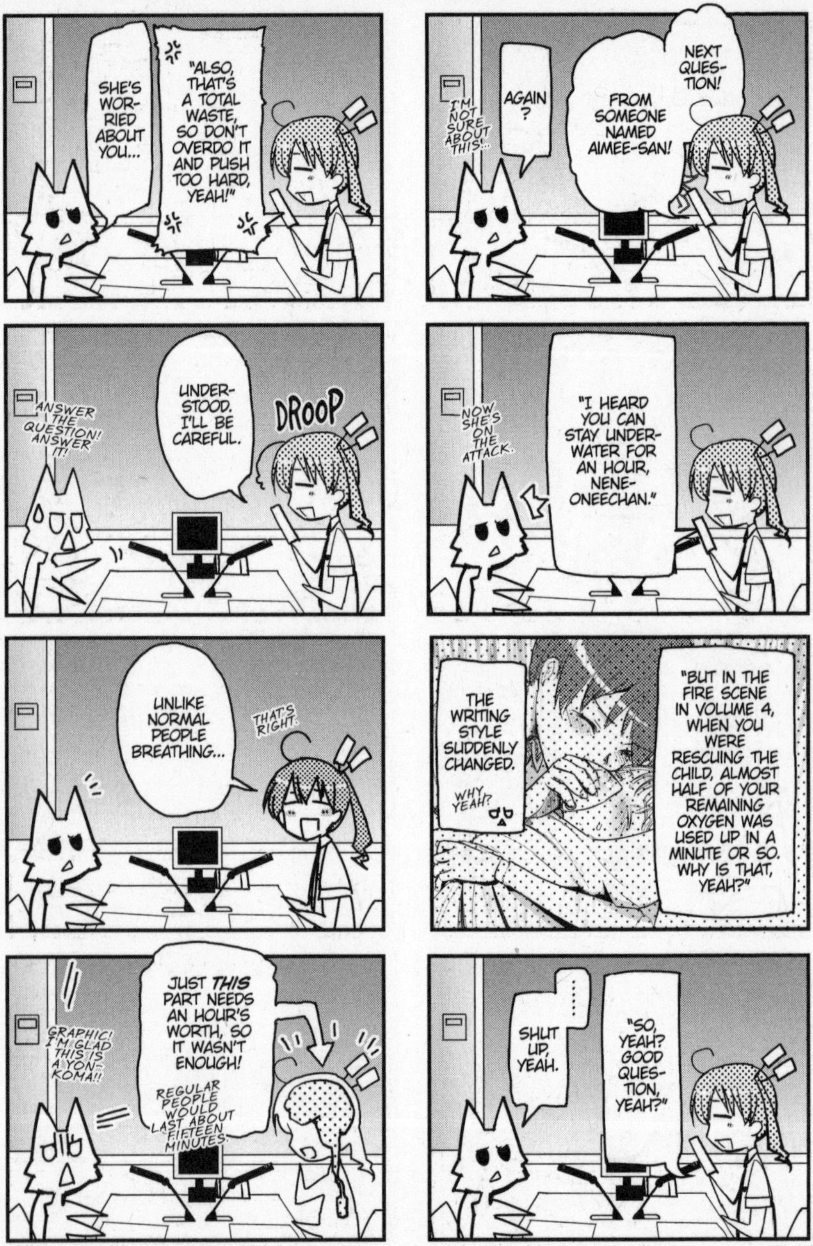
NEXT QUES-TION!
FROM SOMEONE NAMED AIMEE-SAN!
AGAIN?
I'M NOT SURE ABOUT THIS...
"I HEARD YOU CAN STAY UNDER-WATER FOR AN HOUR, NENE-ONEECHAN."
NOW SHE'S ON THE ATTACK.
"BUT IN THE FIRE SCENE IN VOLUME 4, WHEN YOU WERE RESCUING THE CHILD, ALMOST HALF OF YOUR REMAINING OXYGEN WAS USED UP IN A MINUTE OR SO. WHY IS THAT, YEAH?"
THE WRITING STYLE SUDDENLY CHANGED.
WHY, YEAH?
"SO, YEAH? GOOD QUES-TION, YEAH?"
......
SHUT UP, YEAH.
"ALSO, THAT'S A TOTAL WASTE, SO DON'T OVERDO IT AND PUSH TOO HARD, YEAH!"
SHE'S WOR-RIED ABOUT YOU...
DROOP
UNDER-STOOD. I'LL BE CAREFUL.
ANSWER THE QUESTION! ANSWER IT!
THAT'S RIGHT.
UNLIKE NORMAL PEOPLE BREATHING...
JUST THIS PART NEEDS AN HOUR'S WORTH, SO IT WASN'T ENOUGH!
REGULAR PEOPLE WOULD LAST ABOUT FIFTEEN MINUTES.
GRAPHIC! I'M GLAD THIS IS A YON-KOMA!!

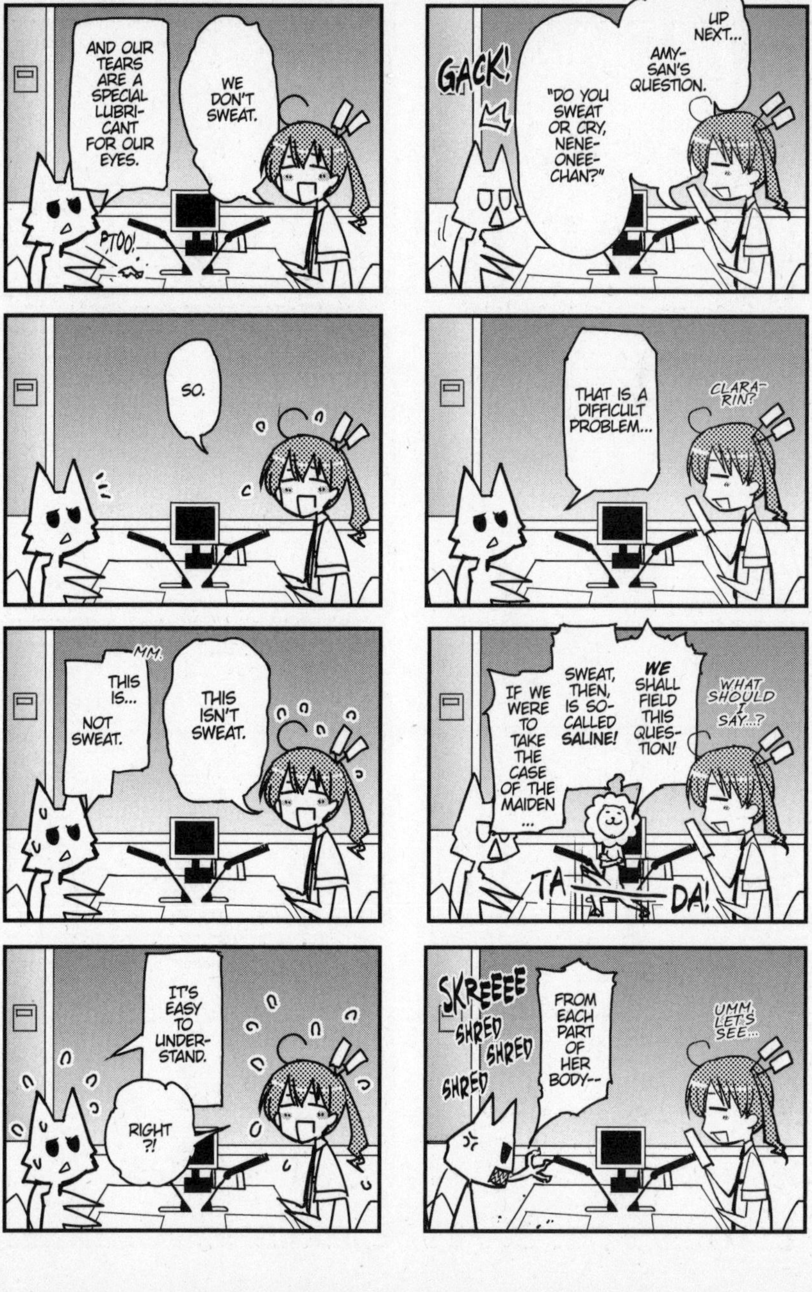
UP NEXT... AMY-SAN'S QUESTION.
"DO YOU SWEAT OR CRY, NENE-ONEE-CHAN?"
GACK!
WE DON'T SWEAT.
AND OUR TEARS ARE A SPECIAL LUBRICANT FOR OUR EYES.
PTOO!
CLARA-RIN?
THAT IS A DIFFICULT PROBLEM...
SO.
WHAT SHOULD I SAY...?
WE SHALL FIELD THIS QUESTION!
SWEAT, THEN, IS SO-CALLED SALINE!
IF WE WERE TO TAKE THE CASE OF THE MAIDEN...
TA-DA!
THIS ISN'T SWEAT.
MM.
THIS IS... NOT SWEAT.
UMM, LET'S SEE...
FROM EACH PART OF HER BODY--
SKREEEE
SHRED SHRED SHRED
IT'S EASY TO UNDERSTAND.
RIGHT?!

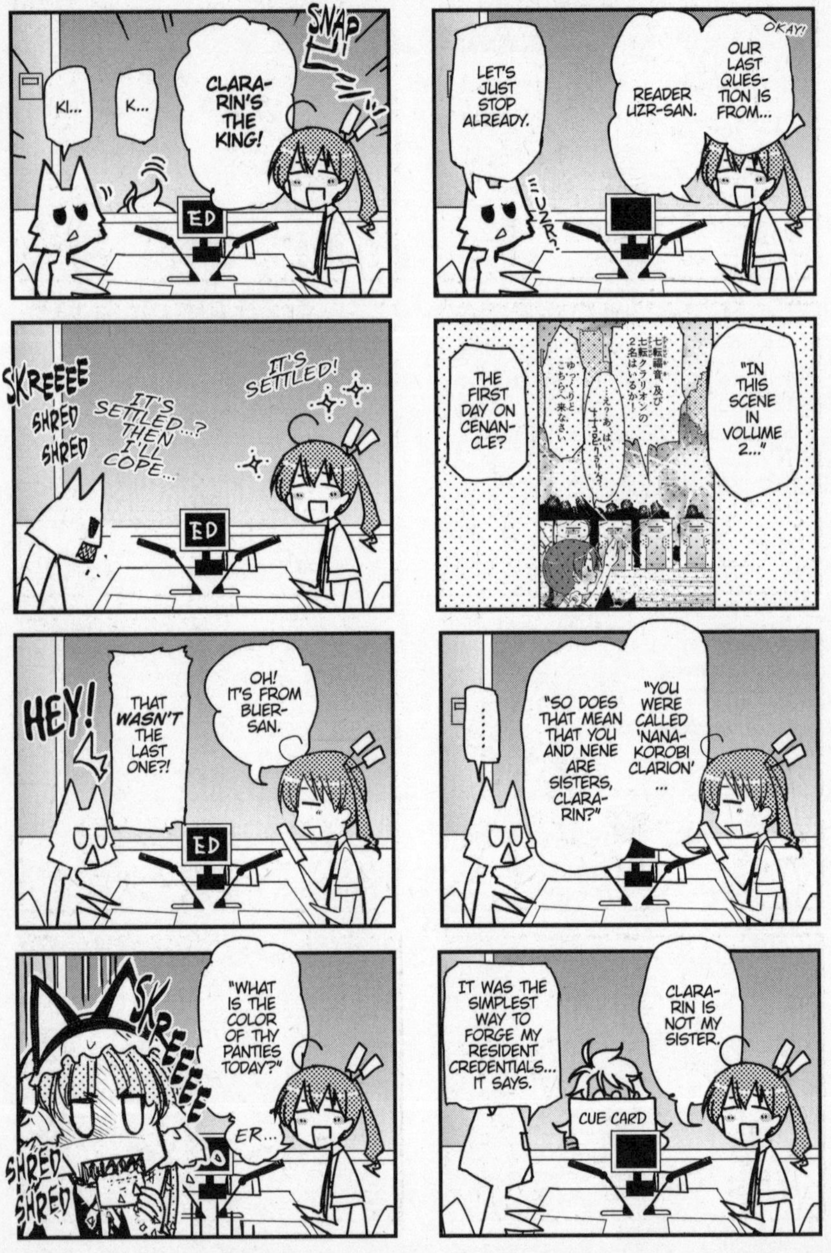
OKAY!
OUR LAST QUES-TION IS FROM...
READER UZR-SAN.
LET'S JUST STOP ALREADY.
UZR?
SNAP
CLARA-RIN'S THE KING!
K...
KI...
"IN THIS SCENE IN VOLUME 2..."
七転福音、及び七転クラリオンの2名はいるか！
ゆっくりとこちらへ来なさい
THE FIRST DAY ON CENANCLE?
IT'S SETTLED!
IT'S SETTLED...? THEN I'LL COPE...
SKREEEEE
SHRED SHRED
"YOU WERE CALLED 'NANA-KOROBI CLARION' ...
"SO DOES THAT MEAN THAT YOU AND NENE ARE SISTERS, CLARA-RIN?"
......
OH! IT'S FROM BUER-SAN.
THAT WASN'T THE LAST ONE?!
HEY!
CLARA-RIN IS NOT MY SISTER.
IT WAS THE SIMPLEST WAY TO FORGE MY RESIDENT CREDENTIALS... IT SAYS.
CUE CARD
"WHAT IS THE COLOR OF THY PANTIES TODAY?"
ER...
SKREEEEEE
SHRED SHRED

ORIGINAL CONCEPT DESIGN NOTES

Original Character Design Sketches

The reason I put off showing you the original design for Nene, one of the main characters, wasn't because I was trying to keep you in suspense. It's just that my design wasn't particularly original. I think all the edges were smoothed down; this is basically an amateur design, with nothing particularly original to speak of.

In fact, one idea that Rikudo-shi opted not to use was that, after Nene got her full-body prosthesis due to illness, her physical therapy facility was destroyed in an avalanche. Between that and the trauma of losing her parents, she would have developed claustrophobia and a fear of the dark, which would have originally prevented her from approaching some traps. Her freezing up would have provided opportunities for her to avoid danger. Maybe Buer's core has that element now?

In my original notes, I wrote, "Nene is always positive and seriously trying hard in any situation. Even if nothing good happens, she gets a gold star for living through it." I frequently create characters with an edge, but I'm not very good at creating characters like Nene. She's where I'm most glad that I asked Rikudo-shi to give the characters makeovers.

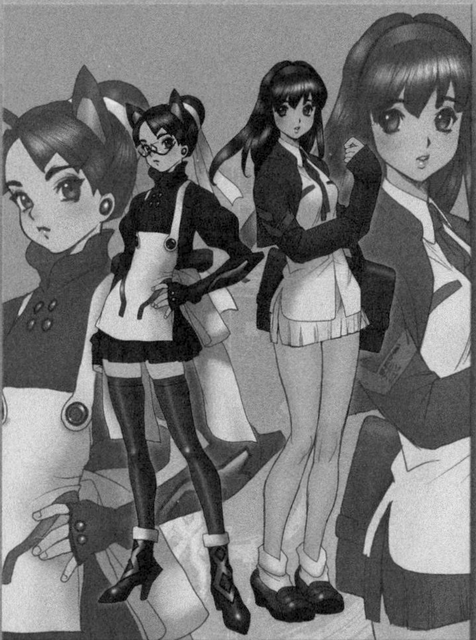

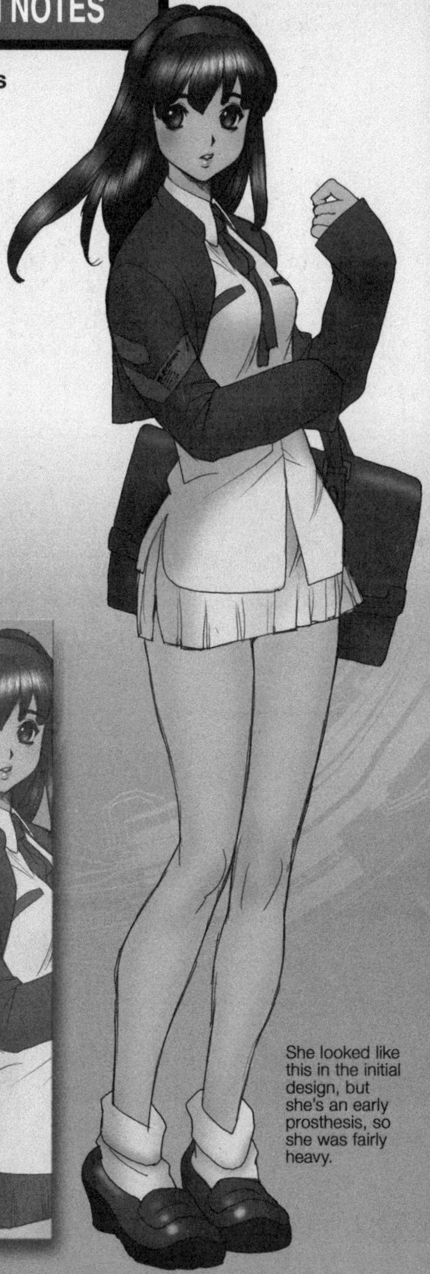

She looked like this in the initial design, but she's an early prosthesis, so she was fairly heavy.

Original Character Design Sketches

These aren't transformations from the Pandora Device; they're just different costumes. The transformations with the Pandora Device and the method of downloading it from Clarion were Rikudo-shi's ideas, rather than elements included in the initial designs. It began with the idea that someone nearby at that time gave him a keyword or an access site, and he downloaded various time-limited software from the network.

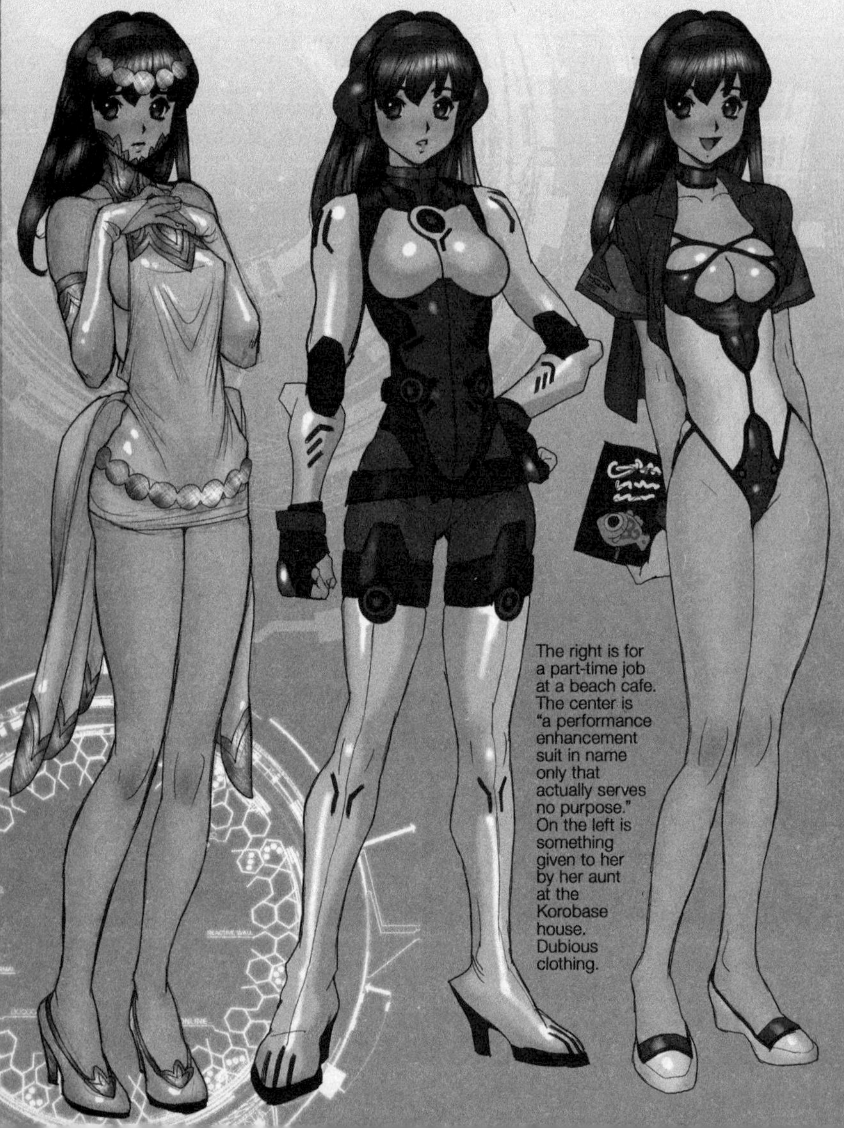

The right is for a part-time job at a beach cafe. The center is "a performance enhancement suit in name only that actually serves no purpose." On the left is something given to her by her aunt at the Korobase house. Dubious clothing.

Greetings! (For the fifth time!)

I mentioned on the previous page that the depictions related to the Pandora Device and the method of connecting with Clarion were Rikudo-shi's ideas, but when I first heard those ideas, I felt like there was already a manga with...not these exact elements, but similar ones, and I was a little unsure about whether to just go ahead as-is, or to propose revisions.

It did occur to me that it could cause problems with the broadcast framework, voluntary restrictions, or overseas development when making it into a movie. But since I couldn't come up with a specific case where there would be a problem, I ultimately didn't propose revisions, in order to prioritize Rikudo-shi's enthusiasm for the work.

Now that we're moving forward with that plan, I think fans might scold me for changes from the movie, which is hard, but I'll just note that on one corner of my desk were alternate plans for when different problems came up, like making the connecting part more like Clarion's cat ears being a connection guide for an aerial tanker. I'd like you to think that if we continue to go forward along this path, there will be no problems from the readers' point of view. I'd also prefer that there be no problems.

I think the pioneer and grand champion of cat ears and apron dress is Yumiko Oshima's *Wata no Kuni Hoshi,* but since this sort of stylization and generalization has been moving ahead in light novels and moe works, I don't see any real problem. Keep fighting, Clarion!

Thinking about the setting of an evil organization's illegal fighting robot, maybe it would have been better to equip her with a short version of Wolverine's claws or something... No, since this was originally an anime plan, I left out any elements that could make it bloody. I forgot. Maybe it's not such a big problem, because there have been a fair number of anime, even on TV, that are bloody or gruesome. But personally, I still worry about it because I've spent years having people working on projects tell me over and over, "don't do it, don't do it." When it's my own project, whatever I do, it's my responsibility, but I think you have to worry about not causing problems for the person you leave the project to.

January 18, 2014
Shirow Masamune

05 STAFF

Original story	Shirow Masamune (in cooperation with Crossroad)
Production	Rikudou Koushi
Composition/Art	Rin Hitotose Rikudou Koushi
Art assistance	Takepon G Unamu Kibayashida
Editing	Koichiro Ochiai (Kadokawa)
Design	Noriyuki Jinguji (Zin Studio)
Special Thanks	Seishinsha Co., Ltd. Prhythm Vision, Inc.

GHOST URN

SEVEN SEAS ENTERTA...

PANDOR...
CRIMSØN...

GHOST URN vol.05

story by **SHIROW MASAMUNE** / art by **RIKUDOU KOUSHI**

TRANSLATION
Jocelyne Allen

ADAPTATION
Ysabet Reinhardt MacFarlane

LETTERING
Roland Amago

LAYOUT
Bambi Eloriaga-Amago

COVER DESIGN
Nicky Lim

PROOFREADER
Janet Houck
Danielle King

PRODUCTION MANAGER
Lissa Pattillo

EDITOR-IN-CHIEF
Adam Arnold

PUBLISHER
Jason DeAngelis

KOUKAKU NO PANDORA volume 5
© Koushi RIKUDOU 2014
© Shirow Masamune 2014
First published in Japan in 2014 by KADOKAWA CORPORATION, Tokyo.
English translation rights arranged with KADOKAWA CORPORATION, Tokyo,
through TOHAN CORPORATION, Tokyo.

Seven Seas books may be purchased in bulk for educational, business, or
promotional use. For information on bulk purchases, please contact Macmillan
Corporate & Premium Sales Department at 1-800-221-7945 (ext 5442)
or write specialmarkets@macmillan.com.

Seven Seas and the Seven Seas logo are trademarks of
Seven Seas Entertainment, LLC. All rights reserved.

ISBN: 978-1-626922-92-1

Printed in Canada

First Printing: July 2016

10 9 8 7 6 5 4 3 2 1

FOLLOW US ONLINE: *www.gomanga.com*

READING DIRECTIONS

This book reads from *right to left*, Japanese style.
If this is your first time reading manga, you start
reading from the top right panel on each page and
take it from there. If you get lost, just follow the
numbered diagram here. It may seem backwards at
first, but you'll get the hang of it! Have fun!!

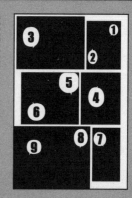